Mary Magdalene, The First Apostle:

The Struggle for Authority

HARVARD THEOLOGICAL STUDIES
51

CAMBRIDGE, MASSACHUSETTS

Mary Magdalene, The First Apostle: The Struggle for Authority

Ann Graham Brock

DISTRIBUTED BY

HARVARD UNIVERSITY PRESS

FOR

HARVARD THEOLOGICAL STUDIES

HARVARD DIVINITY SCHOOL

Mary Magdalene, The First Apostle: The Struggle for Authority

Harvard Theological Studies 51

Series Editors:
François Bovon
Francis Schüssler Fiorenza
Peter B. Machinist

Cover design: Eric Edstam
Cover art: Mary Magdalene and the Apostles. Saint Alban's-Psalter. Dombibliothek Hildesheim HS St. God. 1 (Property of the parish of St. Godehard, Hildesheim, Germany). Written 1123–1135 C.E.; 209 folia=418 pages (27.6 x 18.4 cm).

Brock, Ann Graham.
Mary Magdalene, the first apostle: the struggle for authority / Ann Graham Brock.
    p. cm. -- (Harvard theological studies ; 51)
"Distributed by Harvard University Press for Harvard Theological Studies"
Includes bibliographical references (p.) and index.
ISBN 0-674-00966-5
1. Mary Magdalene, the Apostle, Saint. 2. Peter, the Apostle, Saint. 3. Authority--Religious aspects--Christianity--History of doctrines--Early church, ca. 30–600. 4. Women in Christianity--History--Early church, ca. 30–600. 5. Apostles.
I. Title. II. Harvard theological studies ; no. 51.

BS2485.B3 2003
262'.11'09015--dc21   2002192176

Dedicated with Love and Affection

to

my husband David

and

my mother

Rosa Köhler Graham

Contents

Acknowledgments

In the process of writing my dissertation and turning it into a book, I have many people to whom I am grateful. Without a doubt the first note of appreciation goes to my dissertation committee. I have been incredibly fortunate to have access to the knowledge and insights of four scholars outstanding in their field: Professors François Bovon, Karen King, Helmut Koester, and Elisabeth Schüssler Fiorenza. Each of them contributed their expertise in different but essential ways, including keen insights and helpful, constructive comments throughout earlier drafts. They each gave of themselves and have enriched the entire experience with their support during this undertaking. Additional thanks go to Professors Peter Machinist and Francis Schüssler Fiorenza for reading and approving the manuscript for Harvard Theological Studies and for contributing their thoughtful suggestions as well.

I am especially grateful to Dr. Margaret Studier, who is both managing editor of Harvard Theological Studies and a great friend. She provided personal and professional support with generosity and a wonderful spirit, finding innumerable ways to be indispensable to my life in Cambridge. Special thanks are due Margaret's entire staff: first and foremost the expertise and enthusiasm of Gene McGarry, the thoughtful skill of Lyn Miller, the patient and untiring efforts of Margo McLoughlin, the positive energy of Mindy Newman, and the InDesign and Greek typesetting skills of Greg Goering. I am also thankful for the helpfulness of other readers along the way, such as Cathy Shrum and Khrysso LeFey. Without this help, especially Margaret's, this manuscript would never have reached its final form.

The last few years of researching and writing this dissertation I lived at a distance from Cambridge. I thank also Lieby Bouchard, artist and feeder of the homeless, who along with her husband, Al, opened their hearts to me and often creatively found a place for me to stay whenever I came back to Cambridge to do research. I am thankful as well for the friendship of Gerburg Spiekermann and Yuko Taniguchi, who cared for me in countless ways, including their warmth and hospitality.

The task of doing research was lightened by the skills of staff at various libraries, especially the proficiency of Gene Fox at Episcopal Divinity School, the helpfulness of Gloria Korsman and Laura Whitney at Harvard Divinity School, and the wonderfully supportive staff at Iliff School of Theology. For financial support during this long process I thank Harvard University and the Mellon Foundation dissertation grants, as well as Trinity Lutheran Seminary for their active support of Lutheran students in graduate work.

Finally, I am profoundly grateful to Dr. David R. Brock, my husband and soul mate. He generously and unceasingly provided me with emotional support, technical advice, and compelling spiritual strength to get through the entire process. I owe a huge debt of gratitude to him and to my mother, Rosa Köhler Graham, who, with encouraging phone calls and shared laughter, has provided me with an amazing role model of a woman, a person who balances love and strength well, no matter what hurdles life may bring.

Abbreviations

AB	Anchor Bible
ABD	*Anchor Bible Dictionary.* Edited by D. N. Freedman. 6 vols. New York, 1992.
Acts Andr.	*Acts of Andrew*
Acts Paul	*Acts of Paul*
Acts Pet.	*Acts of Peter*
Acts Phil.	*Acts of Philip*
Acts Phil. Mart.	*Acts of Philip Martyrdom*
Adv. Haer.	Irenaeus, *Adversus Haereses*
AnBib	Analecta biblica
AnBoll	*Analecta Bollandiana*
ANF	*Ante-Nicene Fathers*
ANRW	*Aufstieg und Niedergang der römischen Welt: Geschichte und Kultur Roms im Spiegel der neueren Forschung.* Edited by H. Temporini and W. Haase. Berlin, 1972–.
AsSeign	*Assemblées du Seigneur*
AThR	*Anglican Theological Review*
AUSS	*Andrew University Seminary Studies*
AVer	Actus Vercellenses
Barn.	*Epistle of Barnabas*
BAGD	Bauer, W., W. F. Arndt, F. W. Gingrich, and F. W. Danker. *Greek-English Lexicon of the New Testament and Other Early Christian Literature.* 2d ed. Chicago, 1979.
BCNH	Bibliothèque copte de Nag Hammadi
BCPE	*Bulletin du Centre protestant d'études*
BEvT	Beiträge zur evangelischen Theologie
BG	Papyrus Berolinensis gnosticus
BHG	*Bibliotheca Hagiographica Graece.* Brussels, 1977.

Bib	*Biblica*
BLit	*Bibliothèque liturgique*
BR	*Biblical Research*
BRev	*Bible Review*
BTB	*Biblical Theology Bulletin*
BWANT	Beiträge zur Wissenschaft vom Alten und Neuen Testament
BZ	*Biblische Zeitschrift*
BZNW	Beihefte zur Zeitschrift für die neutestamentliche Wissenschaft
CBPa	Cahiers de Biblia Patristica
CBQ	*Catholic Biblical Quarterly*
CCSA	Corpus Christanorum: Series apocryphorum
CCSG	Corpus Christanorum: Series graeca
CCSL	Corpus Christanorum: Series latina
ChrCent	*Christian Century*
1–2 Clem	*1–2 Clement*
3 Cor.	*3 Corinthians*
CSCO	Corpus scriptorum christianorum orientalium
CSEL	Corpus scriptorum ecclesiasticorum latinorum
CurBS	*Currents in Research: Biblical Studies*
Dial. Sav.	*Dialogue of the Savior*
Did.	*Didache*
DNP	*Der neue Pauly: Enzyclopädie der Antike.* Edited by H. Cancik and H. Schneider. Stuttgart, 1996–.
DRev	*Downside Review*
DT	*Deutsche Theologie*
EBib	Études bibliques
EgT	*Église et théologie*
EHPR	Études d'histoire et de philosophie religieuses
EHS.T	Europäische Hochschulschriften Theologie
EKKNT	Evangelisch-katholischer Kommentar zum Neuen Testament
ETL	*Ephemerides theologicae lovanienses*
EvT	*Evangelische Theologie*
FB	Forschung zur Bibel
FRLANT	Forschungen zur Religion und Literatur des Alten und Neuen Testaments
GCS	Die griechische christliche Schriftsteller der ersten [drei] Jahrhunderte

Gos. Mary	*Gospel of Mary*
Gos. Pet.	*Gospel of Peter*
Gos. Phil.	*Gospel of Philip*
Gos. Thom.	*Gospel of Thomas*
Herm. Sim.	*Shepherd of Hermas, Similitudes*
Herm. Vis.	*Shepherd of Hermas, Visions*
HeyJ	*Heythrop Journal*
Hist. eccl.	Eusebius, *Historia ecclesiastica*
HNT	Handbuch zum Neuen Testament
Hom. Matt.	Chrysostom, *Homiliae in Matthaeum*
HR	*History of Religions*
HSem	Horae semiticae. 9 vols. London, 1908–1912.
HTKNT	Herders theologischer Kommentar zum Neuen Testament
HTR	*Harvard Theological Review*
Ign. *Eph.*	Ignatius, *Letter to the Ephesians*
Ign. *Magn.*	Ignatius, *Letter to the Magnesians*
Ign. *Phld.*	Ignatius, *Letter to the Philadelphians*
Ign. *Rom.*	Ignatius, *Letter to the Romans*
Ign. *Smyrn.*	Ignatius, *Letter to the Smyrnaeans*
Ign. *Trall.*	Ignatius, *Letter to the Trallians*
Int	*Interpretation*
JAC.E	Jahrbuch für Antike und Christentum Ergänzungsband
JBL	*Journal of Biblical Literature*
JECS	*Journal of Early Christian Studies*
JFSR	*Journal of Feminist Studies in Religion*
JR	*Journal of Religion*
JSNT	*Journal for the Study of the New Testament*
JSNTSup	Journal for the Study of the New Testament: Supplement Series
JSSSup	Journal of Semitic Studies: Supplement Series
JTS	*Journal of Theological Studies*
KD	*Kerygma und Dogma*
LD	Lectio divina
LTK	*Lexicon für Theologie und Kirche*
LXX	Septuagint
Mart. Paul	*Martyrdom of Paul*
Mart. Pet.	*Martyrdom of Peter*

Mus	*Muséon: Revue d'études orientales*
NCBC	New Century Bible Commentary
NHC	Nag Hammadi Codices
NHL	*Nag Hammadi Library in English.* Edited by James M. Robinson, 1988.
NHMS	Nag Hammadi and Manichaean Studies
NHS	Nag Hammadi Studies
NIBCNT	New International Biblical Commentary on the New Testament
NJBC	*New Jerome Bible Commentary*
NovT	*Novum Testamentum*
NovTSup	Novum Testamentum Supplements
NPNF¹	*Nicene and Post-Nicene Fathers,* Series 1
NTA	New Testament Abstracts
NTApoc⁵	*New Testament Apocrypha.* English translation edited by R. McL. Wilson. 2 vols. 5th ed. Louisville, Ky.: Westminster/ John Knox, 1991–92.
NTApok³	*Neutestamentliche Apokryphen in deutscher Übersetzung.* Edited by E. Hennecke and W. Schneemelcher. 2 vols. 3d ed. 1959–64.
NTOA	Novum Testamentum et Orbis Antiquus
NTS	*New Testament Studies*
OiC	*One in Christ*
OrChr	*Oriens christianus*
OrSyr	*L'orient syrien*
PG	Patrologia graeca=Patrologiae cursus completus: Series graeca. Edited by J.-P. Migne. 162 vols. Paris, 1857–1886.
PHam	Hamburg Greek Papyrus of the *Acts of Paul*
Pis. Soph.	*Pistis Sophia*
PL	Patrologia latina=Patrologiae cursus completus: Series latina. Edited by J.-P. Migne. 217 vols. Paris, 1844–1864.
PO	Patrologia orientalis. Edited by Graffin-Nau.
Pol. Phil.	Polycarp, *Letter to the Philippians*
POxy	Papyrus Oxyrhynchus
Prot. Jas.	*Protevangelium of James*
PRyl	Papyrus Rylands
PTS	Patristische Texte und Studien
RB	*Revue biblique*
RBén	*Revue bénédictine*

REByz	*Revue d'études byzantines*
RelSRev	*Religious Studies Review*
RevScRel	*Revue des sciences religieuses*
RHPR	*Revue d'histoire et de philosophie religieuses*
RTP	*Revue de théologie et de philosophie*
SBA	Studies in Biblical Archaeology
SBAW	Sitzungsberichte der bayerischen Akademie der Wissenschaften in München
SBL	Society of Biblical Literature
SBLDS	Society of Biblical Literature Dissertation Series
SBLSymS	Society of Biblical Literature Symposium Series
SBS	Stuttgarter Bibelstudien
SBT	Studies in Biblical Theology
SC	Sources chrétiennes
SE	*Studia evangelica*
SEÅ	*Sensk exegetisk årsbok*
SecCent	*Second Century*
SHR	Studies in the History of Religions (supplement to *Numen*)
SJT	*Scottish Journal of Theology*
SNTSMS	Society for New Testament Studies Monograph Series
Soph. Jes. Chr.	*Sophia of Jesus Christ*
SR	*Studies in Religion*
ST	*Studia theologica*
StPatr	Studia patristica
STRev	*Sewanee Theological Review*
TB	Theologische Bücherei
TDNT	*Theological Dictionary of the New Testament.* Edited by G. Kittel and G. Friedrich. Trans. G. W. Bromiley. 10 vols. Grand Rapids, Mich. 1964–1976.
ThH	Théologie historique
THKNT	Theologischer Handkommentar zum Neuen Testament
ThSt	Theologische Studien
ThTo	*Theology Today*
TJT	*Toronto Journal of Theology*
TPINTC	Trinity Press International New Testament Commentaries
TQ	*Theologische Quartalschrift*
TRE	*Theologische Realenzyklopädie*
TS	*Theological Studies*

TTZ	*Trierer theologische Zeitschrift*
TU	Texte und Untersuchungen
TUGAL	Texte und Untersuchungen zur Geschichte der altchristlichen Literatur
TZ	*Theologische Zeitschrift*
VC	*Vigiliae christianae*
VCSup	Supplements to Vigiliae christianae
Vir. ill.	Jerome, *De viris illustribus*
WUNT	Wissenschaftliche Untersuchungen zum Neuen Testament
ZKT	*Zeitschrift für katholische Theologie*
ZNW	*Zeitschrift für die neutestamentliche Wissenschaft und die Kunde der älteren Kirche*
ZTK	*Zeitschrift für Theologie und Kirche*

CHAPTER ONE

The Issue of Apostolic Authority

A postolic authority, without question, was a key issue in the early
Christian churches. It insured that the one carrying the gospel
message was a bona fide messenger. The criteria by which various early
Christian authors attributed apostolic authority to certain followers of
Jesus and not to others in early Christian documents provide insights
into the politics of various factions of the early church. For example,
Mary Magdalene was so esteemed among some early Christians that they
bestowed on her the honorific title, "apostle to the apostles,"[1] and yet
for others she holds no apostolic status at all and is instead known as
a reformed prostitute, a concept for which there is no biblical basis.[2]

What did it take to be an apostle and were women included in that
group? Hippolytus, an early Christian bishop and martyr of Rome (ca.
170–ca. 236), wrote:

> Lest the female apostles doubt the angels, Christ himself came
> to them so that the women would be apostles of Christ and by
> their obedience rectify the sin of the ancient Eve. . . . Christ
> showed himself to the (male) apostles and said to them: . . . "It

---

[1] See Rosemarie Nürnberg, "Apostolae Apostolorum: Die Frauen am Grab als erste
Zeuginnen der Auferstehung in der Väterexegese," in *Stimuli, Exegese und ihre Hermeneutik
in Antike und Christentum* (Fs. Ernst Dassmann; ed. Gary Schöllgen and Clemens Scholten;
JAC.E 23; Münster: Aschendorff, 1996), 228–42, and Elisabeth Schüssler Fiorenza, "Mary
Magdalene: Apostle to the Apostles," *Union Theological Seminary Journal* (April 1975):
22–24. See also ch. 9, below, for further discussion.

[2] This association results from the identification of Mary Magdalene as the unnamed
female sinner (later interpreted as prostitute) of Luke 7:36–50, the passage immediately
preceding Mary Magdalene's introduction into the Gospel of Luke.

is I who appeared to these women and I who wanted to send them
to you as apostles."[3]

This reference to female apostles from a third-century bishop of
Rome indicates that at least in some early Christian circles the definition
of apostle included both genders. Most Christians know the canonical
gospel narratives to which Hippolytus alludes, in which Jesus makes
a resurrection appearance to certain women and sends them out on the
apostolic mission as the first gospel messengers. In fact, they can often
even name the most well known of these women as Mary Magdalene.
Yet, when asked to describe the apostles of antiquity, most Christians
inevitably conjure up an image of "twelve apostles." Although the phrase
"twelve apostles" occurs only twice in the New Testament, the close link
between the terms "twelve" and "apostles" has become so common in
contemporary settings that many Christians consider these words to be
coterminous. This all-male group, however, includes neither the women
just mentioned nor the apostle Paul, one of the most well known and
influential of all the apostles.

This study begins with an inquiry into this conceptual dissonance,
asking on what basis an early Christian figure claimed or received the
title "apostle." Scholars of Paul's epistles have noticed in particular the
connection that Paul forges between his own claim of being an apostle
and the resurrection appearance he received. Other early Christians made
this claim as well, as Hans von Campenhausen explains:

> The emergence within the primitive Church of major determinative
> figures, described indiscriminately in later times as "apostolic," de-
> rives without exception so far as we can judge from the experience
> of the Resurrection, or at the very least stands in a close historical
> and spiritual connection with that experience.[4]

---

[3]Hippolytus, *De Cantico* 24–26, CSCO 264, 43–49; Gerald O'Collins and Daniel
Kendall, "Mary Magdalene as Major Witness to Jesus' Resurrection," *TS* 48 (1987): 632
n. 8.

[4]Hans von Campenhausen, *Ecclesiastical Authority and Spiritual Power in the Church
of the First Three Centuries* (trans. J. A. Baker; Peabody, Mass.: Hendrickson, 1997),
22–23. He writes: "This connection between the apostolate and the resurrection
experience seems to me today even more certain than it did at the time of my essay, 'Der
urchristliche Apostelbegriff' " (p. 22 n. 55). He refers here to his article, "Der urchristliche
Apostelbegriff," *ST* 1 (1947): 96–130; see also Adolf von Harnack, *Die Mission und*

If, therefore, receiving a resurrection appearance was the primary requirement for apostleship, and narratives describe Mary Magdalene not only receiving the first of such appearances but also receiving a divine commission to report the news to others, then why is she not more universally recognized as an apostle? The following investigation seeks to answer that question by examining the ways in which early Christian literature portrays particular disciples as having acquired a special prominence or authority, especially as apostles. It maintains, along with most scholars, that one of the primary means of establishing a bid for status and position in the early church was by receiving a resurrection appearance from Jesus. This investigation also emphasizes the significance of receiving a commissioning. It therefore turns to the concepts of apostleship and resurrection witness to discern religious and political implications in the naming of particular followers of Jesus as "apostles."

Etymology of the Term "Apostle"

Because such a wealth of interpretations has associated itself with the word ἀπόστολος ("apostle") even from the first years of Christianity, scholars continue to debate both the origins and the meaning of the term.[5] Although some scholars trace the early Christian usage of this word back to Greek literature, this connection lacks strength because the history of the word ἀπόστολος in Greek literature is primarily connected with seafaring, where it arose as a description of a type of transport ship and came eventually to refer to the dispatch of a fleet.[6] Only Herodotus, employing the word twice in the sense of "messenger," provides a pre-Christian Greek connection to the meaning of the word in New Testament texts.[7]

Ausbreitung des Christentums in den ersten drei Jahrhunderten (Wiesbaden: VMA, 1924), 332–44.

[5]We shall see in ch. 8 why I disagree with J. Kirk, who claims that there is unity in the diverse presentations of apostolic ministry in the New Testament; see J. Andrew Kirk, "Apostleship since Rengstorf: Towards a Synthesis," *NTS* 21 (1975): 249–64.

[6]Karl Heinrich Rengstorf, "ἀπόστολος," *TDNT* 1 (1993): 407. For a most thorough article on the history of scholarship on the term ἀπόστολος, see Elmar M. Kredel, "Der Apostelbegriff in der neueren Exegese: Historisch-kritische Darstellung," *ZKT* 78 (1956): 169–93, 257–305.

[7]Herodotus 1.21 and 4.38; Francis H. Agnew, "On the Origin of the Term *Apostolos*,"

The term is also rare in Greek Judaism since the Jews were not a seafaring people. Josephus, for example, employs the term once to describe the sending of envoys to Rome (which involved a journey by sea). The Septuagint likewise employs the term only once in describing Ahijah's commission to give a divine message to the wife of King Jeroboam I (3 Kings 14:6).[8]

Some scholars, such as Ernst Käsemann and Karl Rengstorf, trace the concept of "apostle" back to Jewish usage. Käsemann states, "It seems fairly certain that the Semitic idea of sending with an authoritative commission determined the NT understanding of apostle."[9] Von Campenhausen likewise claims a Semitic connection, arguing that

> the very word "apostle" is nothing other than a literal translation of a Jewish legal term with a definite meaning, namely *shaliach* [שָׁלִיחַ], which denotes the person of a plenipotentiary representative, whose task it is to conduct business independently and responsibly for the one who has assigned him these powers for a particular service.[10]

In later rabbinic Judaism this concept is well known; the Hebrew term indicates an authorized messenger who represents the dispatcher.[11]

Since the time of Rengstorf, however, other scholars have called into question this close association of ἀπόστολος with the Hebrew term שָׁלִיחַ.[12] Against the claim of Jewish origins for ἀπόστολος these scholars would cite such passages as Phil 2:25, which refers to Epaphroditus as an

---

CBQ 38 (1976): 49. With the exceptions of Herodotus 1.21 and Plato *Epistulae* 7.346a, the word ἀπόστολος does not commonly appear in the sense of "envoy." In the Hellenistic era, for example, Epictetus applied the concept of the divine envoy to the ideal cynic (*Dissertationes* 3.22.3; 4.8.31), but the term ἀπόστολος does not occur. Hans Dieter Betz, "Apostle," *ABD* 1:309.

 [8]Edwin Hatch and Henry A. Redpath, *A Concordance to the Septuagint* (3 vols. in 2; Grand Rapids, Mich.: Baker, 1987), 1:145. This passage does not occur in the Vaticanus manuscript, indicating that this one usage of the term is more recent than the oldest version of the Septuagint. The term occurs twice in Josephus, but one occurrence is weakly attested. Rengstorf, "ἀπόστολος," 1:413.

 [9]Ernst Käsemann, *Commentary on Romans* (trans. Geoffrey Bromiley; Grand Rapids, Mich.: Eerdmans, 1980), 5–6.

 [10]Campenhausen, *Ecclesiastical Authority and Spiritual Power,* 22.

 [11]Rengstorf, "ἀπόστολος," 1:415–20.

 [12]Holger Mosbech, for example, calls the Semitic origins strongly into question; see "Apostolos in the New Testament," *ST* 2 (1948): 170, 187–88. Schmithals believes that

ἀπόστολος when the congregation sends him with money, but "for such a sending there certainly can have been no Jewish institution to serve as a direct prototype."[13] Rudolph Schnackenburg, one of the scholars who also questions a direct Jewish derivation for ἀπόστολος, suggests an intermediate position instead, proposing "a new Christian coining perhaps by analogy with the Jewish 'envoys.' "[14]

Thus to date no scholarly consensus exists concerning the origin or meaning of ἀπόστολος except in the sense of "someone dispatched or sent on behalf of another." For this particular exploration, the origin of the term is a less decisive factor than its subsequent evolution within early Christian literature, a discussion of which we will begin here — with an

---

the concept of apostle derives from gnosticism, especially the gnostic idea of a redeemer figure. His theory proposes a figure native to the Syrian setting who employed the title "apostle" as a self-designation; a theory that also has not been well received. See Walter Schmithals, *The Office of Apostle in the Early Church* (trans. John E. Steely; Nashville: Abingdon, 1969), 115. Geo Widengren also suggests a wider background for the concept by examining the representation of messengers of God among the Sumerians, Mandaeans, Manichaeans, and Samaritans. See Geo Widengren, *Religionsphänomenologie* (Berlin: de Gruyter, 1969) and idem, "Les origines du gnosticisme et l'histoire des religions," *Le Origini dello Gnosticismo: Colloquio di Messina 13–18 Aprile 1966: Testi e Discussioni* (SHR, *Numen Sup 12*; ed. Ugo Bianchi; Leiden: Brill, 1967), 28–60 (summary in Hans Dieter Betz, *Galatians: A Commentary on Paul's Letter to the Churches* [Philadelphia: Fortress, 1979], 75).

[13]Schmithals, *Office of Apostle*, 102. G. Klein's *Die zwölf Apostel* and the German original of Schmithals' book appeared at the same time. See Günter Klein, *Die zwölf Apostel: Ursprung und Gehalt einer Idee* (FRLANT 77; Göttingen: Vandenhoeck & Ruprecht, 1961). Charles K. Barrett (*The Signs of an Apostle* [London: Epworth Press, 1970], 16) explains that Klein had the advantage of seeing Schmithals's typescript, and that Schmithals viewed Klein's work in time to be able to include in his published work an eight-page appendix in response to Klein.

[14]Rudolf Schnackenburg, "Apostolicity — the Present Position of Studies," *OiC* 6 (1970): 252 n. 17. Apostolic authority in the first century of Christianity also has roots stemming from the verb ἀποστέλλειν, meaning "to send out" under the auspices of authority to speak for someone. This word frequently occurs in the Septuagint in connection with mission. Although the noun ἀπόστολος appears only once in the Septuagint, the verb ἀποστέλλειν occurs more than 700 times "predominantly used where it is a matter of commissioning with a message or a task" (Rengstorf, "ἀποστέλλω," 1:400). Such a basic definition appears among the Church fathers, as in Origen, who says, "Everyone who is sent by someone is an apostle of the one who sent him," including missionaries, delegates, and envoys (*Commentarii in evangelium Joannis*, 32.17; referenced in Betz, "Apostle," *ABD* 1:309).

examination of the qualifications required of an apostle—and explore further in the final chapter on apostleship.[15]

Qualifications for Apostleship

The New Testament affirms the significance of being an apostle in the way this term appears at the beginning of eleven of its epistles.[16] The letters of Paul, the earliest Christian texts, provide especially clear evidence of its significance.[17] In Paul's claim to apostolicity and legitimation, two aspects emerge as essential: 1) witnessing an appearance of the risen Christ, and 2) receiving a divine call or commission to proclaim Christ's message.

Paul's apologetic stance for his apostleship rests foundationally upon the argument that the resurrected Lord indeed appeared to him. He claims apostleship numerous times throughout his epistles and does so primarily on the basis of this resurrection appearance.[18] In 1 Cor 9:1 he writes: "Am I not an apostle? Have I not seen Jesus our Lord?" (οὐκ εἰμὶ ἀπόστολος; οὐχὶ Ἰησοῦν τὸν κύριον ἡμῶν ἑόρακα.[19] Another passage in 1 Corin-

---

[15]See ch. 8, below.

[16]Rom 1:1; 1 Cor 1:1; 2 Cor 1:1; Gal 1:1; Eph 1:1; Col 1:1; 1 Tim 1:1; 2 Tim 1:1; Titus 1:1; 1 Pet 1:1; and 2 Pet 1:1.

[17]Betz, "Apostle," ABD 1:309.

[18]Rengstorf, "ἀπόστολος," 1:407–8; see also Mosbech, "Apostolos," 170; W. D. Davies, "Church Life in the New Testament," Christian Origins and Judaism: The Jewish People: History, Religion, Literature (Philadelphia: Westminster, 1962), 241; Hans Küng, Die Kirche (Freiburg: Herder, 1967), 412; Arnold Ehrhardt, The Apostolic Ministry (Edinburgh: Oliver and Boyd, 1958), 5; Kirk, "Apostleship since Rengstorf," 255; Agnew, "Apostolos," 49–53; idem, "The Origin of the NT Apostle-Concept: A Review of Research," JBL 105 (1986): 75–96; Albert Marie Denis, "L'investiture de la fonction apostolique par 'apocalypse,' " RB 64 (1957): 335–62, 492–515. For further exegetical studies, see Hans Conzelmann, 1 Corinthians (Hermeneia; Philadelphia: Fortress, 1975), 151–52.

[19]Paul refers here to his vision of Christ described in Gal 1:12 and 1 Cor 15:8. In forming the question in 1 Cor 9:1, Paul employs the negative particle οὐ, which anticipates an affirmative answer; see Friedrich Blass and Albert Debrunner, A Greek Grammar of the New Testament and Other Early Christian Literature (trans. and ed. Robert W. Funk; Chicago: University of Chicago, 1961), §427 (2); Conzelmann, 1 Corinthians, 152. Lietzmann believes that this passage is the result of the Cephas group casting doubts on the apostolic rank of Paul; see Hans Lietzmann, An die Korinther (2d ed.; HNT 9; Tübingen: Mohr [Siebeck], 1923), esp. 7, 41: ". . . des Petrus Verhalten wird um so mehr betont, als man ihn vermütlich als Gegenbeispiel eines 'echten' Apostels gegenüber Pls benutzt hatte" (p. 41).

thians underlines the significance of this concept, as Paul, transmitting the resurrection traditions that he received, includes himself among the witnesses of the risen Christ:[20]

παρέδωκα γὰρ ὑμῖν ἐν πρώτοις, ὃ καὶ παρέλαβον, ὅτι Χριστὸς . . . ὤφθη Κηφᾷ εἶτα τοῖς δώδεκα· ἔπειτα ὤφθη ἐπάνω πεντακοσίοις ἀδελφοῖς ἐφάπαξ, ἐξ ὧν οἱ πλείονες μένουσιν ἕως ἄρτι, τινὲς δὲ ἐκοιμήθησαν· ἔπειτα ὤφθη Ἰακώβῳ εἶτα τοῖς ἀποστόλοις πᾶσιν· ἔσχατον δὲ πάντων ὡσπερεὶ τῷ ἐκτρώματι ὤφθη κἀμοί.

For what I received I passed on to you as of first importance: that Christ . . . appeared to Cephas, and then to the Twelve. After that, he appeared to more than five hundred of the brothers and sisters at the same time, most of whom are still living, though some have fallen asleep. Then he appeared to James, then to all the apostles, and last of all he appeared to me also, as to one born out of time. (1 Cor 15:3, 5–8)

Significantly, the context of this passage is not a conversion story recounting how Paul became a Christian, but rather is his claim to apostolicity. The presence of Paul's name among these witnesses is vital because the function of this list "is a matter of demonstrating the authority of certain leaders, specifically named, showing their authority to have been conferred on them by an appearance to them of the risen Lord, and it is a matter of establishing this in the tradition in 'legitimation formulae.' "[21] As such, the names of the disciples are "kept embodied in the tradition because they are seen as demonstrating that the leaders of primitive Christianity received their legitimation, their mandate, their vocation and calling, and their position of full power and authority, from Heaven."[22] That Paul closely connects resurrection appearances and apostolic authority is borne out by the fact that he emphasizes Christ's appearance to him precisely in those letters in which the issue of his claim of apostleship arises (see Gal 1:15; Rom 1:1–5).[23]

---

[20]Conzelmann, *1 Corinthians*, 251–60.

[21]Ulrich Wilckens, *Resurrection: Biblical Testimony to the Resurrection: An Historical Examination and Explanation* (trans. A. M. Stewart; Atlanta: John Knox, 1978), 16.

[22]Wilckens, *Resurrection*, 13. See also Gregory J. Riley, *Resurrection Reconsidered: Thomas and John in Controversy* (Minneapolis: Fortress, 1995), 89 n. 65.

[23]Wilckens, *Resurrection*, 13.

Not only is a resurrection appearance fundamental to being an apostle, but so, too, is the perception of divine initiative in this calling. Von Campenhausen affirms the significance of this connection by explaining, "again and again the decisive factor is the encounter with the Risen Lord, which was frequently both experienced and understood as a special call or commission."[24] Paul's letters, including such passages as Gal 1:11–16 and 1 Cor 15:8–11, indicate that a divine initiative or a commissioning was a vital element in the battle for status and theological authority.[25]

This divine commissioning is especially critical because Paul's use of the term ἀπόστολος exhibits two levels of apostleship: individuals may be sent as representatives of a congregation (as in 2 Cor 8:23),[26] or they may be commissioned by a divine source, as he himself was (Gal 1:1). Paul thus incorporates the phrase "apostle of Christ," and variations upon it, into his epistles and contrasts the divinely ordained position with the function both of innumerable missionaries and also of community apostles (as in Phil 2:25).[27] Paul carefully articulates that he is not one of those apostles who are merely sent by a congregation but is rather an apostle by divine authority: "Paul, an apostle, sent not from humans nor by a human, but by Jesus Christ and God the Father, who raised him from the dead."[28]

Clearly the source of his authority is significant for Paul because he mentions the divine initiative in his calling at the beginning of almost all his epistles. In 1 Cor 1:1, for example, he states that he is "called to be an apostle of Christ Jesus by the will of God" (κλητὸς ἀπόστολος Χριστοῦ Ἰησοῦ διὰ θελήματος θεοῦ). This passage exemplifies how he establishes his legitimacy. He accentuates his position as an apostle in three ways: with the words that he is "called," that he is an apostle "of Jesus Christ," and that he is an apostle "by the will of God," thus emphasizing again the divine role so instrumental in his authority. Likewise in Romans, he reaf-

---

[24]Campenhausen, *Ecclesiastical Authority and Spiritual Power*, 23.

[25]See also 1 Cor 1:1, 17; 2 Cor 12:11–12.

[26]On 2 Cor 8:23b see Victor Paul Furnish (*II Corinthians* [AB 32A; New York: Doubleday, 1984], 425), who prefers to translate the phrase ἀπόστολοι ἐκκλησιῶν as "representatives of the churches" rather than "apostles of the churches" to avoid the implication that these people are apostles in the same sense that Paul is.

[27]Käsemann, *Romans*, 5.

[28]Παῦλος ἀπόστολος οὐκ ἀπ᾽ ἀνθρώπων οὐδὲ δι᾽ ἀνθρώπου ἀλλὰ διὰ Ἰησοῦ Χριστοῦ καὶ θεοῦ πατρὸς τοῦ ἐγείραντος αὐτὸν ἐκ νεκρῶν (Gal 1:1).

firms these themes, describing that he is "called to be an apostle" (κλητὸς ἀπόστολος) and is "set apart for the gospel of God" (ἀφωρισμένος εἰς εὐαγγέλιον θεοῦ [Rom 1:1]). Additional scriptural references to Paul's status as an apostle sent by Jesus Christ occur in Gal 1:1, 1 Cor 1:1, 2 Cor 1:1, and Eph 1:1.

In addition to the Pauline epistles, the book of Acts employs the term "apostle" with great frequency, as it constitutes the "twelve" as a group and portrays them at the foundational beginnings of Christianity. A comparison of usage shows that with respect to the Christian concept of ἀπόστολος, "one fact becomes constantly more clear: in the New Testament we have no unified concept of the 'apostle' but rather a number of definitions which seem to stand in contradiction to one another."[29] Despite the variations in the definition of apostleship, however, there appear to be a few fundamental similarities. The author of Luke–Acts, for example, parallels Paul's claim of divine intervention in the aspect of apostleship, by having the eleven appeal to divine authority to incorporate a new member into this special group. It is therefore not the group who chooses the successor for Judas; rather, the final decision comes through God's guidance by means of casting lots (Acts 1:23–26). Although the author of Acts presents a different definition of apostolicity than Paul does, as we shall see later,[30] there remains nevertheless a fairly consistent portrayal with respect to two crucial elements: the resurrection appearance narrative and the element of divine intervention.

The Role of Resurrection Witness Narratives

Because these appearance traditions were so instrumental in establishing an individual's status as an apostle, it is not surprising that a survey of early Christian resurrection narratives discloses some significant variations among the traditions in their identification of which disciples saw the risen Jesus subsequent to his crucifixion and burial. These appearances served to make an explicit and privileged link between an individual and Jesus, the importance of which cannot be underestimated.

---

[29]Schnackenburg, "Apostolicity," 246; see also Francis H. Agnew, "The Origin of the NT Apostle-Concept," 75–96, esp. 77.

[30]These various definitions are explored further in ch. 8, below.

Jeremias explains that early Christians "rallied around individuals who had a claim to this distinction."[31] Paul provides a written collection of names of those who had authority because they either made a similar claim to a resurrection appearance from Christ or had it made for them (1 Cor 15:3, 6–7). This list of witnesses that Paul received, and in turn transmitted, specifically names Cephas, the twelve, five hundred brothers and sisters, James, and "all the apostles." Some scholars perceive in this passage two parallel, competing lists of witnesses: Cephas and the twelve, and James and all the apostles, reflecting two rival groups centered on either Peter or James.[32] Paul's inclusion of both lists may indicate that he refrains from choosing between them. Whether or not any rivalry existed among the personalities featured in Paul's list, clearly the presence of one's name in a list of resurrection witnesses functioned to legitimize one's authority. Thus early Christian texts tended specifically to highlight the names of one or more followers of Jesus and provide them with a privileged position with respect to the rest of the group.[33] Whether Paul's enumeration represents one list or two,

---

[31]Joachim Jeremias, *Neutestamentliche Theologie. I. Die Verkündigung Jesu* (Gütersloh: Mohn, 1971), 291; John E. Alsup, *The Post-Resurrection Appearance Stories of the Gospel-Tradition: A History-of-Tradition Analysis with Text-Synopsis* (Stuttgart: Calwer, 1975), 63.

[32]Jeremias (*Neutestamentliche Theologie*, 291) discerns traces of this rival tradition concerning James in the *Gospel of the Hebrews* and the Syriac *Didaskalia*. Jeremias concludes, "keine Frage, es sind die radikalen Kreise des palästinischen Judenschristentums, . . . die ihn [Petrus] darum aus der Rolle des Empfängers der Ersterscheinung verdrängt haben." Koester ("Apocryphal and Canonical Gospels," *HTR* 73 [1980]: 105–30) writes of James: "James the righteous occupied a position of authority as the leader of the Christian community in Jerusalem until his martyrdom in AD 62"; in the *Gospel of Thomas*, "Saying 13, however, indicates that the authority of James was superseded by that of Thomas." See Galatians 2, Acts 15:13; 21:18. Hegesippus' report about James the Just is quoted by Eusebius (*Hist. eccl.* 2.23.4–18). A good collection of all early materials about James can be found in Martin Dibelius, *James* (rev. Heinrich Greeven; Hermeneia; Philadelphia: Fortress, 1976), 11–21; other studies on James include John Painter, *Just James: The Brother of Jesus in History and Tradition* (Columbia, S.C.: University of South Carolina Press, 1997); and Josef Blinzler, *Die Brüder und Schwestern Jesu* (SBS 21; Stuttgart: Katholisches Bibelwerk, 1967). Blinzler interprets the brothers mentioned in Mark 6:3 as cousins (p. 119). John Barber Lightfoot (*The Epistle of St. Paul to the Galatians* [Grand Rapids, Mich.: 1957], 252–91), also discusses the issue of whether James is an apostle. For more on the rivalry, see also Wilckens, *Resurrection*, 13; Alsup, *Post-Resurrection Appearance Stories*, 63–64.

[33]The earliest apocryphal acts, for example, tend to highlight only one apostle or disciple. Over time, these texts begin to feature two or even three figures, but this phenomenon tends to be a later development in the genre. See François Bovon, "Jesus' Missionary

however, the most intriguing feature of this authoritative list is that at the time it was transmitted, the terms "twelve" and the "apostles" had not yet become coterminous. The "twelve" came to be identified with the apostolate only after Paul.[34]

Portraying a figure as an apostle forged an authoritative link between that figure and Jesus, and functioned to legitimize the words in the texts that featured that particular apostle. As a result, a comparison of various texts reveals a rivalry for authority. The next several chapters examine the evidence for apostolic rivalry as it appears in the literary representations of early Christian figures, especially those of Mary Magdalene and Peter. In terms of these two figures, a great deal of scholarly work has already been done on each of them, but the research has tended to focus on one of the individuals — on Mary Magdalene[35]

Speech as Interpreted in the Patristic Commentaries and the Apocryphal Narratives," *Texts and Contexts: Biblical Texts in Their Textual and Situational Contexts* (ed. Tord Fornberg and David Hellhom; Oslo: Scandinavian University Press, 1995), 875–76.

[34] Käsemann, *Romans*, 5.

[35] An impressive number of studies and monographs on Mary Magdalene have appeared in recent years. See, for example, Jane Schaberg, *The Resurrection of Mary Magdalene: Legends, Apocrypha, and the Christian Testament* (New York: Continuum, 2002); Susanne Ruschmann, *Maria von Magdala im Johannesevangelium: Jüngerin — Zeugin — Lebensbotin* (Neutestamentliche Abhandlungen 40; Münster: Aschendorff, 2002); Erika Mohri, *Maria Magdalena: Frauenbilder in Evangelientexten des 1. bis 3. Jahrhunderts* (Marburg: Elwert Verlag, 2000); Katherine Ludwig Jansen, *The Making of the Magdalen: Preaching and Popular Devotion in the Later Middle Ages* (Princeton: Princeton University Press, 2000); Silke Petersen, *"Zerstört die Werke der Weiblichkeit!": Maria Magdalena, Salome und andere Jüngerinnnen Jesu in christlich-gnostischen Schriften* (NHMS 48; Leiden: Brill, 1999), with extensive bibliography on pp. 351–71; Antti Marjanen, *The Woman Jesus Loved: Mary Magdalene in the Nag Hammadi Library and Related Documents* (NHMS 40; Leiden: Brill, 1996), also with extensive bibliography; Ingrid Maisch, *Maria Magdalena zwischen Verachtung und Verehrung: Das Bild einer Frau im Spiegel der Jahrhunderte* (Freiburg im Breisgau: Herder, 1996); Esther de Boer, *Mary Magdalene: Beyond the Myth* (Harrisburg, Pa.: TPI, 1997); Mary R. Thompson, *Mary of Magdala: Apostle and Leader* (New York: Paulist Press, 1995); Renate Schmid, *Maria Magdalena in gnostischen Schriften* (Material-Edition 29; Munich: Arbeitsgemeinschaft für Religions- und Welt-anschauungensfragen, 1990); J. Kevin Coyle, "Mary Magdalene in Manichaeism?" *Mus* 104 (1991): 39–55; Maddalena Scopello, "Marie-Madeleine et la tour: *Pistis et sophia*," in *Figures du Nouveau Testament chez les Pères* (CBPa 3; Strasbourg: Centre d'analyse et de documentation patristiques, 1991), 179–96; Carla Ricci, *Mary Magdalene and Many Others: Women Who Followed Jesus* (trans. Paul Burns; Minneapolis: Fortress, 1994); Susan Haskins, *Mary Magdalen: Myth and Metaphor* (New York: Harcourt Brace,

or on Peter,[36] except when they appear together in controversy texts. This research will broaden this study to compare these two figures in conjunction with each other, even in texts in which there is no explicit controversy to see how they fare with respect to apostolic authority.

This study, therefore, deals with what emerges when we find these two figures in the same text. The examination that follows begins by treating six passages that include some of the most well-known accounts of resurrection appearances.[37] It compares and contrasts them specifically with respect to the way the authors portray the primary figures in each text and then widens its scope to evaluate additional noncanonical texts, including some lesser-known Coptic and Syriac versions of resurrection narratives. It was especially the intriguing variations among the primary figures in these resurrection narratives that motivated me to focus on the portrayals of Peter and Mary Magdalene. These are two of the most

---

1993); Richard Atwood, *Mary Magdalene in the New Testament Gospels and Early Tradition* (European University Studies 457; Bern: Peter Lang, 1993); François Bovon, "Le privilège pascal de Marie-Madeleine," *NTS* 30 (1984): 50–62; English translation in François Bovon, *New Testament Traditions and Apocryphal Narratives* (trans. Jane Haapiseva-Hunter; PTMS 36; Allison Park, Pa.: Pickwick, 1994), 147–57, 228–35. A nice summary of Magdalene studies appears in Pamela Thimmes, "Memory and Re-Vision: Mary Magdalene Research since 1975," *CurBS* 6 (1998): 193–226.

[36]Numerous monographs on Peter have appeared in recent years as well. See, for example, Christian Grappe, *Images de Pierre aux deux premiers siècles* (EHPR 75; Paris: Presses Universitaires de France, 1995). Pheme Perkins provides an excellent study in *Peter: Apostle for the Whole Church* (Columbia, S.C.: University of South Carolina Press, 1994). See also Terence Smith, *Petrine Controversies in Early Christianity: Attitudes Toward Peter in Christian Writings of the First Two Centuries* (WUNT 2.15; Tübingen: Mohr [Siebeck], 1985). Throughout his book Smith admirably covers a vast expanse of material and sources offering numerous nuggets of material. See his list for more on the lives of Peter (including references he makes to other lists on pp. 1–2). See also Raymond E. Brown, Karl Donfried, and J. Reumann, eds., *Peter in the New Testament* (Minneapolis/ New York: Augsburg/Paulist Press, 1973). It might have been of more scholarly value had it included more than just the canonical texts in its examination of the role of Peter. Other resources include: Chrysostom Frank, "Petrine Texts in Byzantine Homilies on the Dormition," *Eastern Churches Journal* 6 (1999): 67–84; Carston Thiede, *Simon Peter: From Galilee to Rome* (Grand Rapids, Mich.: Academie Books, 1988); Jacques Dupont, "Les discours de Pierre," in *Nouvelles Études sur les Actes des apôtres* (LD 118; Paris: Cerf, 1984), 58–111; Oscar Cullmann, *Peter: Disciple, Apostle, Martyr: A Historical and Theological Study* (2d ed.; Philadelphia: Westminster, 1962).

[37]Mark 16:1–8; Matt 28:1–10; Luke 24:1–35; John 20:1–18; *Gos. Pet.* 12–14 [50–60], and 1 Cor 15:3–8.

prominent and perhaps the most polemically charged figures in early Christian history, and as a result, many of the discrepancies among the resurrection narratives involve them.[38] This focus will build on research in New Testament scholarship that has uncovered aspects of many patriarchal tendencies within certain branches of early Christianity and their attempts to suppress the significance of women's leadership roles, especially that of Mary Magdalene.[39]

The following survey of particular resurrection narratives is not exhaustive but rather aims at revealing certain discernible patterns in the portrayal of leadership positions. It does so by comparing and contrasting the texts in terms of one particular aspect: the means by which authors portray early Christian figures as having the basis for apostolic authority. This survey can only begin the process of recognizing the complexity of the issues on both a literary and a historical level in the development of apostolic authority. Therefore, even though numerous types of authority existed within early Christian circles,[40] this investigation focuses specifically upon the authority to be an apostle—that is, the authority of being an eyewitness who is thus uniquely qualified to preach or proclaim the good news of a new age in Jesus Christ.

The overall methodology of this book relies on a two-pronged approach to these ancient texts—a literary-rhetorical analysis combined with a historical-critical approach. Each method of inquiry provides clues essential to an understanding of both early literary representations of the apostles and of the implications for how those representations model authoritative leadership roles in the lives of early Christians. A literary analysis of texts assists in determining how the various characters function in a narrative—what roles they play, how they are portrayed, and to whom they are subordinate. By means of this methodology, one may

---

[38]I include, however, brief examinations of the leadership roles of Paul, Philip, and the Beloved Disciple, for reasons explained in chs. 3, 7, and 8.

[39]See Rudolf Pesch, *Das Markusevangelium: Kommentar zu Kap. 8, 27–16, 20* (HTKNT 2/2; Freiburg: Herder, 1977), 545. See also Elisabeth Schüssler Fiorenza's groundbreaking book, *In Memory of Her: A Feminist Theological Reconstruction of Christian Origins* (New York: Crossroad, 1983), which opened the eyes of many to a new understanding of early Christian history and the role of women in it; Elaine Pagels, *The Gnostic Gospels* (New York:Vintage Books, 1981); Bovon, "Mary Magdalene's Paschal Privilege," 50–62.

[40]Types of authority in the early Christian communities included that of prophet, teacher, elder, and bishop (see 1 Cor 12:28).

discern what a given text overtly or covertly appears to be persuading its audience to believe.[41]

This book will examine the portrayals of early Christian leaders in a wide variety of texts because these representations are useful in reconstructing the history of the rhetoric of early Christian leadership. It will further seek to identify through a programmatic presentation of various understandings of apostolic authority the faulty presuppositions and biases that have led to misinterpretations in the past. By combining a revised understanding of the qualifications for apostlehood with an appreciation of certain tendencies within the various appearance narratives, this study aims to illuminate how various leadership roles are either highlighted or marginalized.[42]

This study employs historical-critical analysis to gain insight into the temporal and geographical contexts from which these early Christian texts emerged. The research offered below aims at a critical reconstruction of early Christian history, especially the life settings of the narratives that describe the roles of early Christian leaders following Jesus' death. This examination into the function of authority in the early stages of Christianity concurs with the findings of scholars who by the nineteenth century had already discerned a certain competition among various apostolic figures in the texts in which they were portrayed. These New Testament scholars include leading figures such as Ferdinand Christian Baur and the Tübingen school, followed later by Walter Bauer, Hans von Campenhausen, and others. [43] These scholars gathered substantial evidence to show that

---

[41]For more on rhetorical criticism and/or narrative criticism, see Elisabeth Schüssler Fiorenza, *Rhetoric and Ethic: The Politics of Biblical Studies* (Minneapolis: Fortress, 1999), who differs methodologically from George A. Kennedy, *New Testament Interpretation through Rhetorical Criticism* (Chapel Hill: University of North Carolina Press, 1984). Mark Allen Powell provides a good summary of various methodologies in his book, *What is Narrative Criticism?* (Minneapolis: Fortress, 1990). In general, rhetorical critics seek to discover how a work of literature practices the art of persuasion and achieves its particular effects.

[42]This research builds upon the type of methodology and concepts set forth in Elisabeth Schüssler Fiorenza's work, including a hermeneutics of suspicion and a hermeneutics of remembrance. See, for instance, her *Bread Not Stone: The Challenge of Feminist Biblical Interpretation* (Boston: Beacon, 1984), 15–18, 108, as well as *Rhetoric and Ethic*, 50, 93.

[43]For more on these topics, see Walter F. Bauer, *Orthodoxy and Heresy in Earliest Christianity* (ed. Robert Kraft and Gerhard Krodel; trans. members of the Philadelphia Seminar on Christian Origins; Philadelphia: Fortress, 1971); Campenhausen, *Ecclesiastical Authority and Spiritual Power.*

the early Christian church did not exist as a unified body but rather consisted of distinctive, competing groups that associated themselves with different foundational figures and various theologies. The following study builds upon such foundational scholarship, employing historical-critical method in order to continue to investigate the bases upon which apostolic authority was established and the channels through which it was transmitted. At the time in which many of these earlier scholars were working, however, gender was not a focus for analysis. My own research seeks to push beyond some of these foundational efforts on apostolic authority by delving more deeply into the impact of gender issues on early Christian leadership roles.[44] With the discovery of the Nag Hammadi texts, even more examples of competition among early Christian leaders have come to the fore. Rather than reviewing and summarizing the significant research here, a summary and review of findings will appear in the sections as we touch on each text.

Summary

This book examines instances in which authors chose individual figures from the narratives of Jesus' disciples and represented those figures as apostles, thus allowing each author to claim apostolic derivation for his or her message. It explains how using the name of a particular apostle operated as a persuasive tool in the polemics and apologetics circulating among early Christians.[45]

Gregory of Antioch (d. 593) portrays Jesus as appearing to Mary Magdalene and the other Mary at the tomb and saying to them: "Be the first teachers to the teachers. So that Peter who denied me learns that I can also choose women as apostles" (πρῶται γίνεσθε τῶν διδασκάλων διδάσκαλοι. μαθέτω Πέτρος ὁ ἀρνησάμενός με ὅτι δύναμαι καὶ γυναῖκας ἀποστόλους χειροτονεῖν).[46] This sixth-century quotation

---

[44]With respect to the apostolic role of Mary Magdalene, I am employing what Schüssler Fiorenza calls a "hermeneutics of remembrance." See Schüssler Fiorenza, *Bread Not Stone*, 20.

[45]Campenhausen, *Ecclesiastical Authority and Spiritual Power*, 15.

[46]Gregory of Antioch, *Oratio in Mulieres Unguentiferas. XI*, PG 88.1863–64. See Haskins, *Mary Magdalen*, 92. For more on Peter see also Robert Murray, *Symbols of Church and Kingdom: A Study in Early Syriac Tradition* (Cambridge: Cambridge University Press, 1975), 217.

shows that women's right to be apostles continued to be defended over the centuries. The following chapters ask why it is specifically Peter's name that Gregory of Antioch singles out for convincing on the question of women's apostolicity: Is it merely because Peter represents the leadership of a whole group, or is it because in some way Peter's name specifically comes to the forefront in the issue of gender exclusivity in the matter of teaching and preaching? The following research addresses this question. Because the authority to preach and proclaim the word is still denied to women in certain Christian circles today, this is a historical question with ongoing relevance for our time.[47]

The history of the concept of apostolic authority reflects a legacy of contradictory views within the Christian Church, evident from the earliest documents and continuing into the present.[48] Even the canon itself does not privilege any one opinion, but instead preserves a certain diversity — a diversity mirrored in noncanonical texts as well. Ultimately, however, despite the differences, the preponderance of traditions displays consistency with respect to the importance of receiving a resurrection appearance and a divine calling as key criteria in the attribution of apostleship. This research explores not only the discrepancies among the various canonical and noncanonical texts but also their implications for apostolic authority with regard to Mary Magdalene and others, including Peter.

---

[47]This aspect of eligibility for preaching became relevant for me in my own faith journey when my husband and I decided to make the commitment to go to a Lutheran seminary (Missouri Synod). Ironically, the seminary was prepared to ordain my husband, who had only recently become a Lutheran after I invited him to church; but I, who had been a Lutheran all my life, was refused the right to pursue a Master of Divinity for gender reasons. We subsequently transferred to a Lutheran synod (now the ELCA) that does ordain both women and men for ministry. This incident sparked my interest in the question of the authority to preach. Thus, along with others who approach this issue from multiple perspectives, including liberation theology and experiential approaches, I bring questions from my own current social location as an academic who is trained in historical and literary criticism.

[48]Karen King points out, "In every century including our own, history records women exercising leadership in Christian communities, and in every century that leadership has been contested, beginning in the early church and continuing through contemporary battles over the ordination and ministry of women." See her essay, "Prophetic Power and Women's Authority: The Case of the *Gospel of Mary* (Magdalene)," in *Women Preachers and Prophets through Two Millennia of Christianity* (ed. Beverly Mayne Kienzle and Pamela J. Walker; Berkeley: University of California Press, 1998), 21.

The study thus begins with a focus upon the Gospel of Luke, asking: Since Luke is the only canonical gospel that includes an individual resurrection appearance to Peter, does the special emphasis on Peter in this gospel have a corresponding effect upon the portrayal of Mary Magdalene's status? The same question applies to the Gospel of John, but with respect to the Beloved Disciple. What, if any, effect does the particularly high Johannine esteem of the Beloved Disciple have on the portrayals of Peter and Mary Magdalene?

After comparing and contrasting the roles of Peter and Mary in Luke and John (the two gospels showing the most disparity with respect to apostolic choices), the study examines Matthew and Mark, along with the *Gospel of Peter,* with respect to how each gospel lays the groundwork for apostolic authority in its resurrection narrative. In particular, it compares the resurrection narratives in these texts by noting the presence or absence of a commissioning, which, in addition to an appearance of Jesus, is another key element in establishing authority for leadership positions. This research will therefore compare portrayals of figures specifically named in resurrection traditions, noting which figures receive the first appearance, which receive either a Christophany or an angelophany, which receive a commissioning, and which do not.

The discoveries of new texts, including those from Nag Hammadi, give scholars completely new insights into the diversity of early Christianity. Especially intriguing among these texts are those that portray in narrative form a conflict featuring the figures of Peter and/or Mary Magdalene. An analysis of the roles of these two figures in texts such as the *Gospel of Thomas*, the *Gospel of Mary*, and *Pistis Sophia* raises questions concerning the representation of women in leadership roles. How does the conflict portrayed in a literary text reflect perspectives on apostolic authority, including that of Mary Magdalene or Peter? While these controversy scenes often appear in second- and third-century texts, this research delves into the roots of some of the controversy, present already in the first century in the divergence of early resurrection narratives. Texts such as these that did not become part of the canon provide illuminating details in the legends and traditions surrounding certain apostolic figures. A comparison of two apparently similar texts, the *Acts of Peter* and the *Acts of Paul,* shows that in drawing on the authority of Peter and Paul respectively, these two contemporaneous texts differ drastically in terms of what they advocate, especially with respect to leadership roles for men and women.[49]

The figure or figures whom an author chooses to promote or demote in a text can provide insight into that author's loyalties within the diversity of early Christianity. In fact, even in the process of translating a text into another language, sometimes the status or even the identity of the key actor in a narrative changes. Certain resurrection appearance narratives, for example, that otherwise closely resemble one another, vary with respect to the names of the recipient or recipients of the appearance. Thus certain Syriac and Coptic texts, interestingly, portray not Mary Magdalene but Mary, the mother of Jesus, conversing with Jesus in the garden in his first resurrection appearance. The next section, therefore, examines which texts portray different recipients of the first resurrection appearances and suggests possible reasons for such changes.

Finally, this study returns once again to the initial question of the definition of apostleship and highlights the most important differences even within the New Testament concerning the qualifications necessary for being an apostle. It specifically examines the concept of the "twelve apostles" and compares it to the portrayals of other early church leaders who could and did qualify to be called an apostle. It will look intensively at two early traditions of apostolic authority concerning Mary Magdalene and Peter and the path each eventually took.

---

[49]Apocryphal texts such as these, although similarly named in genre are not necessarily similar, "L'impression qui se dégage des différentes études examinées est que nos textes ne correspondent exactement à aucun genre de la littérature antique." Jean-Daniel Kaestli, "Les principales orientations de la recherche sur les Actes apocryphes des apôtres," in *Les Actes apocryphes des apôtres: christianisme et monde païen* (ed. François Bovon et al.; Geneva: Labor et Fides, 1981), 49–67; esp. 67.

CHAPTER TWO

Apostolic Authority in the Gospel of Luke

This chapter will demonstrate how the role of Mary Magdalene as a resurrection witness in the Gospel of Luke differs significantly from her role as a resurrection witness in the other canonical gospels. It is Luke alone among the canonical gospels that claims that the risen Lord first appeared exclusively to Peter. This significant difference provides the strongest evidence for the thesis that the Gospel of Luke attempts to establish and defend the primacy of Peter over the other apostles.[1] The Gospel of Luke rather consistently differs from the other gospels by privileging Peter in its portrayal of the disciples. Applying the methodology of redaction criticism reveals how the author of Luke shapes traditions and source material to enhance the standing of Peter. The evangelist shapes those traditions in three discernible ways: by supplementing the Petrine tradition with material found nowhere else,[2] by omitting source material unfavorable to Peter, and by modifying extant narratives about him. Thus, among the canonical gospel writers,

---

[1]Cullmann, *Peter*, 23–26; Pesch, *Das Markusevangelium*, 2:545. Schüssler Fiorenza (*In Memory of Her*, 51) states, "The Lukan stress on Peter as the primary Easter witness must be situated within the early Christian discussion of whether Peter or Mary Magdalene is the first resurrection witness." See also Perkins, *Peter*, 84.

[2]For texts on the *Sondergut* in Luke, see Karl Bornhäuser, *Studien zum Sondergut des Lukas* (Gütersloh: Bertelsmann, 1934); Gerd Petzke, *Das Sondergut des Evangeliums*

Luke's unique presentation of Peter as the recipient of an individual resurrection appearance is the keystone of the evangelist's overall program for enhancing the status of Peter as a leader of the early church. I begin with a detailed examination of that program, turning then to a consideration of its effect on the portrayal of Mary Magdalene in the Gospel of Luke. Finally, I relate Luke's portrayal of Mary Magdalene to the roles assigned to women in the gospel as a whole.

Lukan Supplementation of Traditions about Peter

Beginning with the introduction of Peter into discipleship, the author of Luke–Acts assigns to Peter more prominence than the other three canonical gospels do. First, this author provides a significantly more developed account of Peter's call than either Matthew or Mark. Mark's version requires only three verses to depict Jesus calling both Simon Peter and his brother Andrew to discipleship (Mark 1:16–18). Matthew's version likewise requires only three verses and depicts Jesus calling them both (Matt 4:18–20). Luke's version, on the other hand, requires a full eleven verses to depict the incident (Luke 5:1–11)[3] and focuses specifically on Simon Peter while not mentioning Andrew once, despite the significant increase in narrative detail.

---

nach Lukas (Zürcher Werkkommentare zur Bibel; Zürich: Theologischer Verlag, 1990); and Kim Paffenroth, *The Story of Jesus according to L* (JSNTSup 147; Sheffield: Sheffield Academic Press, 1997).

[3]The focus is so completely on Peter in these eleven verses that James and John, though mentioned in passing in v. 10 of this passage, are also not specifically called as they are in Matthew and Mark. For more on the calling see François Bovon, *Das Evangelium nach Lukas* (3 vols.; Zürich: Benziger/Neukirchen-Vluyn: Neukirchener Verlag, 1989–96), 1: 227–36; I. Howard Marshall, *The Gospel of Luke: A Commentary on the Greek Text* (Grand Rapids, Mich.: Eerdmans, 1978), 199–206; Samuel O. Abogunrin, "The Three Variant Accounts of Peter's Call: A Critical and Theological Examination of the Texts," *NTS* 31 (1985): 587–602; Jindřich Mánek, "Fishers of Men," *NovT* 2 (1958): 138–41; Günter Klein, "Die Berufung des Petrus," *ZNW* 58 (1967): 1–44; Rudolf Pesch, "La rédaction lucanienne du logion des pêcheurs d'hommes (Lc. V, 10c)," *ETL* 46 (1970): 413–32; Klaus Zillessen, "Das Schiff des Petrus und die Gefährten vom anderen Schiff," *ZNW* 57 (1966): 137–39; George E. Rice, "Luke's Thematic Use of the Call to Discipleship," *AUSS* 19 (1981): 51–58; Heinz Schürmann, "La promesse à Simon-Pierre: Lc 5, 1–11," *AsSeign* 36 (1974): 63–70; Jean Delorme, "Luc V.1–11: Analyse structurale et histoire de la rédaction," *NTS* 18 (1971/1972): 331–50.

When Jesus addresses Simon Peter in Luke 5, proclaiming that "from now on you will catch people," the "you" is expressed by a grammatically singular verb, ἔσῃ (v. 10). Thus in this passage Jesus singles out Peter from the group, whereas in the parallel passages in both Matthew (4:19) and Mark (1:17), Jesus states "I will make you (ὑμᾶς) fishers of people," using the plural pronoun to include all the disciples. Moreover, only in Luke does Jesus specifically pick Simon's boat and then ask for him to push out a little from the land (v. 3). This Lukan passage continues by describing Simon Peter's recognition of the divinity of Jesus. As Pheme Perkins notes, "When Peter responds to the miraculous catch with the confession of his own sinfulness (Luke 5:8), he acknowledges the holiness of God present in Jesus (cf. Isa. 6:5)."[4] Luke portrays Peter's confession here as an exhibition of Peter's astuteness in response to the teaching and miracles, and only in Luke does Peter make a confession of faith at this point.

Another example of the Lukan gospel's use of supplementary material to emphasize Peter's primacy occurs in its account of Jesus' prediction of Peter's denial. All three synoptic gospels record Jesus' prediction that Peter will deny him, but only in Luke does Jesus speak the words that mitigate the prediction.[5] Here Jesus bestows on Peter a special commission that is not granted to the other disciples, telling him: "But I have prayed for you (περὶ σοῦ) in order that your faith may not fail. And when you have turned back, strengthen your brothers."[6] In this additional material that only Luke offers, Jesus proclaims his ongoing support for Peter rather than a condemnation of Peter's behavior.

---

[4]Perkins, *Peter*, 84. Some scholars believe Luke 5:1–11 to be a misplaced appearance story, especially because of its close resemblance to the narrative at the lake in John 21 and the end of the *Gospel of Peter*.

[5]Luke sometimes adds to the Markan source sentences, such as this one, that promise leadership to Peter. Sometimes these additions explain the disciples' actions. See Perkins, *Peter*, 84; Martin Dibelius, *Die Formgeschichte des Evangeliums* (3rd ed.; Tübingen: Mohr [Siebeck], 1959), 201.

[6]ἐγὼ δὲ ἐδεήθην περὶ σοῦ ἵνα μὴ ἐκλίπῃ ἡ πίστις σου· καὶ σύ ποτε ἐπιστρέψας στήρισον τοὺς ἀδελφούς σου (Luke 22:32). The σοῦ (a singular pronoun) in the text "limits the interest of Jesus to Peter who is to be the means by which the other disciples will be strengthened" (Marshall, *Luke*, 821). "Lk 22:31f. stand apart from the rest of the tradition, and therefore the saying is open to the suspicion of reflecting a theological development" (ibid., 819).

The rhetorical effect of Jesus' words is to highlight Peter's role by indicating that, despite his weakness, Peter is the one he has chosen to strengthen the others. By placing these words in the narrative, the author provides a redemption for Peter's actions even before the denial takes place.[7] The incident of the denial, therefore, which could have served to diminish Peter's status as a leader among the disciples, is recast as an opportunity for Jesus to express his support of Peter in anticipation of the crisis of Jesus' crucifixion.

The Lukan gospel also provides a few minor additions to the traditions concerning Peter, again singling him out in the incident of the woman with a flow of blood. In Mark, when this woman touches Jesus and he asks who touched him, the reply comes from "his disciples" (5:31). In Luke, however, it is Peter alone who replies to the question (Luke 8:45).[8] Elsewhere, in both Matthew (24:44) and Luke (12:40) Jesus notes that the Son of Man will arrive at an unexpected hour. At this point in Jesus' discourse only Luke gives Peter a speaking part: "Lord, are you saying this parable to us or to everyone?" (12:41). Peter's question concerning parables is almost certainly a Lukan redaction,[9] providing Peter with additional dialogue and thus more prominence in the text. Lastly, in Matthew and Mark, Jesus sends either "the disciples" (Matt 26:17) or "two of his disciples" (Mark 14:13) to prepare the Passover meal, but Luke's gospel supplements the known tradition by specifically naming Peter as one of the two (Luke 22:8).[10]

Lukan Omission of Traditions about Peter

Not only does the Lukan evangelist supplement the gospel tradition with pro-Petrine material, but it appears that this author also frequently

[7]Eta Linnemann, "Die Verleugnung des Petrus," *ZTK* 63 (1966): 1–32. Linnemann does not believe in the historicity of Peter's denials but believes that the story about Peter is simply a concretizing of the general denial of all the disciples. While this is possible, it does not explain why it is always specifically Peter's name that is singled out in connection with the denial. Even the *Acts of Peter*, a pro-Petrine text, refers to Peter's denial (*Acts Pet.* 7).

[8]For more on Peter as spokesperson, see Dupont, "Les discours de Pierre," 58–111, esp. 108–9.

[9]Bovon, *Lukas*, 2:324; Brown, Donfried, and Reumann, eds., *Peter*, 114.

[10]Christopher F. Evans, *Saint Luke* (TPINTC; London: SCM, 1990), 778; Marshall, *Luke*, 791.

removes or mitigates any synoptic tradition concerning Peter that could be interpreted to his detriment. For instance, one of the most potentially damaging descriptions of Peter's behavior in the synoptic gospels follows Jesus' prediction of the crucifixion. All three synoptic gospels agree closely on the wording of that prediction:

Gospel of Mark:	**Gospel of Matthew:**	**Gospel of Luke:**
δεῖ τὸν υἱὸν τοῦ ἀνθρώπου πολλὰ παθεῖν καὶ ἀποδοκιμασθῆναι ὑπὸ τῶν πρεσβυτέρων καὶ τῶν ἀρχιερέων καὶ τῶν γραμματέων καὶ ἀποκτανθῆναι καὶ μετὰ τρεῖς ἡμέρας ἀναστῆναι.	δεῖ αὐτὸν εἰς Ἱεροσόλυμα ἀπελθεῖν καὶ πολλὰ παθεῖν ἀπὸ τῶν πρεσβυτέρων καὶ ἀρχιερέων καὶ γραμματέων καὶ ἀποκτανθῆναι καὶ τῇ τρίτῃ ἡμέρᾳ ἐγερθῆναι.	δεῖ τὸν υἱὸν τοῦ ἀνθρώπου πολλὰ παθεῖν καὶ ἀποδοκιμασθῆναι ἀπὸ τῶν πρεσβυτέρων καὶ ἀρχιερέων καὶ γραμματέων καὶ ἀποκτανθῆναι καὶ τῇ τρίτῃ ἡμέρᾳ ἐγερθῆναι.
the Son of Man must suffer many things and be rejected by the elders, chief priests and scribes, and he must be killed and after three days rise again. (8:31)	he must go to Jerusalem and suffer many things at the hands of the elders, chief priests and scribes, and he must be killed and on the third day be raised. (16:21)	the Son of Man must suffer many things and be rejected by the elders, chief priests and scribes, and he must be killed and on the third day be raised. (9:22)

Following this prediction, however, there is a significant difference between the description of events by Mark and Matthew as opposed to that of Luke.

Gospel of Mark:	**Gospel of Matthew:**	**Gospel of Luke:**
καὶ προσλαβόμενος ὁ Πέτρος αὐτὸν ἤρξατο ἐπιτιμᾶν αὐτῷ.	καὶ προσλαβόμενος αὐτὸν ὁ Πέτρος ἤρξατο ἐπιτιμᾶν αὐτῷ λέγων, ἵλεώς σοι, κύριε· οὐ μὴ ἔσται σοι τοῦτο.	[no parallel]

| Peter took him aside and began to rebuke him. (8:32b) | Peter took him aside and began to rebuke him. "Never, Lord!" he said. "This shall never happen to you!" (16:22) |

Mark and Matthew agree that Peter rebuked Jesus, but Luke has no such narrative, even though the agreement in the previous text indicates that they are working from a common tradition. In Mark and Matthew, Jesus in turn rebukes Peter:

Gospel of Mark:	**Gospel of Matthew:**	**Gospel of Luke:**
ὁ δὲ ἐπιστραφεὶς καὶ ἰδὼν τοὺς μαθητὰς αὐτοῦ ἐπετίμησεν Πέτρῳ καὶ λέγει, ὕπαγε ὀπίσω μου, Σατανᾶ, ὅτι οὐ φρονεῖς τὰ τοῦ θεοῦ ἀλλὰ τὰ τῶν ἀνθρώπων.	ὁ δὲ στραφεὶς εἶπεν τῷ Πέτρῳ, ὕπαγε ὀπίσω μου, Σατανᾶ· σκάνδαλον εἶ ἐμοῦ, ὅτι οὐ φρονεῖς τὰ τοῦ θεοῦ ἀλλὰ τὰ τῶν ἀνθρώπων.	[no parallel]

| But when he turned and looked at his disciples, he rebuked Peter and said, "Get behind me, Satan! You do not have in mind the concerns of God, but the concerns of humans." (8:33) | But he turned and said to Peter, "Get behind me, Satan! You are a stumbling block to me because you do not have in mind the concerns of God, but the concerns of humans." (16:23) |

Luke not only sharply departs from the other synoptics by omitting Peter's rebuke of Jesus; more significantly, Luke omits the harsh rebuke that Peter receives in turn from Jesus that includes, in both Mark and Matthew, the hint of a demonic force operating through Peter.[11] Luke has exorcised from his account both Peter's objectionable behavior and the verb ἐπιτιμάω, "to rebuke."

---

[11]Bovon, *Lukas*, 1:476–80; Joseph A. Fitzmyer, *The Gospel According to Luke* (2 vols.; AB 28–28a; Garden City, N. Y.: Doubleday, 1985), 1:613–21; Marshall, *Luke*, 237–40; Evans, *Luke*, 369–71.

Curiously, the Lukan text immediately following the rebuke once again closely parallels the wording of the Markan source material:

Gospel of Mark:	Gospel of Matthew:	Gospel of Luke:
εἴ τις θέλει ὀπίσω μου ἀκολουθεῖν, ἀπαρνησάσθω ἑαυτὸν καὶ ἀράτω τὸν σταυρὸν αὐτοῦ καὶ ἀκολουθείτω μοι.	εἴ τις θέλει ὀπίσω μου ἐλθεῖν, ἀπαρνησάσθω ἑαυτὸν καὶ ἀράτω τὸν σταυρὸν αὐτοῦ καὶ ἀκολουθείτω μοι.	εἴ τις θέλει ὀπίσω μου ἔρχεσθαι, ἀρνησάσθω ἑαυτὸν καὶ ἀράτω τὸν σταυρὸν αὐτοῦ καθ' ἡμέραν, καὶ ἀκολουθείτω μοι.
"if anyone wishes to come after me, he must deny himself and take up his cross and follow me." (8:34)	"if anyone wishes to come after me, he must deny himself and take up his cross and follow me." (16:24)	"if anyone wishes to come after me, he must deny himself and take up his cross daily and follow me." (9:23)

Since there are no reasons to assume that the author of Luke worked from a defective copy of Mark or that the preserved Lukan gospel itself is defective, it appears that the omission is deliberate on Luke's part.[12]

Likewise, when the synoptics record Jesus' prediction that Peter will deny him, Mark and Matthew agree on Peter's response to the prediction:

Gospel of Mark:	Gospel of Matthew:	Gospel of Luke:
ἐὰν δέῃ με συναποθανεῖν σοι, οὐ μή σε ἀπαρνήσομαι.	κἂν δέῃ με σὺν σοὶ ἀποθανεῖν, οὐ μή σε ἀπαρνήσομαι.	[no parallel]

[12]Marshall judges Luke's omission of Markan material as "doubtlessly deliberate." Marshall, *Luke*, 364. Marshall provides five possible reasons for the omission, none of which, however, is Luke's desire to portray Peter more positively. His possibilities are: (1) The omitted section is repetitious of earlier material and does not materially add to the presentation of Jesus as the Messiah. (2) Luke had to omit material from Mark in order to accommodate his own extra material within a book of convenient length. (3) More positively, Luke wished to move straight from the feeding miracle (and the preceding incidents) to the christological confession that was aroused by it. (4) It is possible that Luke knew of a tradition which joined together the feeding miracle and Peter's confession, as in John 6; note, however that John 6 retains the story of Jesus walking on the water. (5) Possibly also Luke wished to maintain the unity of the scene in Galilee and to avoid Mark's description of Jesus' work in Gentile territory.

"Even if I have to die with you, I will never deny you." (14:31)	"Even if I have to die with you, I will never deny you." (26:35)

Intriguingly, in Luke this statement is absent as well. Perhaps the omission is an example of Luke's avoidance of having Peter emphatically state a position that according to tradition proves to be wrong.[13] We will see below that Luke employs this avoidance technique elsewhere, as in the account of Jesus' prediction of Peter's denial.

Although Jesus regularly rebukes Peter in Mark and Matthew, nowhere in Luke does Jesus ever actually rebuke him. For instance, although both Matthew and Mark portray Jesus as specifically chiding Peter for sleeping in the garden, Luke presents the tradition differently:

Gospel of Mark:	Gospel of Matthew:	Gospel of Luke:
καὶ ἔρχεται καὶ εὑρίσκει αὐτοὺς καθεύδοντας, καὶ λέγει τῷ Πέτρῳ, Σίμων, καθεύδεις οὐκ ἴσχυσας μίαν ὥραν γρηγορῆσαι.	καὶ ἔρχεται πρὸς τοὺς μαθητὰς καὶ εὑρίσκει αὐτοὺς καθεύδοντας, καὶ λέγει τῷ Πέτρῳ, οὕτως οὐκ ἰσχύσατε μίαν ὥραν γρηγορῆσαι μετ' ἐμοῦ.	καὶ ἀναστὰς ἀπὸ τῆς προσευχῆς ἐλθὼν πρὸς τοὺς μαθητὰς εὗρεν κοιμωμένους αὐτοὺς ἀπὸ τῆς λύπης, καὶ εἶπεν αὐτοῖς, τί καθεύδετε; ἀναστάντες προσεύχεσθε, ἵνα μὴ εἰσέλθητε εἰς πειρασμόν.
And he came and found them [his disciples] sleeping. "Simon," he said to Peter, "are you asleep? So could you not keep watch for one hour?" (14:37)	Then he returned to his disciples and found them sleeping. "Could you men not keep watch with me for one hour?" he asked Peter. (26:40)	When he rose from prayer and went back to the disciples, he found them sleeping from sorrow. "Why are you sleeping?" he asked them. "Get up and pray so that you may not fall into temptation." (22:45–46)

---

[13]Another possibility is that Luke is choosing to follow a different source at this point.

Mark and Matthew give similar accounts of this rebuke with Jesus specifically singling out Peter. The Lukan text states merely that Jesus addresses "them" and speaks to the disciples as a group.[14] This omission of Peter's name in Luke belongs to a consistent pattern whereby the author programmatically alters traditional material to present Peter in the best possible light. Additional omissions also occur in Luke, but these are some of the most significant ones.[15]

Lukan Modification of Traditions about Peter

Sometimes Luke deals with unflattering source material concerning Peter not by omitting it but by modifying it. One such modification of Petrine material by Luke occurs in the account of the transfiguration. Although the Markan account that Peter "did not know what to say, for they were terrified"[16] indicates that he reacted out of ignorance and

---

[14]The way in which the author of Luke improves the portrayal of the disciples, especially Peter, also becomes apparent at the Mount of Olives. In Mark, Jesus finds them "sleeping" (14: 37); in Matthew, Jesus also finds them "sleeping" (26:40); only in Luke does the author add the small explanatory note that Jesus finds them "sleeping for sorrow (κοιμωμένους ἀπὸ τῆς λύπης)" (22:45). Fitzmyer parallels this explanation to another Lukan explanation of Peter's uncomprehending remark in 9:33e (see Mark 9:6). Fitzmyer (*Luke*, 2:1442) includes additional information on the Greek word λύπη, a cardinal passion related to sin and guilt, which Luke attributes only to the disciples; this gospel excises any mention of Jesus' emotions.

[15]Luke also omits Jesus' cursing of the fig tree and Peter's calling attention to it. One might argue that the efforts of the author of Luke to present the character of Peter more positively are merely part of an overall effort to improve the impression of the group of disciples that includes Peter. Luke, for example, omits the mention of the disciples' flight at the time of the crucifixion, as recorded in Mark and Matthew. However, the author's alterations do not always improve the status of the disciples as a whole. The author of Luke still has the disciples ask a question that could be interpreted as a misunderstanding, for example, but does not mention Peter by name in the incident. Thus when Peter, James, John, and Andrew ask "when the Temple will be destroyed" (13:3)—the question could be interpreted as a misunderstanding on the part of these disciples—but in Luke the question is posed by an anonymous "they" (21: 7). As mentioned, at the Mount of Olives, Luke's Jesus still rebukes the disciples for sleeping, but does not specifically mention Peter's name. Nor do the other individual disciples receive the kind of increase in positive emphasis that Peter does in Luke. Andrew, Peter's brother, is actually less significant in the Gospel of Luke; he does not appear in the healing of Peter's mother-in-law as he does in Mark's version (Mark 1:29, Luke 4:38) and is altogether missing from Luke's narrative of Peter's calling (Luke 5:1–11). See Brown, Donfried, and Reumann, eds., *Peter in the New Testament*, 112.

[16]οὐ γὰρ ᾔδει τί ἀποκριθῇ, ἔκφοβοι γὰρ ἐγένοντο (9:6).

fear, the Lukan account shifts away from the fear and subtly softens the text saying simply that Peter "did not know what he said."[17] The author of Luke modifies source material from Mark in numerous other instances, including the prediction of Peter's denial. In this case, the words of Jesus' prediction with the cock crowing is very similar across all three texts, but Luke's portrayal of Peter's response again differs significantly:

Gospel of Mark:	Gospel of Matthew:	Gospel of Luke:
ὁ δὲ Πέτρος ἔφη αὐτῷ, εἰ καὶ πάντες σκανδαλισθήσονται, ἀλλ᾽ οὐκ ἐγώ.	ἀποκριθεὶς δὲ ὁ Πέτρος εἶπεν αὐτῷ, εἰ πάντες σκανδαλισθήσονται ἐν σοί, ἐγὼ οὐδέποτε σκανδαλισθήσομαι.	ὁ δὲ εἶπεν αὐτῷ, κύριε, μετὰ σοῦ ἕτοιμός εἰμι καὶ εἰς φυλακὴν καὶ εἰς θάνατον πορεύεσθαι.
Peter declared, "Even if all fall away, I never will." (14:29)	Peter replied, "Even if all fall away, I will never fall away." (26:33)	But he replied, "Lord I am ready to go with you to prison and to death." (22:33)

The words of Peter as recorded by both Matthew and Mark are, of course, according to tradition ultimately proven wrong. In Luke, however, Peter does not mistakenly claim that he will not make such a betrayal. The words that the author of Luke places on Peter's lips are, "Lord, I am ready to go with you to prison and to death." These are words that agree with certain early Christian traditions about Peter's career after the resurrection. Here again is another example of how the alterations or omissions that the author of Luke imposes upon the source material serve to represent Peter in a better light.

Confirmation of this pattern of representation appears in the ongoing narrative of Peter's denial in the courtyard:

---

[17]μὴ εἰδὼς ὃ λέγει (9:33). Perkins, *Peter,* 84–85. On this passage, see also Bovon, *Lukas,* 1:497–98.

Gospel of Mark:	Gospel of Matthew:	Gospel of Luke:
ὁ δὲ ἤρξατο ἀναθεμα- τίζειν καὶ ὀμνύναι ὅτι οὐκ οἶδα τὸν ἄνθρωπον τοῦτον ὃν λέγετε.	τότε ἤρξατο καταθε- ματίζειν καὶ ὀμνύειν ὅτι οὐκ οἶδα τὸν ἄνθρωπον.	ἄνθρωπε, οὐκ οἶδα ὃ λέγεις.
He began to call down curses on himself and he swore, "I do not know this man you are talking about." (14:71a)	Then he began to call down curses on him- self and he swore, "I do not know the man." (26:74a)	"Man, I do not know what you are talking about!" (22:60a)

Both Mark and Matthew record that Peter denied that he knew Jesus and cursed or swore when he did so. Luke's response again departs from the other two synoptic gospels by omitting the cursing and replacing it with the innocuous phrase of Peter not understanding what the questioner is talking about. Perkins points out that this phrasing shields Peter from actually articulating that he did not know Jesus.[18] The result in Luke is a softening of the intensity of Peter's misguided denials, which are so strongly portrayed in the other two gospels. Thus the pattern of Luke's improvement of Peter's representation is easily discernible throughout the gospel, but it is nowhere more significant than in the portrayal of an exclusive resurrection appearance to Simon Peter, which marks the culmination of the Lukan program.

The Most Significant Supplementary Tradition in Luke (24:33–34)

The reference to Jesus' exclusive resurrection appearance to Simon Peter (24:33–34) is peculiar to Luke among the canonical gospels and is the most outstanding example of the prominence of Peter in this gospel.[19] Given the syntactical awkwardness of this reference, embedded in the well-known passage describing the travelers on the road to Emmaus, it is worth quoting in full:

[18]Perkins, *Peter*, 86.

[19]Paul Schubert, "The Structure and Significance of Luke 24," *Neutestamentliche Studien für Rudolf Bultmann* (BZNW 21; Berlin: Töpelmann, 1954), 169.

[33] καὶ ἀναστάντες αὐτῇ τῇ ὥρᾳ ὑπέστρεψαν εἰς Ἰερουσαλήμ, καὶ εὗρον ἠθροισμένους τοὺς ἕνδεκα καὶ τοὺς σὺν αὐτοῖς, [34] λέγοντας ὅτι ὄντως ἠγέρθη ὁ κύριος καὶ ὤφθη Σίμωνι.

[33] They got up and returned at once to Jerusalem. And they found the eleven and those with them, gathered together [34] and saying, "The Lord has risen indeed and has appeared to Simon."

A source-critical analysis shows that by the time this section appears in the Gospel of Luke, the use of Mark as a source has been discontinued. [20] The material in this passage, then, is either a Lukan composition or a tradition that comes from "L," the body of special source material found only in Luke. [21] The language of the text strongly suggests that it is a Lukan composition, [22] as the vocabulary of verses 33 and 35 is thoroughly Lukan. [23] Guillaume indicates that the passage is Lukan in narrative, vocabulary, style, structure, and topics. [24] Not only is the language Lukan, but the text is filled with Lukan theological motifs. [25]

---

[20] Wolfgang Dietrich, *Das Petrusbild der lukanischen Schriften* (BWANT 5, Heft 14; Stuttgart: Kohlhammer, 1972). This monograph presents an in-depth study of Peter in Luke–Acts, with a portrayal of the psychological development of Peter.

[21] Fitzmyer, *Luke*, 2:1554. "L" is not necessarily a single source. "The diversity of the special materials included in Luke's Gospel warns against the assumption of just one major special source for Luke," writes Helmut Koester (*Ancient Christian Gospels: Their History and Development* [Philadelphia: Trinity Press, 1992], 337). See also Richard J. Dillon, *From Eye-Witnesses to Ministers of the Word: Tradition and Composition in Luke 24* (AnBib 82; Rome: Biblical Institute Press, 1978), 69–155. Because of the Lukan stamp in vocabulary and themes, the passage does not appear to be a later redaction.

[22] Joachim Jeremias, *Die Sprache des Lukasevangeliums: Redaktion und Tradition im Nicht-Markusstoff des dritten Evangeliums* (Göttingen: Vandenhoeck & Ruprecht, 1980), 319–20.

[23] Evans, *Luke*, 914.

[24] Jean-Marie Guillaume, *Luc interprète des anciennes traditions sur la résurrection de Jésus* (EBib; Paris: Gabalda, 1979), 69–81.

[25] Fitzmyer, *Luke,* 2:1557–59. Among the vocabulary words that are Lukan is the use of the label, "the eleven." Not counting the Markan appendix (16:14), "the eleven" appears in five places in the New Testament; with only one Matthean exception (Matt 28:16), the remainder of the references are in Lukan material: Luke 24:9, 33, and Acts 1:26, 2:14. See Joseph Plevnik, "'The Eleven and Those with Them' according to Luke," *CBQ* 40 (1978): 205–11. Another indication of Lukan provenance is the use of the word κύριος. Although the title of "Lord" as a designation of Jesus is almost entirely absent from Matthew and Mark (except in the vocative case, which is nontechnical), it is one of the most common designations of Jesus in Luke. "It occurs in the narrative for the first time in Luke 7:13, and thereafter some sixteen times,

Vincent Taylor analyzes the episode in detail, noting the characteristic Lukan vocabulary and constructions, and concludes that "Luke has embellished an existing tradition with unusual freedom."[26]

The text of the Emmaus encounter contains numerous puzzling aspects. For instance, this passage portrays the two disciples running all the way back to Jerusalem to share their experience, and yet they are not the first ones to speak in their meeting with the eleven. Instead, the eleven preempt the Emmaus pair with news of their own. The group tells the two disciples from Emmaus that "the Lord has risen and has appeared to Simon."[27] Only secondarily, then, do the two disciples share their experience on the road to Emmaus, thereby giving primacy to the report of a resurrection appearance of Jesus to Simon Peter.[28] The accusative form of the participle λέγοντας ("saying") indicates that it is the gathered group that reports the appearance of Jesus to Simon. The alternate reading λέγοντες preserved by Codex D, however, makes the participle nominative, thus indicating that the Emmaus travelers report to the gathered group that "the Lord has risen and has appeared to Simon"—as in fact a reader might expect them to do. On the other hand, Peter is not present at the Emmaus encounter, and it is unclear how the two disciples would know that Jesus has appeared to him also. The textual variation between λέγοντας and λέγοντες highlights the awkwardness of this text.

The only other possible canonical reference to a solitary appearance to Peter is 1 Cor 15:5, where he heads the list of witnesses. It is uncertain whether Luke knew the account of an appearance to Peter alone from the formula in 1 Corinthians (which Paul says he received from tradition) or

---

always in non-Marcan sections" (Marshall, *Luke*, 166). It is uncertain whether Luke has taken over the use of the title from his sources (see Friedrich Rehkopf, *Die lukanische Sonderquelle* [WUNT 5; Tübingen: Mohr, 1959], 95); and Ferdinand Hahn, *Christologische Hoheitstitel: Ihre Geschichte im frühen Christentum* (4th ed.; FRLANT 83; Göttingen: Vandenhoeck & Ruprecht, 1974], 88–91) or has introduced it himself (so Philipp Vielhauer, *Aufsätze zum Neuen Testament* [TB 31; Munich: Kaiser, 1965], 154–56). "The fact that the title is not introduced by Luke into Marcan material strongly suggests that his usage rests to some extent upon his sources" (Marshall, *Gospel of Luke*, 166).

[26]Vincent Taylor, *The Passion Narrative of St. Luke: A Critical and Historical Investigation* (ed. O. E. Evans; SNTSMS 19; Cambridge: University Press, 1972), 109–12; see also Fitzmyer, *Luke*, 2:1555.

[27]Fitzmyer, *Luke*, 2:1559.

[28]Roland Meynet, *L'Évangile selon Saint Luc: Analyse rhétorique* (2 vols.; Paris: Cerf, 1988), 2:237.

whether he received it as an isolated tradition.[29] Whatever the case may be, what is interesting about Luke 24:34 is that Luke asserts here, in awkward syntax, the temporal priority of the appearance to Simon (Peter)—"despite the apparent priority of the appearance on the way to, and at, Emmaus."[30] It appears that the theological agenda of the author takes precedence over the narrative flow of the story. This singling out of Peter gives him the status of primacy among those who receive a resurrection appearance from Jesus. This factor, along with the supplementation, omission, and modifications of many other traditions, shows that Luke represents Peter more prominently and more favorably than any other canonical gospel. It is likewise probably no accident that Peter is the last of the twelve to be mentioned by name in the Gospel of Luke and the first of the twelve to be mentioned by name in Acts.[31] In summary, the status of Peter is portrayed with such prominence in the Gospel of Luke that it can legitimately be described as a pro-Petrine text.[32]

The Portrayal of Mary Magdalene in the Gospel of Luke

Because the Gospel of Luke assigns Jesus' first resurrection appearance to Peter, Mary Magdalene correspondingly loses the primacy that she holds as a resurrection witness in the other canonical gospels, especially Matthew and John.[33] It is thus worth examining how the portrayal of

---

[29]Evans, *Luke*, 915.

[30]Ibid.

[31]Brown, Donfried, and Reumann, eds., *Peter in the New Testament*, 128.

[32]The book of Acts has often been considered a pro-Pauline text, especially since the majority of chapters (7, 9–28) feature him and his missionary activity. If one evaluates this text on the basis of apostolic authority, however, this book clearly gives the primacy to Peter not only over Philip and John, but significantly over Paul as well. One sees this diminishment of Paul's status in Acts especially in comparison to the two claims that Paul makes for himself in his epistles: his status as an apostle and his priority as a missionary to the Gentiles. Both of these elements are diminished in Acts.

[33]Mark is not included in the resurrection appearance comparisons above because it is generally accepted that Mark probably ends at 16:8, on the basis of the earliest and most reliable texts. If so, it does not contain a resurrection appearance by Jesus, but only an epiphany from a young angelic being who commissions the women to tell the news, to which the women react by fleeing the tomb. Both variant additions to this ending attempt to correct whatever point Mark was making if indeed the text ended there. The Gospel of Mark will be discussed further in regards to the commissioning in ch. 4, below.

Mary Magdalene fares respectively in the rest of this gospel. A comparison with the other early Christian gospels indicates that the Lukan author has significantly shaped the Magdalene tradition. When presenting material concerning Mary Magdalene, Luke often parallels Matthew and Mark but diminishes her position among the disciples in subtle ways. For instance, both Mark and Matthew portray the women, including Mary Magdalene, as watching Jesus' crucifixion from afar, and both gospels identify them as women who had followed Jesus from Galilee, ministering to *him*—that is, to Jesus alone (Mark 15:41; Matt 27:55).[34] Interestingly, the Lukan text introduces Mary Magdalene along with the other women much earlier in the narrative than either Matthew or Mark but describes the women as ministering to "them"—that is, to the disciples (Luke 8:3).[35] Schaberg argues that Luke's portrayal of the women ministering to the disciples is consistent with his general tendency to subordinate the roles that the women among Jesus' followers may fill.[36] In Luke, Mary Magdalene is introduced into the gospel as someone who has been healed and who contributes financial support; in other words, she models what this author represents as appropriate roles for women: beneficiaries and benefactors, not leaders.

Another example of Lukan manipulation of material occurs in Luke's description of the women at the cross. In Luke, Mary Magdalene stands at the foot of the cross as she does in Mark (15:40), Matthew (27:56), and John (19:25). Luke, however, does not at this point in the narrative (23:49) name these women at the cross, referring to them merely as the women who had followed him from Galilee (Luke names them only later, coming back from the tomb [24:10], as noted below). Also, only the Lukan narrative of the passion scene portrays others standing with the women, thereby reducing the women's role as the lone witnesses to Jesus' death. Although the other gospels describe the male disciples as fleeing, the Lukan version places additional characters into the crucifixion

---

[34]For the symbolic use of the verb, see also Matt 8:15 and the discussion in Elaine Mary Wainwright, "The Gospel of Matthew," in *A Feminist Commentary*, vol. 2 of *Searching the Scriptures* (New York: Crossroad, 1994), 648–49.

[35]Jane Schaberg, "How Mary Magdalene Became a Whore," *BRev* 8 (1992): 32. Evans interprets Luke: "It also establishes the function of women disciples as material care and not preaching and healing" (Evans, *Luke*, 367); David C. Sim, "The Women Followers of Jesus: The Implications of Luke 8:1–3," *HeyJ* 30 (1989): 51–62.

[36]Schaberg, "How Mary Magdalene Became a Whore," 32.

scene, writing, "But all his acquaintances, including the women who had followed him from Galilee, stood at a distance, watching these events."[37] Not only are the words "all his acquaintances" or "all those known to him" not present in the parallels in Mark and Matthew, but, as Schaberg argues, Luke seems to have added the words "all his acquaintances" into the narrative, as suggested by another grammatical difficulty, the lack of subject-verb agreement between these "acquaintances" and what they were doing. Luke's female witnesses, along with "all his acquaintances," stand on the hill "watching" (ὁρῶσαι), but where context now expects a masculine plural participle in agreement with the male acquaintances, the Lukan text still preserves the feminine plural participle that stands in the source.[38]

In Luke, Mary Magdalene also watches as Jesus is laid in the tomb (Mark 15:46–47, Matt 27:59–61; Luke 23:55). Up until the resurrection scene, the Lukan changes in the presentation of Mary Magdalene are noticeable but arguably relatively minor. Such is not the case for the pivotal moment in the narrative, however, when the Lukan author introduces one of the most significant differences with respect to the resurrection appearances. In Luke's gospel, Mary Magdalene encounters only two messengers at the sepulchre scene and not the resurrected Jesus himself. Luke reports that she and the women accompanying her see only "two men in dazzling clothes" (24:4).[39]

Another significant difference occurs in Luke's subsequent portrayal of the interaction of the women with the rest of the disciples. The author of Luke does not present the words of Mary Magdalene in the form of a kerygmatic statement in the same way that Mary announces the news in the Gospel of John (20:18). The kerygmatic statement in Luke occurs instead on the lips of the two messengers in the previous scene. They

---

[37]εἰστήκεισαν δὲ πάντες οἱ γνωστοὶ αὐτῷ ἀπὸ μακρόθεν, καὶ γυναῖκες αἱ συνακολουθοῦσαι αὐτῷ ἀπὸ τῆς Γαλιλαίας, ὁρῶσαι ταῦτα (23:49).

[38]See Jane Schaberg, "Luke," in *The Women's Bible Commentary* (ed. Carol A. Newsom and Sharon H. Ringe; Louisville, Ky.: Westminster/John Knox, 1992), 290. See also Barbara E. Reid, *Choosing the Better Part? Women in the Gospel of Luke* (Collegeville, Ind.: Liturgical Press, 1996), 200. Although it is possible that the feminine plural participle may be the result of the verb agreeing with the nearest of two or more subjects (see Smyth, *Greek Grammar,* §966), the normal construction demands that when "persons are of different gender, the masculine prevails" (§1055).

[39]Fitzmyer, *Luke,* 2:1544; Marshall, *Luke,* 885; Evans, *Luke,* 894.

say, "He is not here, but has risen! Remember how he told you, while he was still in Galilee: 'The Son of Man must be delivered into the hands of sinners, be crucified and on the third day rise again' " (24:6–7).[40] Luke's account of the women's interaction with the other disciples states only that "[they] told these things to the apostles" (24:10).[41] Moreover, the Lukan author waits until this point to mention who these women are by name: ἡ Μαγδαληνὴ Μαρία καὶ Ἰωάννα καὶ Μαρία ἡ Ἰακώβου ("Mary Magdalene, Joanna, and Mary the mother of James" [24:10]).

Moreover, the disciples' response to the report of what happened is harsher in Luke than in the other gospels. In fact, Luke uses λῆρος, which means "futile nonsense" or "idle talk" and occurs only here in the New Testament, to describe the disciples' opinion of the women's words.[42] The reaction among the disciples is thus one of unbelief—with the exception of Peter, whom the Lukan author portrays as making the first step toward faith by running to the tomb and wondering what had happened (24:12).[43]

Finally, the most important aspect of the differences among these accounts is that in the course of all these events, Luke provides no commissioning of the women to go and tell anyone the news of the resurrection. In the other three gospels either Jesus or the messenger(s) send Mary Magdalene alone or with the other women to proclaim the news. This commissioning is noticeably absent in Luke, a factor that significantly reduces Mary's status as a resurrection witness. This absence bears implications for early Christian history because Luke never provides divine justification for women to preach. In the Gospel of Luke, therefore, Mary Magdalene does not hold the same status as she does in the gospels of Matthew or John.

---

[40]Fitzmyer, *Luke*, 2:1545; Marshall, *Luke*, 886–87; Evans, *Luke*, 895–96.

[41]In full: καὶ ὑποστρέψασαι ἀπὸ τοῦ μνημείου ἀπήγγειλαν ταῦτα πάντα τοῖς ἕνδεκα καὶ πᾶσιν τοῖς λοιποῖς. ἦσαν δὲ ἡ Μαγδαληνὴ Μαρία καὶ Ἰωάννα καὶ Μαρία ἡ Ἰακώβου· καὶ αἱ λοιπαὶ σὺν αὐταῖς. ἔλεγον πρὸς τοὺς ἀποστόλους ταῦτα ("When they came back from the tomb, they told all these things to the eleven and to all the others. It was Mary Magdalene, Joanna, Mary the mother of James, and the others with them who told this to the apostles" [Luke 24:9–10]).

[42]Other examples of definitions include: "trash" and "trumpery." See Henry George Liddell and Robert Scott, *Greek-English Lexicon* (Oxford: Clarendon, 1968), 1046.

[43]Michael D. Goulder, *Luke: A New Paradigm* (JSNTSup 20; 2 vols.; Sheffield: JSOT Press, 1989), 2:777; Evans, *Luke*, 899: "this verse is omitted by D, the Old Latin mss a b d e l r, Marcion, some mss of the Palestinian Syriac, the Arabic Diatessaron and by Eusebius in half of his references." This verse, however, contradicts Luke 24:24b that "some of those who were with us went to the tomb."

As a result Luke is the least helpful of the canonical gospels in justifying the apostolic status of Mary Magdalene or other women.

Portrayal of Other Female Disciples in the Gospel of Luke

Indeed, the representation of Mary Magdalene described above is symptomatic of the overall representation of female followers in the Lukan gospel. Corresponding to the diminishment of Mary Magdalene's role as resurrection witness in this gospel is Luke's overall diminishment of women's roles as early Christian leaders.

Based on the amount of material about female characters that this author presents, some scholars have previously argued that Luke has a high regard for women's roles in early Christianity.[44] A comparison of the four canonical gospels shows that the Gospel of Luke holds the distinction of presenting the highest number of verses concerning women—a total of forty-two passages, twenty-three of which are unique to Luke.[45] Luke's unique emphasis on female roles is often accomplished by pairing narratives about men with narratives about women.[46] Examples of such Lukan pairings include the parables of the man with the mustard seed and the woman with the leaven (13:18–21) and the parables of the man searching for his lost sheep and the woman searching for her lost coin (15:4–10), as well as the accounts of the raisings of the widow's only son and Jairus' only daughter (7:12; 8:42). Although these pairings may lead one to assume the presence in this gospel of an egalitarian attitude towards

---

[44]Leonard Swidler (*Biblical Affirmations of Women* [Philadelphia: Westminster, 1979], 280–81) states, "In sum it can be said that beyond the evidence that clearly points to the fact that Jesus himself was a vigorous feminist, Luke's Gospel reflects this feminism most intensely of all the Gospels." Loretta Dornish (*A Woman Reads the Gospel of Luke* [Collegeville, Ind.: Liturgical Press, 1996], 36) describes how Luke "puts these women and especially Mary at the center of the drama as it begins."

[45]Swidler, *Biblical Affirmations,* 255.

[46]Helmut Flender, *St. Luke, Theologian of Redemptive History* (trans. Reginald H. and Ilse Fuller; translation of *Heil und Geschichte in der Theologie des Lukas* [1965]; Philadelphia: Fortress, 1967), 9–10; Schaberg, "Luke," 279; Joachim Jeremias, *The Parables of Jesus* (New York: Scribner, 1963), 90; Constance F. Parvey points out, "Jeremias (*The Parables of Jesus*) recognizes the similarities of the stories, but he does not suggest that their differences are due to different audiences of women and men." See her "The Theology and Leadership of Women in the New Testament," in *Religion and Sexism* (ed. Rosemary Radford Ruether; New York: Simon & Schuster, 1974), 149 n. 40.

men's and women's roles, a closer look reveals that Luke's pairings are not necessarily supportive of women's leadership roles.[47] Indeed, some scholars have perceived the opposite: the Gospel of Luke typically portrays women in the role of followers: "it deftly portrays them as models of subordinate service, excluded from the power center of the movement and from significant responsibilities."[48]

An example of a Lukan pairing of male and female characters in which a female character fares less well by comparison may be found in the successive narratives about Simeon and Anna at the temple (2:25–35 and 36–38). Indeed, Anna is one of the strongest female characters in Luke. Of the widow Anna, the text relates that "she spoke about him [Jesus] to all who were looking forward to the redemption of Jerusalem."[49] Anna, unlike Simeon, however, has no canticle and the Spirit is not said to be with her, although by contrast three times the text refers to the Spirit empowering Simeon (vv. 25, 26, 27) and attributes two canticles to him.[50] Anna receives three verses as opposed to the eleven allotted to Simeon. With respect to Anna's role, Luke stresses her silent witness, as well as the great length of her widowhood and her continual presence, fasting and praying, in the Temple.[51] Luke's portrayal of Anna displays the strategy evident in the gospel as a whole of providing "female readers with female characters as role models: prayerful, quiet, grateful

[47]Schaberg, "Luke," 278. In Luke–Acts the apostles are all male and generally do not have wives. Nor are the sons and daughters of the kingdom married or given into marriage. Since Philip, the name of one of the twelve, was known to have had four daughters, some scholars believe therefore that this primary figure was subsequently represented by two figures in Acts—one who was an apostle and another known as the Evangelist, thus making it Philip the Evangelist who had four virgin daughters who were prophetesses. Koester suggests that Luke's program of hidden asceticism is closely related to his judgment on the position of women. (The name Philip thus appears in two lists, such as in the list of the Twelve in Mark 3:18; Matt 10:3; Luke 6:14; Acts 1:13, also in John 1:43–48, 6:5–7, 12:21–22, 14:8–9, as well as in the list of the Seven in Acts 6:5 plus the narratives in Acts 8:4-40, and again in 21:8–9.)

[48]Schaberg, "Luke," 275. See also Schüssler Fiorenza, *In Memory of Her*, 151–54. They both improve upon Eugene H. Maly, "Women and the Gospel of Luke," *BTB* 10 (1980): 99–104.

[49]ἐλάλει περὶ αὐτοῦ πᾶσιν τοῖς προσδεχομένοις λύτρωσιν Ἰερουσαλήμ (v. 38).

[50]Schaberg, "Luke," 279.

[51]She is "presumably in the outer court, the only part of the precincts women were allowed to enter." This portrait of Anna may provide a hint of the importance of the ministry of widows in the early church, but it does not elaborate on the nature of that ministry. Schaberg, "Luke," 283.

women, supportive of male leadership."[52] In the process, notes Schaberg, Luke restricts women's roles to what is acceptable to the conventions of the imperial world: "The Gospel attempts to meet various needs, such as instructing and edifying women converts, appeasing the detractors of Christianity, and controlling women who practice or aspire to practice a prophetic ministry in the church."[53]

Luke omits the narrative of the anointing at Bethany that appears in Mark 14:3–9, Matt 26:6–13, and John 12:1–8. This gospel presents instead a somewhat parallel narrative that the author places earlier, during Jesus' Galilean ministry (7:36–50). Such a placement effectively diminishes the prophetic significance of the woman's anointing as an event foreshadowing the passion narrative.[54] Luke's version also changes the emphasis from the anointing "to the emotional extravagance of the woman's actions, on Jesus acceptance of the touch of such a person, and on her being forgiven."[55]

Other representations of women in Luke include the contrasting of Mary and Martha, in which Jesus praises Mary for quietly sitting and listening (Luke 10:38–42).[56] This research highlights only a few examples of the most relevant aspects to the portrayal of women as leaders in this gospel, but many scholars have pointed out other examples of Luke's shaping and diminishment of women's roles.[57]

---

[52]Schüssler Fiorenza, *In Memory of Her*, 50; Schaberg, "Luke," 275.

[53]Schaberg, "Luke," 275.

[54]Schüssler Fiorenza argues that having the woman in the narrative be a "woman of the city, a sinner" was probably the work of the Lukan author. One of the emphases in Luke is the stress on Jesus calling sinners to repentance. See Schüssler Fiorenza, *In Memory of Her*, 128–29.

[55]Schaberg, "Luke," 286.

[56]Schüssler Fiorenza explains that the depiction of Martha "serving at table" reflects the diaconate of table ministry while Mary is praised for quietly listening to the word of Jesus. See Schüssler Fiorenza, *In Memory of Her*, 165; also, idem, "A Feminist Critical Interpretation for Liberation: Martha and Mary: Luke 10:38–42," *Religion and Intellectual Life* 3 (1986), 21–35, esp. 31.

[57]Elisabeth Schüssler Fiorenza, *Jesus: Miriam's Child, Sophia's Prophet* (New York: Continuum, 1994); Luise Schottroff, Silvia Schroer, and Marie-Theres Wacker, *Feminist Interpretation: The Bible in Women's Perspective* (trans. Martin and Barbara Rumscheidt; Minneapolis: Fortress, 1998); Schaberg, "Luke," 275–92; Lilia Sebastiani, *Tra/Sfigurazione. Il personaggio evangelico di Maria di Magdala e il mito della peccatrice redenta nella tradizione occidentale* (Brescia: Queriniana, 1992); Martin Hengel, "Maria Magdalena und die Frauen als Zeugen," in *Abraham unser Vater: Juden und Christen im Gespräch über die Bibel* (Fs. Otto Michel; Leiden: Brill, 1963), 243–56; Ricci, *Mary Magdalene and Many Others*, 51–110; Turid Karlsen Seim, *The Double Message: Patterns of Gender in Luke–Acts*

Summary

The Gospel of Luke exhibits a programmatic heightening of Peter's prominence among all the disciples. Moreover, the special status of Peter in Luke sets this gospel apart from the other three gospels in the canon. The author includes special material about Peter not present elsewhere, including his individualized calling (5:1–11), his role in the miraculous catch of fish (5:4–7), his role as one of two disciples commanded to prepare the Passover Meal (22:8), and his commissioning by Jesus to strengthen the other disciples (22:31–32). The author of Luke omits traditions that are not status-enhancing, such as Peter's rebuke of Jesus (no Lukan parallel to Mark 8:32b and Matt 16:22), Jesus' subsequent rebuke of Peter (no Lukan parallel to Mark 8:33 and Matt 16:23), and Jesus' specifically scolding of Peter for sleeping in the garden (no Lukan parallel to Mark 14:37 and Matt 26:40). In addition to these differences in the tradition, the Gospel of Luke also presents modifications of Markan tradition that without exception enhance the portrayal of Peter. These modifications include changes in Peter's words at the prediction of the denial, the absence of any false promises on Peter's part, and the absence of any swearing or calling down a curse on himself during the denial. Lastly, this preferential treatment of Peter in the third gospel appears most clearly in Luke's supplementation of other canonical Petrine tradition with the mention of a resurrection appearance made exclusively to Peter in 24:34.

All of these elements work together in the Lukan presentation of Peter to raise him to a higher status than he occupies in any of the other

---

(Edinburgh: T&T Clark, 1994). For those that perceive Luke's treatment of women more positively, see Swidler, *Biblical Affirmations of Women*, 280–81; Ben Witherington III, "On the Road with Mary Magdalene, Joanna, Susanna, and Other Disciples—Luke 8:1–3," *ZNW* 70 (1979): 243–48, Susanne Heine, *Frauen der frühen Christenheit: Zur historischen Kritik einer feministischen Theologie* (Göttigen: Vandenhoeck & Ruprecht, 1986; ET: *Women and Early Christianity: Are the Feminist Scholars Right?* [trans. John Bowden; London: SCM, 1987]), who has a "corrective" to the feminist angle; E. Jane Via, "Women in the Gospel of Luke," in *Women in the World's Religions: Past and Present* (ed. Ursula King; New York: Paragon House, 1987), 38–55. Via supports Swidler's hypothesis that the author of Luke could have been a woman (p. 50).

canonical gospels.[58] It is my contention that it is not merely coincidence that the Gospel of Luke, the most pro-Petrine of the canonical gospels, is also the one in which the witness of Mary Magdalene is most diminished. In Luke, Mary Magdalene is portrayed as witnessing two messengers at the sepulchre scene instead of witnessing the resurrected Jesus himself. Furthermore, in contrast to the other three canonical gospels, only Luke refuses her a commission to spread the news of the resurrection, and only Luke refers to the resurrected Lord appearing to Peter alone. The following chapters will continue to argue that a direct and perceptible pattern governs the way in which early Christian authors represent these two figures in relation to each other. The next chapter, dealing with the Gospel of John, will show a significantly different representation of the relative status of Mary Magdalene and Peter.

[58]The significance of the figure of Peter for the author of Luke–Acts is further confirmed in Acts where he acts as the spokesperson for the group, the chief apostle, and the first to convert a Gentile.

CHAPTER THREE

Apostolic Authority in the Gospel of John

Further comparison of early Christian texts with respect to primacy and apostolic authority indicates that their emphases upon certain early disciples vary significantly. For instance, among the four descriptions of the role of Peter in the New Testament gospels, the two most strikingly different portrayals of Peter's prominence occur in the gospels of Luke and John. As the previous chapter has shown, the Gospel of Luke provides special material not appearing in other known sources that elevates Peter to a position of greater prominence among the disciples than that which he occupies in the other gospels. This chapter focuses on the Gospel of John and compares its treatment of Peter to its treatments of the Beloved Disciple and Mary Magdalene, assessing the implications of these treatments for the respective authority and status of the three figures.

The Portrayal of Peter

The gospels of John and Luke each portray the figure of Peter differently at key points in the gospels, including the call narrative, the special selections of disciples, and the Last Supper. The following examination will indicate that Peter appears in only five chapters in the Gospel of John (chapters 1, 6, 13, 18, and 20 [plus 21[1]]), and in each scene Peter's role lacks the prominence or esteem he carries in Luke.

The initial appearance of Peter in the Johannine narrative occurs in the first chapter as Jesus gathers his disciples. Already at this point, a hint of a

[1]Chapter 21 and reasons for considering it to be a supplement to the gospel are discussed later in this chapter.

secondary status for Peter appears, in that he is not the first disciple to be mentioned or to be called (as he is in Mark [1:16–18], Matthew [4:18–20], and Luke [5:1–9]). In fact, in the Gospel of John, Peter does not specifically receive a call from Jesus at all. Nor does Jesus take the initiative to find Peter. Rather, Andrew is the disciple who has the first contact with Jesus and who subsequently relates his experience to his brother Simon. Even though the beginning of this episode focuses on Andrew, making the action revolve around him, his discovery, and his announcement, the manner of Andrew's initial identification in the text betrays the possibility that Peter may have been more well known than Andrew even to the Johannine author. At this point in the gospel neither Andrew nor Simon Peter has yet been introduced, but when the author identifies Andrew, it is in terms of his relation to his brother: "Andrew the brother of Simon Peter" (1:40). In John it is only through Andrew's initiative that Simon Peter comes to Jesus: "The first thing Andrew did was to find his own brother Simon and tell him, 'We have found the Messiah,' that is, the Christ. And he brought him to Jesus" (1:41–42).

The figure of Peter does not appear again until chapter 6. Some scholars contend that despite the failings of Peter, this disciple does indeed hold a position of prominence in John merely by virtue of the fact that Peter acts as the spokesperson for the group when Jesus asks if they too wish to go away (6:67).[2] Peter's response, taking the form of a confession, seems to uphold the status he acquires in Luke by being the most outspoken of the group. The Johannine portrayal of Peter's confession, however, does not carry the same christological significance that it does in Matthew, Mark, or Luke. These texts display some interesting variations in Peter's response to Jesus' inquiry, "But who do you say that I am?" In Mark, Peter answers: "You are the Christ" (Mark 8:29). Likewise, in Matthew, Peter answers: "You are the Christ, the Son of the living God" (Matt 16:16). Peter answers similarly in Luke: "The Christ of God" (Luke 9:20). In the Gospel of John, however, these words of confession announcing the true identity of Jesus (including his divinity) come not from the lips of Peter but from Martha. In response to Jesus' explanation concerning the resurrection, Martha confesses: "I believe that you are the Christ, the Son of God" (11:27a).

[2]Rudolf Schnackenburg, *The Gospel According to St. John* (3 vols.; New York: Crossroad, 1982), 2:77; Rudolf Bultmann, *The Gospel of John: A Commentary* (trans. G. R. Beasley-Murray; Philadelphia: Westminster, 1971), 450; Joseph N. Sanders, *A Commentary on the Gospel According to St. John* (Peabody, Mass.: Hendrickson, 1968), 198–99.

In John, by contrast, the following words present Peter's understanding of the identity of Jesus: "You have the words of eternal life. And we believe and have come to know that you are the Holy One of God" (6:69). Comparing the words of Martha's confession to Peter's in this gospel, one finds that although Peter's words do comprise a faith confession, they are significantly paler than the confession of Martha (or Thomas in this gospel, or the confession of Peter himself as portrayed in the other gospels). Scholars have argued that for a text such as the Johannine gospel, given its strong emphasis on the preexistence and divinity of Jesus, these words appear to be lacking as a christological confession.[3] The words: "the holy one of God" (ὁ ἅγιος τοῦ θεοῦ) could even designate a prophet, not necessarily the "Son of God."[4] The only other two sites where this appellation, "the holy one of God," occurs in the gospels are in Mark 1:24 ("What do you want with us, Jesus of Nazareth? Have you come to destroy us? I know who you are—the Holy One of God!") and the parallel in Luke 4:34;[5] in both gospels the phrase comes from the lips of a demon or unclean spirit.

As Bultmann points out, Peter confesses Jesus neither as the Messiah, nor as Son of Man; neither as the "Son," nor as "him whom God sent," nor even as the σωτήρ, but as the "holy one of God": "thus none of the customary messianic or saviour or redeemer titles from the Jewish or Hellenistic-Gnostic tradition is chosen, but a designation which has no recognisable tradition at all as a messianic title."[6] Numerous textual variants later attempt to refashion the words of Peter's confession to place them in closer agreement with Martha's words in John 11:27, or with

---

[3]For example, see Sandra M. Schneiders, "Women in the Fourth Gospel and the Role of Women in the Contemporary Church," *BTB* 12 (1982): 41. Likewise in the *Gospel of Thomas*, Peter's confession of Jesus' identity appears to be somewhat inadequate (*Gos. Thom.* 13).

[4]Bultmann and Brown explain that the "holy one of God" can designate a prophet or someone set apart. The phrase "the holy one of God" or "the holy one of the Lord" appears to refer in the Hebrew Bible to those consecrated to God; see Judg 13:7 and 16:17 and Raymond E. Brown, *The Gospel According to John* (AB 29–30; 2 vols; Garden City, N.Y.: Doubleday, 1966–1970), 1:298. In the New Testament, 1 John 2:30 and Rev 3:7 describe Jesus as ὁ ἅγιος, but in neither instance are we confronted with a title; the meaning is not, "he who is the Holy One," but "he who is holy." Likewise, "Christians in their eschatological consciousness call themselves ἅγιοι (Rom 1:7, 8:27, etc.)." See Bultmann, *John*, 449 n. 5, and Brown, *John*, 1:298.

[5]The next closest terminology is Acts 2:27 which contains the word ὅσιον "holy one," not "holy one of God."

[6]Bultmann, *John*, 449.

Mark 8:29, Matt 16:16, or Luke 9:20, "but on the original form of the text, attested by ℵ and Δ, there can be no doubt."[7]

Jesus' response to Peter's confession in John is noteworthy because there follows no acknowledgment that Peter has offered an acceptable answer; there are no words of high praise from Jesus or a request for secrecy as one might have expected from reading other gospels. Instead John portrays Jesus replying to Peter's confession with the enigmatic words, "Did I not choose you, the 'twelve,' and one of you is a devil?" (6:70).[8] Brown points out that Peter's connection with the concept of the "twelve" is known from numerous ancient texts, especially the book of Acts, and with this diminution of Peter comes also a diminution of the status of the "twelve." Moreover, only in this section of the Gospel of John is the group described as the "twelve" (6:67, 70, and 71).[9] As Alsup remarks, "This in itself is of considerable interest since the confession of Peter in the synoptic tradition is not associated with the term the Twelve at all, but rather οἱ μαθηταί, but more than this we see that the confession is insoluably connected to the betrayal prophecy in John, i.e., the editorial comment of vs. 71 points to the fundamental reason for the use of the Twelve here at all: the *betrayer* was one of them."[10] The Johannine text never portrays Jesus choosing the "twelve," but the author does reveal

---

[7]Ibid., 449 n. 2.

[8]Graydon Snyder contends that if one considers "the source of Peter's confession and the Markan response to this confession, 'Get behind me, Satan,' it is difficult to avoid reading here a reference to Peter's later denial." Although that reading is prevented by the following verse (6:71), which explicitly states that Judas, son of Simon Iscariot, was meant, "even there the rare use of son of Simon Iscariot gives one the feeling the author is toying with our imaginations, or a redactor has redirected the charge from Peter to Judas. . . . Taken alone it is merely interesting; taken in the context of eight other passages with a similar intent, it appears as a sly attack on the validity of Peter's confession—at least as representative of the disciples." See Graydon F. Snyder, "John 13:16 and the Anti-Petrinism of the Johannine Tradition," *BR* 16 (1971): 11. Others who have discerned anti-Petrinism in John include Arthur H. Maynard, "The Role of Peter in the Fourth Gospel," *NTS* 30 (1984): 531–48; and Savvas Agourides, "Peter and John in the Fourth Gospel," in *SE* 4 (ed. Frank L. Cross; Berlin: Akademie, 1968), 3–7.

[9]John 6:71 appears to be an editorial comment on the preceding verse: "He meant Judas, the son of Simon Iscariot, who, though one of the 'twelve,' was later to betray him." In addition, Judas Thomas, the one who had to feel Jesus' hands, is identified as one of the "twelve" in John 20:24–28.

[10]Alsup, *Post-Resurrection Appearance Stories*, 151–52.

knowledge of traditions not introduced or explained in the text. Peter speaks as the spokesperson of these "twelve."

The third appearance of Peter in the Gospel of John is at the footwashing scene at the Last Supper, in which the author portrays Peter as the disciple who vocally misunderstands Jesus' message. "The purpose of this narrative form is to engage the reader in an imaginary dialogue with Jesus, whereby false and shallow notions of faith are identified and corrected by Jesus, thus exposing error and realigning the belief of the reader in more adequate directions," writes Paul N. Anderson.[11] The dynamic of this text supports the claim of the Russian literary critic, Mikhail Bakhtin, that "misunderstanding in the novel—or any narrative—*always* serves a rhetorical function."[12] Peter's misguided objection to Jesus' actions prompts Jesus to reply: "You do not realize now what I am doing, but later you will understand" (13:7). The ensuing misunderstanding provokes Peter to reply unequivocally in return: "you shall never wash my feet" (13:8). Moreover, this misunderstanding earns Peter a warning from Jesus: "Unless I wash you, you have no part with me" (13:8).[13]

This episode featuring Peter also includes the one use of the term "apostle" (ἀπόστολος) in the Gospel of John: "I tell you the truth, no servant is greater than his master, nor is an apostle greater than the one who sent him" (13:16). Considering how frequently Peter's name is associated with the term "apostle" in early Christian literature, especially in Luke–Acts, it is significant that this term is used in John only in this one passage—a dialogue with Peter that conveys a warning about status. Scholars conjecture that since both the Gospel of John and the Johannine epistles rarely if ever use the term "apostle" (especially in reference to the "twelve"), a term used by most other authors of the New Testament, it seems that this general avoidance of the word is significant and most likely deliberate.[14]

[11]Paul N. Anderson, "The *Sitz im Leben* of the Johannine Bread of Life Discourse and Its Evolving Context," *Critical Readings of John 6* (ed. R. Alan Culpepper; Leiden: Brill, 1997), 17.

[12]See Mikhail Bakhtin, "Forms of Time and Chronotope in the Novel," in *The Dialogic Imagination* (ed. Michael Holquist; Austin, Tex.: University of Texas Press, 1981), 164.

[13]Smith, *Petrine Controversies in Early Christianity*, 145.

[14]See also James D. G. Dunn, *Unity and Diversity in the New Testament: An Inquiry into the Character of Earliest Christianity* (2d ed.; London: SCM, 1990), 119. Contra his evaluation is Kevin Quast, *Peter and the Beloved Disciple: Figures for a Community*

In the Gospel of John, interestingly, Peter never appears as part of a select group of two or three disciples designated for special revelation, such as in the Transfiguration Narrative, which is absent from this text. In the portrayal of the Last Supper, the author of John explicitly places Peter in a secondary role to the Beloved Disciple, a figure referred to by that appellation only in this gospel. That the Beloved Disciple holds the most esteemed position in John is evident from the place of honor the Beloved Disciple occupies next to Jesus at the last meal. In the description of this event, Peter's distance from Jesus in this scene, in fact, requires him to signal to the Beloved Disciple when Peter has a question for Jesus (John 13:24).

In this same chapter, Peter possesses another speaking part. He asks Jesus, "Lord, why can't I follow you now? I will lay down my life for you" (13:37). This sentence is actually contrary to fact in that Peter is not on this night ready to lay down his life for Jesus; precisely the opposite is true as seen in Jesus' immediate response, "Will you lay down your life for me?" (13:38), followed by the warning of Peter's betrayal. Therefore, this text too places Peter in a less than ideal position. Compare this to Mark, followed closely by Matthew, in which Peter states, "Even though they all fall away, I will not" (Mark 14:29, Matt 26:33). As we have seen in the previous chapter, the Lukan parallel improves Peter's speech to make his claim one that actually comes true:[15] that he is willing to go to "prison and to death" (22:33), a statement that later traditions concerning Peter indicate did eventually come to pass.[16] Thus, while the author of Luke eliminates the irony of Peter's words in Mark and Matthew, the author of John heightens that irony.

The fourth appearance of Peter in John is at the arrest and trial of Jesus (18:10–27). Nothing in this section attributes to Peter any special prominence, although only in John is he named as the one who cuts off

---

in Crisis (JSNTSup 32; Sheffield: JSOT Press, 1989), 23. He refers to a scholar even further along the spectrum, John J. Gunther ("The Relation of the Beloved Disciple to the Twelve," *TZ* 37 [1981]: 129–48), who states, "Anyone especially loved by Jesus would necessarily gravitate toward *membership* in the Twelve" (142). Such an evaluation indicates the hegemony that this group of the "twelve" holds in the minds of so many New Testament scholars.

[15]This recasting of his response shows that Peter understands the implication of Jesus' words. See Perkins, *Peter,* 85.

[16]As reflected in the pro-Petrine addition in John 21:18.

the right ear of the high priest's slave (v. 10).[17] At Peter's misreading of the situation, Jesus rebukes him to put away his sword (v. 11). After the soldiers had taken Jesus away, both Simon Peter and the "other disciple,"[18] the one known to the high priest, follow Jesus. Only in John is it "the other disciple" (ὁ μαθητὴς ὁ ἄλλος) who makes it possible for Peter to enter the court of the high priest (v. 16). Peter then denies being one of Jesus' disciples (vv. 17, 25, and 27). Peter makes his fifth and final appearance in the Gospel of John (not counting the appendix of chapter 21) at the empty tomb (20:3–10).

In this resurrection narrative Mary Magdalene arrives and announces that the tomb is empty: "So she came running to Simon Peter and the other disciple, the one Jesus loved, and said, 'They have taken the Lord out of the tomb, and we don't know where they have put him!' "[19] As a result of this announcement, two disciples, Peter and "the other disciple" (ὁ ἄλλος μαθητής) go to the tomb, find it empty, and return puzzled. Because they meet neither an angel nor Jesus, this text grants Peter nothing special in terms of authority or recognition.

> [3] ἐξῆλθεν οὖν ὁ Πέτρος καὶ ὁ ἄλλος μαθητὴς καὶ ἤρχοντο εἰς τὸ μνημεῖον. [4] ἔτρεχον δὲ οἱ δύο ὁμοῦ· καὶ ὁ ἄλλος μαθητὴς προέδραμεν τάχιον τοῦ Πέτρου καὶ ἦλθεν πρῶτος εἰς τὸ μνημεῖον, [5] καὶ παρακύψας βλέπει κείμενα τὰ ὀθόνια, οὐ μέντοι εἰσῆλθεν. [6] ἔρχεται οὖν καὶ Σίμων Πέτρος ἀκολουθῶν αὐτῷ, καὶ εἰσῆλθεν εἰς τὸ μνημεῖον, καὶ θεωρεῖ τὰ ὀθόνια κείμενα, [7] καὶ τὸ σουδάριον, ὃ ἦν ἐπὶ τῆς κεφαλῆς αὐτοῦ, οὐ μετὰ τῶν ὀθονίων κείμενον ἀλλὰ χωρὶς ἐντετυλιγμένον εἰς ἕνα τόπον. [8] τότε οὖν εἰσῆλθεν καὶ ὁ ἄλλος μαθητὴς ὁ ἐλθὼν πρῶτος εἰς τὸ μνημεῖον καὶ εἶδεν καὶ ἐπίστευσεν· [9] οὐδέπω γὰρ ᾔδεισαν τὴν γραφὴν ὅτι δεῖ αὐτὸν ἐκ νεκρῶν ἀναστῆναι. [10] ἀπῆλθον οὖν πάλιν πρὸς αὐτοὺς οἱ μαθηταί.

---

[17] Matt 26:51 and Mark 14:47 also record that the ear of the servant of the high priest was cut off. The Gospel of Luke adds that it is the right ear of the high priest but does not say who did it (Luke 22:60).

[18] I understand this "other disciple" not to be the Beloved Disciple as some scholars have argued. There is no reference to this disciple being the "beloved one," nor any reason to believe that it is the Beloved Disciple.

[19] τρέχει οὖν καὶ ἔρχεται πρὸς Σίμωνα Πέτρον καὶ πρὸς τὸν ἄλλον μαθητὴν ὃν ἐφίλει ὁ Ἰησοῦς καὶ λέγει αὐτοῖς· ἦραν τὸν κύριον ἐκ τοῦ μνημείου καὶ οὐκ οἴδαμεν ποῦ ἔθηκαν αὐτόν (20:2).

[3]So Peter and the other disciple started for the tomb. [4]Both were running, but the other disciple outran Peter and reached the tomb first. [5]He bent over and looked in at the strips of linen lying there but did not go in. [6]Then Simon Peter, who was behind him, arrived and went into the tomb. He saw the strips of linen lying there, [7]as well as the burial cloth that had been around Jesus' head. The cloth was folded up by itself, separate from the linen. [8]Finally the other disciple, who had reached the tomb first, also went inside. He saw and believed. [9]For they still did not understand from Scripture that Jesus had to rise from the dead. [10]Then the disciples went back to their homes. (John 20:3–10)

Maynard points out that the indication that Peter was following (ἀκολουθῶν [v. 6]) the other disciple probably carries more than merely a literal descriptive sense. He observes, "Since the term 'to follow' is a technical term for becoming a disciple in the Fourth Gospel, it is probable that it is here used to subordinate Peter"[20] to the other disciple. One could argue that status is communicated in v. 8 by the words that describe the reaction of "the other disciple" (ὁ ἄλλος μαθητὴς) as seeing and believing after entering the tomb: "Finally the other disciple, who had reached the tomb first, also went inside. He saw and believed." The intriguing feature of this scene is that it does not concentrate its attention upon Peter but specifically describes only the reaction of the other disciple upon entering the tomb. Even more puzzling is the interpretive issue: what exactly did the other disciple see and believe? Although this statement could possibly mean that this other disciple achieved a resurrection faith, some scholars, such as George MacRae, for instance, have called such an interpretation into question. MacRae points out the exegetical problem in claiming that what the other disciple "saw and believed" was the resurrection. He suggests a different interpretation: "In light of other statements in the Gospel (see, e.g., the comment on 16:30), we may suppose he believed that Jesus had indeed returned to the Father, as he had promised. This is what constitutes true christological faith in the Fourth Gospel. Thus the resurrection as such is not (yet) the object of faith."[21]

---

[20]Maynard, "The Role of Peter in the Fourth Gospel," 540; also Charles K. Barrett, *The Gospel According to St. John: An Introduction with Commentary and Notes on the Greek Text* (2d ed.; Philadelphia: Westminster, 1978), 563.

[21]George W. MacRae, *Invitation to John: A Commentary on the Gospel of John with Complete Text from the Jerusalem Bible* (Garden City, N.Y.: Image Books, 1978), 219.

Since the verb πιστεύω, "to believe (in) something," can also mean "to be convinced of something,"[22] scholars have also proposed that John 20:8 means no more than that the other disciple "became convinced that Mary Magdalene had spoken the truth when she reported that the tomb was empty."[23] Such an interpretation has a long history, including Augustine, who also understood that what the other disciple saw and believed was Mary's report. St. Augustine wrote:

> "And he saw and believed." Here some, by not giving due attention, suppose that John believed that Jesus had risen again; but there is no indication of this from the words that follow. For what does he mean by immediately adding, "For as yet they knew not the scripture, that He must rise again from the dead"? He could not then have believed that He had risen again, when he did not know that it was necessary for Him to rise again. What then did he see? What was it that he believed? What but this, that he saw the sepulchre empty, and believed what the woman had said, that He had been taken away from the tomb? "For as yet they knew not the scripture, that He must rise again from the dead."[24]

As Augustine's attentive reading of the text shows, it is definitely not clear from the remark in John that what the disciple "saw and believed" is actually a reference to Jesus' resurrection. Along those same lines are certain modern scholars as well, such as Ernst von Dobschütz, who argues

---

Also, James H. Charlesworth, *The Beloved Disciple: Whose Witness Validates the Gospel of John?* (Valley Forge, Pa.: TPI, 1995), 108.

[22]Bauer, *Greek English Lexicon,* s.v. "πιστεύω."

[23]Brown, Donfried, and Reumann, eds., *Peter in the New Testament,* 137 n. 294.

[24]Augustine, "Homilies on the Gospel of John," in 7:436; Latin is from *Sancti Aurelii Augustini: In Iohannis evangelium Tractatus CXX.* CCSL 36:664. "et uidit, inquit, et credidit. hic nonnulli parum adtendentes, putant hoc Iohannem credidisse, quod Iesus resurrexit; sed quod sequitur, hoc non indicat. quid sibi enim uult quod statim adiunxit: nondum enim sciebant scripturam, quia oportet eum a mortuis resurgere? non ergo eum credidit resurrexisse, quem nesciebat oportere resurgere. quid ergo uidit? quid credidit? uidit scilicet inane monumentum, et credidit quod dixerat mulier, eum de monumento esse sublatum. nondum enim sciebant scripturam, quia oporteret eum a mortuis resurgere. et ideo quando id ab ipso Domino audiebant, quamuis apertissime diceretur, consuetudine audiendi ab illo parabolas, non intellegebant, et aliquid aliud eum significare credebant. sed ea quae sequuntur in sermonem alium differamus."

that what the disciples saw and believed was anything but an Easter faith,[25] especially in light of the juxtaposition of the next verse ("for they still did not understand from Scripture that Jesus had to rise from the dead" [v. 9]), which, as Augustine pointed out, further calls into question the interpretation that this is a belief in the resurrection. If this "other disciple" had come to a resurrection belief, then the subsequent verse carries with it an almost contradictory sense when it describes the reaction of the two disciples and that they still did not understand that Jesus had to rise. In other words, it is quite possible that what this disciple believed when he saw the tomb was Mary's report.[26]

Because it is relevant here for the portrayal of Peter in this gospel, it must be noted that whatever it was that the other disciple "saw and believed"—whether it was a belief in the resurrection or a belief that the corpse was gone—the text excludes Peter's name from this reaction: the passage specifically indicates by using verbs in the singular form that it was the other disciple who saw and believed. Interestingly, when this passage goes on to explain that they still did not understand from Scripture that Jesus had to rise from the dead, the narrative reverts to plural verb forms, thus designating both disciples. In neither case does this verse add to the status of Peter in any way in the gospel as a whole.

Not only does this gospel *not* indicate a special position for Peter, but it also does not show any particular esteem for the term "apostles" as a designation for the group surrounding Jesus. In the Gospel of John, Jesus does not specifically call Peter and does not specifically choose Peter as

[25]Dobschütz claims, "Das rätselhafte 'er sah und glaubte' ist alles andere als Osterglaube." See Ernst von Dobschütz, *Ostern und Pfingsten* (Leipzig: Hinrichs, 1903), 7. If the reaction of the other disciple is indeed a belief in the resurrection, then one must ask what the following verse is intended to explain: "they still did not understand from Scripture that Jesus had to rise from the dead"? Nauck states, "Alle Schwierigkeiten verschwinden in dem Augenblick, wo man sich entschließt, das ἐπίστευσεν in 20:8 nicht auf die Entstehung des Osterglaubens zu beziehen, sondern es so zu verstehen: er überzeugte sich von dem Tatbestand, die Leiche war nicht da." See Wolfgang Nauck, "Die Bedeutung des leeren Grabes für den Glauben an den Auferstandenen," *ZNW* 47 (1956): 243–67, esp. 254.

[26]Minear states that this other disciple does not at this point in the narrative believe that Jesus has resurrected. He explains, "In a similar way, verse 10 excludes the possibility that this text refers to faith in the resurrection: 'then the disciples went back to their homes.'" Paul S. Minear, "'We don't know where . . .' John 20:2," *Int* 30 (1976): 127. Likewise Charlesworth (*Beloved Disciple*, 77) asks if scholars have dealt sufficiently with the contextual force of 20:9.

a member of a select group of two or three disciples. Peter vocally expresses his misunderstanding of the footwashing and must ask the Beloved Disciple for information at the Last Supper. Moreover, when Peter runs to the empty tomb, he receives no special resurrection appearance from Jesus. This lackluster portrayal of Peter changes, however, in chapter 21 of the Gospel of John.

John 21: The Reinstatement of Peter

The most notable text for evaluating Peter's role in John's gospel is found in chapter 21, a chapter that most scholars believe to be an appendix or later addition.[27] In this supplementary chapter the positions of authority held by certain of the disciples change significantly, perhaps as the result of a later redactor's attempt to represent an effort by the Johannine community to unite with the church at large.[28] The chapter is regarded as a later addition to the gospel for a number of reasons. The words at the end of John 20 give the impression that this is the conclusion of the book: "Jesus did many other miraculous signs in the presence of his disciples, which are not recorded in this book. But these are written that you may believe that Jesus is the Christ, the Son of God, and that by believing you may have life in his name" (vv. 30–31).

In this final scene in John 21 the attitude represented in the text is significantly more positive toward Peter, as the redactor acknowledges Peter's authority. One can easily perceive the rehabilitative effort of this appendix, especially as it enhances the status of Peter in a way not previously seen in John. For instance, this chapter specifically depicts Peter bringing in the net that overflows with fish and yet remains unbroken (21: 11). The total number of fish — 153 — no doubt has some symbolic value unknown to us, but is perhaps an allusion to success in evangelization.[29] Whatever the meaning, this description of the scene portrays the entire

[27]Numerous scholars consider chapter 21 to be an appendix, including Brown, *John*, 2:1079; and Bultmann, *John*, 700–6. Bultmann's commentary includes an analysis of the different vocabulary and style of this additional chapter. See also Jean Zumstein, "Der Prozess der Relecture in der johanneischen Literatur," *NTS* 42 (1996): 394–411, esp. 403–4.

[28]Brown, *John*, 2:1082.

[29]Augustine advances the theory that the number 153 is the triangulated number of 17. For other possible explanations of the number, see Jindřich Mánek, "Fishers of Men," *NovT* 2 (1958): 141.

group of disciples fishing, but then focuses only on Peter, who single-handedly pulls in the net in obedience to Jesus' request.

This chapter subsequently again singles out Peter as the one with whom Jesus has a one-to-one conversation (vv. 15–23), and in this dialogue Peter at last receives a special commissioning from Jesus. Jesus specifically commands Peter to feed his lambs and shepherd his sheep. Some scholars have recognized this three-part commissioning as a redemption of Peter's three-part denial.[30] This dialogue functions to impart a special commissioning for Peter as a leader for the group, placing the future ministerial leadership firmly in the hands of Peter with divine authorization. Thus, this additional chapter accomplishes in a few verses that which did not occur in the entire Gospel of John: it attributes a special and unique position to Peter not previously held in John. It must be noted, however, that even though Peter's status is significantly higher in this conciliatory Johannine appendix, it nevertheless still does not supercede that of the Beloved Disciple, as the following section indicates.[31]

The Portrayal of the Beloved Disciple

The author of the Gospel of John portrays the ideal of discipleship in the figure of a disciple called "the one whom Jesus loved" (ὃν ἠγάπα ὁ Ἰησοῦς) using the Greek word ἀγαπάω,[32] a description most often translated as "the Beloved Disciple."[33] The Gospel of John explicates three levels with respect to faith: those with no faith, those with faith but at an inadequate level, and the kind of faith demonstrated by the

---

[30]Cullmann, *Peter*, 204. Contra the rehabilitation concept are Spitta, Goguel, and Bultmann. Bultmann (*John,* 712) states that this scene "provides no hint of a relation to the account of the denial."

[31]"Hence the author of chapter 21 lauds Peter, but concludes that he was no Beloved Disciple" (Charlesworth, *Beloved Disciple,* 435 n. 18).

[32]The phrase, using the verb ἀγαπάω, occurs in John 13:23 and John 19:26. The account of the race to the tomb in ch. 20, however, uses a different verb (φιλέω) to describe the disciple who is loved. Therefore, because it is not absolutely certain that it refers to the same person, I will treat the descriptions as references to two different individuals.

[33]Scholars who argue that a historical figure stands behind John's Beloved Disciple include: Oscar Cullmann, *Der johanneische Kreis: Sein Platz im Spätjudentum, in der Jüngerschaft Jesu und im Urchristentum: Zum Ursprung des Johannesevangeliums* (Tübingen: Mohr [Siebeck] 1975), 67–88; Raymond Brown, *Community of the Beloved Disciple* (New York: Paulist, 1979), 31–34; Charlesworth, *Beloved Disciple,* 12–24, 425.

Beloved Disciple, who recognizes the true nature of Jesus, including both his divinity and his preexistence. In John this model disciple holds the position of honor at the Last Supper (13:23) and even more so at the cross when all of the other male disciples flee (19:26).

At the final gathering of the disciples for the Last Supper, the Beloved Disciple is positioned beside Jesus, reclining so that his head lies on Jesus' bosom (ἐν τῷ κόλπῳ τοῦ Ἰησοῦ [13:23]). This position echoes a passage in the first chapter in which Jesus himself is described as "the one who is in the bosom of the Father" (ὁ ὢν εἰς τὸν κόλπον τοῦ πατρός [1:18]).[34] This passage portrays Jesus in this privileged position with respect to the Father, receiving revelation. The Johannine author positions the Beloved Disciple similarly to indicate his privileged position in receiving from Jesus the revelation contained in the Farewell Discourses. The Beloved Disciple then functions as a decisive link in the transmission of revelation and therefore is endowed with the highest authority.[35]

The term "the Beloved Disciple" next appears in the narrative of the crucifixion (τὸν μαθητὴν . . . ὃν ἠγάπα [19:26]). Although many of the other disciples have scattered, the Beloved Disciple is described as faithfully standing at the foot of the cross along with the mother of Jesus, his mother's sister, and Mary Magdalene. In these verses the Johannine author portrays a significant directive from Jesus to Mary and the Beloved Disciple: "When Jesus saw his mother and the disciple whom he loved standing nearby, he said to his mother, 'Woman, here is your son,' and to the disciple, 'Here is your mother' " (19:26–27a). This formation of a new familial bond is followed by the remark that "From that time on, this disciple took her into his home" (19:27b). Although it is possible to understand this scene in a straightforward way, as some scholars have, interpreting the last sentence as simply the act of a concerned son to ensure that his mother will now have someone to care for her in her old age and in his absence, an alternative and perhaps even more powerful understanding of this scene is to interpret that this interaction now effectively portrays

---

[34]François Bovon, "The Gospel according to John, Access to God, at the Obscure Origins of Christianity," *Diogenes* 146 (1990): 36–50.

[35]Ignatius draws a similar parallel between God and the Son and the Son and the bishop. See Ign. *Eph.* 5.1: "For in a short time I had such fellowship with your bishop as was not human but spiritual, how much more blessed do I consider you who are mingled with him as the Church is with Jesus Christ and as Jesus Christ is with the Father, so that all things are harmonious in unison!" (ANF 1:51).

Mary adopting the Beloved Disciple as her son: "Woman, here is your son." Rhetorically, the Beloved Disciple's becoming the "son of Mary" thus entitles him to be the one who follows most closely in the footsteps of Jesus and who continues the mission and ministry that Jesus began.

Cullmann argues that the tensions in the text between the two figures of the Beloved Disciple and Peter represent the way in which the Johannine traditions, represented by the Beloved Disciple, significantly differ from the traditions of the "twelve," represented by Peter.[36] Raymond Brown likewise argues, "In counterposing their hero over against the most famous member of the Twelve, the Johannine community is symbolically counterposing itself over against the kinds of churches that venerate Peter and the Twelve"[37] In Jesus' reference to "other sheep" who also belong to his fold (John 10:16), the Johannine Christians recognize a reference to churches which derive their tradition from Peter.[38]

Even in chapter 21, the chapter that rehabilitates the position of Peter, the Beloved Disciple maintains an elevated status.[39] For instance, at the beginning of the chapter, the Beloved Disciple, not Peter, first recognizes Jesus and identifies him to Peter: "Then the disciple whom Jesus loved said to Peter, 'It is the Lord!' "[40] When Peter later inquires about the fate of the Beloved Disciple, Jesus responds, "If I want him to remain until I return, what is that to you?" (v. 22). Whether these words suggest a slight hint of rebuke for Peter is not clear, but it is clear that Jesus still remains

[36]"Die fast durchgehende Konfrontierung zwischen Petrus und dem Lieblingsjünger, die die beiden Jünger zugleich als sich ergänzend und doch mit einer gewissen Bevorzugung des Lieblingsjüngers zusammenstellt, entspricht ganz und gar der Tatsache, daß das *ganze* Evangelium, auch abgesehen von den genannten Stellen, eine Theologie und Traditionen bezeugt, die von denen der Zwölfergruppe verschieden sind, die hinter der synoptischen Tradition steht und als deren Sprecher dort Petrus erscheint" (Cullmann, *Der johanneische Kreis*, 76).

[37]Brown, *Community of the Beloved Disciple*, 83.

[38]Ibid., 90.

[39]"Die ambivalente Beziehung, die wir im Johannes-Evangelium zwischen Petrus, dem Repräsentanten der übrigen Urgemeinde, und dem 'Lieblingsjünger' feststellen werden, spiegelt sehr genau das doppelte Bestreben des johanneischen Kreises wider: einerseits Festhalten bewußter Eigenständigkeit, andererseits Überzeugung von der Notwendigkeit der gegenseitigen Ergänzung im Interesse der Gemeinsamkeit" (Cullmann, *Der johanneische Kreis*, 60).

[40]λέγει οὖν ὁ μαθητὴς ἐκεῖνος ὃν ἠγάπα ὁ Ἰησοῦς τῷ Πέτρῳ· ὁ κύριός ἐστιν (v. 7).

supportive of the Beloved Disciple.[41] So in response to Peter's question concerning the Beloved Disciple, Jesus is portrayed as defending this disciple by saying he planned for him not to die a martyr's death.

The Gospel of John portrays the Beloved Disciple in key positions: in the place of honor at the Last Supper and at the foot of the cross, where he is the only male disciple who has not fled. If the conversation between Jesus and the Beloved Disciple and Mary, Jesus' mother, in the crucifixion narrative depicts an adoption scene, then this text grants him even more authority. Thus in a number of ways the Beloved Disciple holds a significantly higher status than Peter in this gospel.[42]

The Portrayal of Mary Magdalene and Other Female Leadership

We have seen that the Gospel of Luke devotes considerably more space to women than the other canonical gospels do, but Luke tends to portray the women as followers, not as leaders. John's gospel, on the other hand, develops several models of strong female leadership. These narratives include Jesus' encounter with the Samaritan woman at the well, his anointing by Mary at Bethany, Martha's confession of his identity, and the witness of Mary Magdalene to his resurrection. Moreover, interestingly, John's gospel never offers a list of the traditional exclusively all-male group of twelve disciples, as do the synoptic gospels (Matt 10:2–4, Mark 3:1–19, Luke 6:14–16), Acts (1:13), the *Epistula Apostolorum,*[43] and the *Questions of Bartholomew.*[44]

---

[41]Contra Quast (*Peter and the Beloved Disciple*, 114), who says, "In no place is Peter criticized or devalued. Perhaps, the 'other disciple' is meant, in a certain sense, to be 'up-valued' even, by way of Peter's authority." See also Rudolf Schnackenburg, "Der Jünger, den Jesus liebte," in *EKKNT: Vorarbeiten* (Zürich: Neukirchener Verlag, 1970), 2:104; Schnackenburg, *John,* 3:314.

[42]Agourides, "Peter and John in the Fourth Gospel," 6. Agourides explains that Jesus did not appear to the Beloved Disciple (as he did later to the "twelve"), because he did not *need* to see Jesus. See also Quast, *Peter and the Beloved Disciple*, 114.

[43]*Epistula Apostolorum* in *The Apocryphal New Testament: A Collection of Apocryphal Christian Literature in an English Translation* (ed. J. Keith Elliott; Oxford: Clarendon, 1993), 555–88.

[44]*Questions of Bartholomew* in Jean-Daniel Kaestli, ed., "Questions de Barthélemy," *Écrits apocryphes chrétiens,* 267–95; and Elliott, *Apocryphal New Testament,* 652–72.

The Samaritan woman at the well is only one example of the significance accorded to women in this gospel, as she is the one who begins
the Christian mission in Samaria (4:1–45). Adele Reinhartz notes, "Her
initial contact with Jesus marks one of the few occasions in the Gospel in
which a dialogue between Jesus and another character does not become
a monologue for Jesus alone."[45] With the ἐγώ εἰμι formula Jesus reveals
his divine identity to her directly.[46]

Martha's role in this gospel also exhibits John's positive portrayal of
women. Martha declares her recognition of Jesus' divinity in a way that
Peter earlier in chapter 6 did not.[47] In John 11 Martha confesses, "Yes,
Lord; I believe that you are the Christ, the Son of God, the one who is
coming into the world" (v. 27). Martha makes this confession even before
Jesus raises Lazarus from the dead. This sequence gains significance in
light of Jesus' later remark to Thomas: "Have you believed because you
have seen me? Blessed are those who have not seen and yet believe"(20:
29).[48] Jesus speaks these words after Thomas makes the highest christological confession of the gospel. In the same chapter containing Martha's
confession, Judas complains against Mary's action of anointing Jesus with
expensive ointment, but Jesus defends her (11:54–12:11). As Schüssler
Fiorenza observes, the author of John thereby contrasts Mary, "the true
female disciple," with Judas, "the unfaithful male disciple."[49]

We have seen above how the Johannine author diminishes Peter's stature in the first twenty chapters of the gospel in the ways that narratives are
presented or reshaped. Conversely, the Johannine author goes further than
the synoptic gospels in portraying Mary Magdalene as an active figure in
the narrative toward the end of the gospel. The Johannine account not only
represents her as the first recipient of an appearance of the resurrected
Lord, but even more significantly, it highlights her role by excluding any

---

[45]Adele Reinhartz, "The Gospel of John," in *A Feminist Commentary* (vol. 2 of
Searching the Scriptures; ed. Elisabeth Schüssler Fiorenza; New York: Crossroad, 1994),
2:573.

[46]Ibid.

[47]With respect to Martha's confession Raymond Brown ("Roles of Women in the Fourth
Gospel," *TS* 36 [1975]: 693) suggests, "Giving to a woman a role traditionally associated
with Peter may well be a deliberate emphasis on John's part. . . ."

[48]Reinhartz, "Gospel of John," 2:581.

[49]Ibid., 2:583. Mary "is the positive counterpart to Judas; the true female disciple is an
alternative to the unfaithful male disciple." (Schüssler Fiorenza, *In Memory of Her*, 330).

mention of the other female visitors to the empty tomb named in the synoptic gospels. The possibility is strong that 20:2 reflects a tradition that originally included other female witnesses, because although this gospel specifies only her name, the announcement that she makes to the other disciples employs a first-person plural verb: "So she came running to Simon Peter and the other disciple, the one Jesus loved, and said, 'They have taken the Lord out of the tomb, and we do not know (οὐκ οἴδαμεν) where they have put him!'" Thus, even though the scene depicts Mary alone, her announcement uses the plural "we," suggesting that an earlier version of this narrative included other women with her.

The first verse of the chapter reads: "Early on the first day of the week, while it was still dark, Mary Magdalene went to the tomb and saw that the stone had been removed from the entrance" (John 20:1). In this section of John 20:1–18, seams in the story indicate that the present shape of the narrative is not its original form. Numerous scholars have suggested that John 20:2–10 has been inserted into the material, because there is a discontinuity between verses 10 and 11.[50] After the two disciples depart in v. 10, Mary is still standing outside of the tomb, alone as she was in v. 1, and crying as if nothing had happened in the previous verses. It is only in v. 11 that Mary looks into the tomb. Moreover, the plural "we don't know" of v. 2 is even more incongruous in light of Mary's later statement to the angels in v. 13: "I don't know where they have put him." Verse 11 thus flows much more logically immediately after v. 1, suggesting that in an earlier form of this narrative, Mary finds the tomb empty and then immediately experiences a resurrection epiphany. Such a chronology would parallel the sequence of events in other resurrection announcement stories featuring Mary Magdalene. Thus numerous scholars agree that the text as it stands now in the Gospel of John is not an original unity.[51] The discontinuity in sequence and the two seams between v. 1 and v. 2 and between v. 10 and v. 11 strongly suggest that the scene of Peter and the other disciple running to the tomb is an interpolation.

---

[50]Brown, *John*, 2:983, 995.

[51]Bultmann, *John*, 681; Otto Michel, "Ein johanneischer Osterbericht," in *Studien zum Neuen Testament und zur Patristik: Festschrift für Erich Klostermann* (TU 77; Berlin: Akademie-Verlag, 1961), 35; Brown, *John*, 2:983. The recent book by Susanne Ruschmann, goes into great detail on this particular passage, including a semantic analysis (Ruschmann, *Maria von Magdala im Johannesevangelium*, 108–20).

Assuming that vv. 2–10 consist of interpolated material, the narrative of the appearance to Mary would have read approximately as follows[52]:

¹ τῇ δὲ μιᾷ τῶν σαββάτων Μαρία ἡ Μαγδαληνὴ ἔρχεται πρωῒ σκοτίας ἔτι οὔσης εἰς τὸ μνημεῖον καὶ βλέπει τὸν λίθον ἠρμένον ἐκ τοῦ μνημείου. . . . ¹¹ Μαρία δὲ εἰστήκει πρὸς τῷ μνημείῳ ἔξω κλαίουσα. ὡς οὖν ἔκλαιεν, παρέκυψεν εἰς τὸ μνημεῖον ¹² καὶ θεωρεῖ δύο ἀγγέλους ἐν λευκοῖς καθεζομένους, ἕνα πρὸς τῇ κεφαλῇ καὶ ἕνα πρὸς τοῖς ποσίν, ὅπου ἔκειτο τὸ σῶμα τοῦ Ἰησοῦ. ¹³ καὶ λέγουσιν αὐτῇ ἐκεῖνοι· γύναι, τί κλαίεις; λέγει αὐτοῖς ὅτι ἦραν τὸν κύριόν μου, καὶ οὐκ οἶδα ποῦ ἔθηκαν αὐτόν. ¹⁴ ταῦτα εἰποῦσα ἐστράφη εἰς τὰ ὀπίσω καὶ θεωρεῖ τὸν Ἰησοῦν ἑστῶτα καὶ οὐκ ᾔδει ὅτι Ἰησοῦς ἐστιν. ¹⁵ λέγει αὐτῇ Ἰησοῦς· γύναι, τί κλαίεις; τίνα ζητεῖς; ἐκείνη δοκοῦσα ὅτι ὁ κηπουρός ἐστιν λέγει αὐτῷ· κύριε, εἰ σὺ ἐβάστασας αὐτόν, εἰπέ μοι ποῦ ἔθηκας αὐτόν, κἀγὼ αὐτὸν ἀρῶ. ¹⁶ λέγει αὐτῇ Ἰησοῦς· Μαριάμ. στραφεῖσα ἐκείνη λέγει αὐτῷ Ἐβραϊστί ραββουνι (ὃ λέγεται διδάσκαλε). ¹⁷ λέγει αὐτῇ Ἰησοῦς· μή μου ἅπτου, οὔπω γὰρ ἀναβέβηκα πρὸς τὸν πατέρα·

¹Early on the first day of the week, while it was still dark, Mary Magdalene went to the tomb and saw that the stone had been removed from the entrance. . . . ¹¹but [this "but" (δέ) and the repetition of Mary's name are probably redactional accommodations to the interpolated material] Mary stood outside the tomb crying. As she wept, she bent over to look into the tomb ¹²and saw two angels in white, seated where Jesus' body had been, one at the head and the other at the foot. ¹³They asked her, "Woman, why are you crying?" "They have taken my Lord away," she said, "and I don't know where they have put him." ¹⁴At this, she turned around and saw Jesus standing there, but she did not realize that it was Jesus. ¹⁵"Woman," he said, "why are you crying? Who is it you are looking for?" Thinking he was the gardener, she said, "Sir, if you have carried him away, tell me where you have put him, and I will get him." ¹⁶Jesus said to her, "Mary." She turned toward him and cried out in Aramaic, "Rabboni!" (which means Teacher). ¹⁷Jesus said, "Do not hold on to me, for I have not yet returned to the Father."[53]

---

[52]Alsup contends that the angelophany to Mary in Matthew probably had been a narrative of a Christophany. See Alsup, *Post-Resurrection Appearance Stories*, 110.

[53]Riley (*Resurrection Reconsidered*, 98 n. 86) states that a "simple reading (and my own opinion), without an abnormal view of the Greek [μή μου ἅπτου, οὔπω γὰρ ἀναβέβηκα πρὸς

In this resurrection appearance Christ goes on to dispatch Mary to the others: "Go instead to my brothers [and sisters?] and tell them, 'I am returning to my Father and your Father, to my God and your God.' "[54] In the next verse, Mary complies: "Mary Magdalene went to the disciples with the news: 'I have seen the Lord!' And she told them that he had said these things to her."[55]

If indeed vv. 2–10 consist of material interpolated into the text, as they appear to be, one must ask why the figure of Peter appears in this narrative at all. A number of explanations are possible. The interpolation may merely be the incorporation of a tradition similar to the one in Luke (24:12 or 24) in which Peter comes to the tomb, sees that it is empty, and leaves again in a puzzled state. Perhaps the author has heard the competing version that portrays Peter as the first resurrection witness and this interpolation communicates this awareness of an alternative narrative concerning Peter, places him at the site, but specifically chooses to focus upon the protophany to Mary Magdalene, even to the exclusion of the other women.[56] In any case, the interpolation provides the presence of two male disciples or witnesses who serve to corroborate Mary Magdalene's report that the tomb was empty.[57]

In John, Mary Magdalene ultimately does not appear to have a greater role than the Beloved Disciple, but she does appear to have a more sig-

---

τὸν πατέρα], would allow the sentences to mean: 'Let go of me now, for I need to go to my Father, and you need to go to the other disciples. . . . ' This implies that Mary has embraced Jesus and is then told to go to the other disciples, as in Matt 28:9–10."

[54] πορεύου δὲ πρὸς τοὺς ἀδελφούς μου καὶ εἰπὲ αὐτοῖς· ἀναβαίνω πρὸς τὸν πατέρα μου καὶ πατέρα ὑμῶν καὶ θεόν μου καὶ θεὸν ὑμῶν (20:17b).

[55] ἔρχεται Μαριὰμ ἡ Μαγδαληνὴ ἀγγέλλουσα τοῖς μαθηταῖς ὅτι ἑώρακα τὸν κύριον, καὶ ταῦτα εἶπεν αὐτῇ (20:18).

[56] I am indebted to Helmut Koester for this insight (verbal communication).

[57] Charlesworth explains, "The need for shoring up Mary Magdalene's report seems rather obvious; thus, both Peter and the Beloved Disciple are presented as the two male witnesses needed to establish the fact that the tomb was empty." He continues, "The author of the GosJn knew Jewish law and even stated the requisite statute: 'in your torah it is written that the witness of two men is true' (8:17). . . . Few scholars have seen the importance of presenting two males as witnesses to what Mary reported; but Marsh [*Gospel of John* (New York: Viking, 1968), 631] wisely stated that the author of the GosJn 'now tells how Peter and the Beloved Disciple come and witness the fact of the empty tomb' " (Charlesworth, *Beloved Disciple*, 97–98).

nificant one than Peter. In this gospel she is single-handedly responsible for sharing the resurrection news with the others, a role that later earns her the title, *apostola apostolorum* ("apostle of the apostles").[58] Her portrayal as the first resurrection witness in John coincides well with the way that the Gospel as a whole portrays female characters in leadership roles spreading the good news.[59]

Summary

The Gospel of John clearly privileges the figure of the Beloved Disciple in this text, thus presenting a significant instance in early Christian literature in which a figure is not subordinated to Peter, a figure who over time gains great authority in Christian history. Peter's role is conversely diminished on numerous occasions in the gospel. Jesus does not call Peter; he makes no positive statement in response to Peter's confession; he does not single him out as a member of an inner circle of disciples; and he makes no individual resurrection appearance to him, as he does in Luke. Rather, the Gospel of John provides opportunities for other figures, such as the woman at the well, Martha, and finally Mary Magdalene to be faithful evangelists and witnesses to Christ.

Moreover, the Gospel of John likewise privileges the figure of Mary Magdalene over that of Peter. Rather than being one of two or several women at the tomb, in this gospel she, alone among the women, and indeed alone among all the disciples, is singled out to receive an individual resurrection appearance from Christ. Moreover, she also receives a commissioning from Christ to go tell the others what she has seen and heard. The next chapter explores further the significance and implications of the receipt of such a commissioning or divine authorization to spread the good news.

---

[58]This title is discussed in more detail in the last chapter.

[59]Schüssler Fiorenza, *In Memory of Her*, 316–30. Raymond Brown, "Appendix II: Roles of Women in the Fourth Gospel," *The Community of the Beloved Disciple*, 183–98; idem, "Roles of Women in the Fourth Gospel," *TS* 36 (1975): 688–99.

CHAPTER FOUR

Portrayals of Apostolic Witness:
The Gospels of Mark and Matthew
versus the *Gospel of Peter*

The previous chapters have argued that a figure's prestige and authority are increased when he or she is depicted in a narrative as the recipient of a resurrection appearance from Jesus. A comparison of resurrection reports in early Christian literature shows that the discrepancies concerning recipients of resurrection appearances do not fall neatly into predictable categories, such as "canonical" and "noncanonical" or "orthodox" and "heretical." We have seen that even within the New Testament itself, the gospels of Luke and John present contradictory portrayals of the first resurrection appearances of Jesus. Indeed, we have seen that an inverse relationship obtains between the two gospels insofar as Luke magnifies Peter and diminishes Mary, while John magnifies Mary and diminishes Peter. This inverse relationship may reflect competing perspectives on the authority and standing of these two figures in the early church. If indeed some competition between proponents of Peter and Mary Magdalene concerning their status as apostolic witnesses occurred, then texts that assign special prominence to Peter, such as the *Gospel of Peter,* may preserve further traces of such competition in their treatment of Mary. This chapter, therefore, compares three additional resurrection narratives — the gospels of Mark and Matthew and the *Gospel of Peter* — to the gospels of Luke and John with respect to their accounts of the first resurrection appearances.

This chapter also examines the way in which a figure's authority is further enhanced in such a narrative if the encounter also includes a commissioning from Jesus. This chapter therefore examines how Peter and

Mary Magdalene fare as recipients of commissionings. Although Rengstorf rightly points out that "the apostles receive their religious impress from him who commissions them, and in such a way that the commission itself is the main thing, not its bearers,"[1] I maintain that the identity of those chosen to bear commissions is just as significant, especially with respect to apostolic authority.

Mary and Peter in the Gospels of Mark and Matthew

The New Testament records four commissionings of Mary: one in Mark, two in Matthew, and one in John, each with its own distinctive variations. In the first of these four resurrection narratives and commissionings, the Gospel of Mark, a "young man . . . dressed in a white robe"[2] tells Mary Magdalene and two other women: "But go, tell his disciples and Peter that he is going before you to Galilee; you will see him there just as he told you."[3] This narrative in Mark is filled with enigmatic elements and in many ways raises more questions than it answers. Even the exact ending of the gospel is unclear because the text breaks off suddenly after 16:8 with the particle γάρ. Greek sentences that end with this word are rare indeed.[4] If the gospel was meant to end with 16:8, perhaps the author felt that narrating a commissioning and the announcement from a heavenly messenger that Christ is risen and no longer there would provide sufficient evidence of the resurrection itself; the author chose to focus, rather, on the commissioning of the women to evangelize to the "disciples and to Peter." The specific reference to Peter is curious; it could be that he is being singled out as leader, or it could be that, as Anderson suggests, "The singling out of Peter recalls his denial."[5] Another unusual element of the gospel's conclusion is that the text specifies Mary Magdalene and the other women as witnesses,

---

[1] Rengstorf, "apóstolos," TDNT: Abridged in One Volume, 71.

[2] νεανίσκον καθήμενον ἐν τοῖς δεξιοῖς περιβεβλημένον στολὴν λευκήν (v. 5). As Hugh Anderson (The Gospel of Mark [NCBC; Grand Rapids, Mich.: Eerdmans, 1976], 355) explains, "Mark's reserve toward the supernatural is evident from the way he introduces quite simply a young man, who is none-the-less clearly an 'angel', a white robe being the traditional garb of heavenly beings (cf. 2 Mac. 3:26, 33; Rev. 7:9, 13f.)."

[3] ἀλλὰ ὑπάγετε εἴπατε τοῖς μαθηταῖς αὐτοῦ καὶ τῷ Πέτρῳ ὅτι προάγει ὑμᾶς εἰς τὴν Γαλιλαίαν· ἐκεῖ αὐτὸν ὄψεσθε, καθὼς εἶπεν ὑμῖν (16:7).

[4] Anderson, Mark, 353.

[5] Ibid., 357.

but then relates that they "said nothing to anyone because they were afraid."[6] This last part of Mark ends before portraying a resurrection appearance of Jesus, but not without the promise of his appearance in Galilee. The desire to see this promise fulfilled has spawned the addition of at least two variant endings: vv. 9–10 (the so-called "shorter ending") and vv. 9–20 (the "longer ending"). Both endings are clearly later additions.[7] Significant for this study is the fact that the climax of the gospel in vv. 1–8, discounting the secondary endings, includes the crucial commissioning of three women—Mary Magdalene, Mary the mother of James, and Salome—to go and tell the other disciples what they have seen. Despite their fear, it is clear that they did spread the news, as the very existence of the Gospel of Mark demonstrates.

The resurrection narrative in the Gospel of Matthew goes into considerably more detail.[8] One of the noteworthy elements of the scene in this gospel is its bestowal upon Mary Magdalene and the women of not one but two commissionings to spread the news. The angel first commissions Mary to tell the "disciples" (μαθηταί), and then Jesus commissions Mary to tell the "brothers" (ἀδελφοί). These two accounts of a commissioning appear to be independent of one another.[9] One account resembles the

---

[6]καὶ οὐδενὶ οὐδὲν εἶπαν, ἐφοβοῦντο γάρ (16:8).

[7]Regarding the longer ending of Mark, Anderson (*Mark*, 358) writes: "Some of the best MSS of Mark end at 16:8. Many others include these verses [i.e., the longer ending supplied later by 16:9-20]. But in vocabulary, style, and content they are unquestionably non-Marcan, and have a distinct flavour of the second century." Likewise with the shorter ending: "Unlike the [longer ending], it was obviously written with the express purpose of providing the necessary conclusion to what its author took to be an otherwise incomplete Gospel" (ibid., 361).

[8]τότε λέγει αὐταῖς ὁ Ἰησοῦς· μὴ φοβεῖσθε· ὑπάγετε ἀπαγγείλατε τοῖς ἀδελφοῖς μου ἵνα ἀπέλθωσιν εἰς τὴν Γαλιλαίαν, κἀκεῖ με ὄψονται (28:10). See Keith Howard Reeves, *The Resurrection Narrative in Matthew: A Literary-Critical Examination* (Lewiston: Mellen Biblical Press, 1993); Elaine Mary Wainwright, *Towards a Feminist Critical Reading of the Gospel according to Matthew* (BZNW 60; Berlin: de Gruyter, 1991); Janice Capel Anderson, "Matthew: Gender and Reading," *Semeia* 28 (1983): 3–27; W. F. Albright and C. S. Mann, *Matthew* (AB 26; Garden City, N.Y.: Doubleday, 1971), 366.

[9]Walter Grundmann, *Das Evangelium nach Matthäus* (5th ed.; THKNT 1; Berlin: Evangelische Verlagsanstalt, 1981), 568 n. 4: "Die beiden Erzählungen sind nicht voneinander abhängig, sondern in ihnen gestaltet sich eine Maria-Magdalena-Tradition, aus deren Wurzel beide unabhängig voneinandergewachsen sind." See also Alsup, *Post-Resurrection Appearance Stories*, 208.

commissioning scene in the Gospel of Mark ("Go and tell the disciples
. . .")[10] while the other parallels the scene found in John ("Go and tell
my brothers . . .").[11] In the two gospels in which Jesus himself supplies
the commission to Mary to spread the news, he directs her in both cases
to speak to the ἀδελφοί (John 21:23 and Matt 28:10).

Matthew's presentation of Peter in the Gospel of Matthew places the
disciple in an ambiguous position.[12] As Brown writes, "Matthew is the
Evangelist who gives Peter the most exalted role as the recipient of the
keys of the kingdom of heaven (16:19), but Matthew would never make
Peter first in the kingdom. That is a primacy specifically denied even to
members of the Twelve (20:20–26)."[13] As Kingsbury explains, compared
to Mark, the Gospel of Matthew "lends greater prominence of both a positive and negative sort, to the figure of Peter."[14] For instance, Matthew's
Jesus blesses Peter with the power to bind and loose (16:17–19),[15] but
Matthew's Jesus also subsequently rebukes Peter and refers to him as
"Satan," and only in Matthew does Jesus label Peter a "stumbling block"
(σκάνδαλον, 16:23). Matthew thus displays a tendency to include mul-

---

[10]καὶ ταχὺ πορευθεῖσαι εἴπατε τοῖς μαθηταῖς αὐτοῦ ὅτι ἠγέρθη ἀπὸ τῶν νεκρῶν,
καὶ ἰδοὺ προάγει ὑμᾶς εἰς τὴν Γαλιλαίαν, ἐκεῖ αὐτὸν ὄψεσθε· ἰδοὺ εἶπον ὑμῖν
(28:7).

[11]πορεύου δὲ πρὸς τοὺς ἀδελφούς μου καὶ εἰπὲ αὐτοῖς· ἀναβαίνω πρὸς τὸν πατέρα
μου καὶ πατέρα ὑμῶν καὶ θεόν μου καὶ θεὸν ὑμῶν (John 20:17b). The Greek word ἀδελ-
φοίς can designate either a group of "brothers" or a group of "brothers and sisters."

[12]Jack Dean Kingsbury, "The Figure of Peter in Matthew's Gospel as a Theological
Problem," *JBL* 98 (1979): 67–83.

[13]Brown, "Roles of Women in the Fourth Gospel," 694 n. 16.

[14]Kingsbury, "The Figure of Peter in Matthew," 69.

[15]Ibid. See also Paul Hoffmann, "Der Petrus-Primat im Matthäusevangelium," *Neues
Testament und Kirche* (Fs. R. Schnackenburg; ed. J. Gnilka; Freiburg: Herder, 1974),
94–114; Eduard Schweizer, *Matthäus und seine Gemeinde* (SBS 71; Stuttgart: Katholisches
Bibelwerk, 1974), 42–44, 151–55; Max Wilcox, "Peter and the Rock: A Fresh Look at
Matthew xvi. 17–19," *NTS* 22 (1975/76): 73–88. See also Ulrich Luz, *Das Evangelium
nach Matthäus* (EKKNT 1.2; 4 vols.; Zürich: Benziger/Neukirchen-Vluyn: Neukirchener
Verlag, 1990), 450–83; Joseph A. Burgess, *A History of the Exegesis of Matthew 16:
17–19 from 1781 to 1965* (Ann Arbor, Mich.: Edwards Brothers, 1976). Some scholars
argue that this may be another example of the retrojection of veneration onto figures in
the text. Campenhausen (*Ecclesiastical Authority and Spiritual Power,* 17; see also 129)
for example, argues, "The famous saying that the whole Church is to be built on Peter is
simply inconceivable in the mouth of Jesus, and in all probability reflects a situation in
which expansion has already gone beyond the ambit of the primitive community."

tiple traditions, seen best in the inclusion of both the angelophany and the christophany received by Mary, as well as both the tradition identifying Mary Magdalene as the first resurrection witness and the tradition noting Peter as a primary leader.[16]

Although Matthew displays more inclusivity of both Peter and Mary traditions than either Luke or John does, it is still apparent that Matthew attributes different amounts of prominence and authority to each of the two figures in the passion narrative. Here one finds that Matthew records both an angelophany and a christophany to Mary Magdalene, as well as her commissioning by Jesus, while Peter receives neither by name. Matthew's last reference to Peter is in the account of his denial of Jesus (26:75); his name does not appear again, even when Jesus sends his disciples out into the world (28:16–20).

As already mentioned, this crucial element of the commissioning of Mary Magdalene through either an angelophany or a christophany is absent from the Gospel of Luke. It is also absent from the *Gospel of Peter*. The following section will show that with respect to the granting of apostolic status, the Gospel of Luke and the apocryphal *Gospel of Peter* have more in common with each other than Luke has with the other three canonical gospels, insofar as they both feature Peter, not Mary, as a primary recipient of a resurrection appearance. Indeed, both gospels demonstrate a marked tendency to exclude women from positions of authority.[17]

Portrayals of Peter and Mary in the *Gospel of Peter*

A comparison of the *Gospel of Peter* with the Gospel of Luke demonstrates that texts with pro-Petrine tendencies significantly differ in their portrayal of Mary's status from those texts in which Peter holds a diminished position. The text recognized as the *Gospel of Peter* was known only from allusions to it in patristic sources[18] until the discov-

---

[16]Matthew also transmits the two miraculous feedings (of the five thousand [14:13–21] and of the four thousand [15:32–39]) from Mark, which Luke does not.

[17]Another parallel between these texts occurs in an actual resurrection scene mentioned both in Luke (24:51) and the *Gospel of Peter* (10.39–40).

[18]Patristic references provide evidence of a document specifically called *The Gospel of Peter*. See, for example, Serapion of Antioch, preserved in Eusebius (*Hist. eccl.* 6.12.3–6); Origen, *Comm. on Matt.* Vol. 10, chapter 17; Jerome, *Vir. Ill.* 1 and the *Decretum Gelasianum*. "Un évangéliste qui écrit sous le nom de Pierre ne pouvait manquer de mettre en

ery of a Greek fragment in the late nineteenth century at Akhmim in Egypt.[19] It is undoubtedly a pro-Petrine text as it portrays Peter not only witnessing the entire resurrection event, but also narrating the text as a whole. Peter describes Jesus' resurrection and begins to relate a resurrection appearance to himself and others: "I, Simon Peter and my brother Andrew took our nets and went to the sea. . . ."[20] Unfortunately, the manuscript breaks off a few words later.

Despite the relatively early date of the *Gospel of Peter,* in the first or early second century,[21] its accounts of resurrection appearances show signs

---

plein jour la prééminence du chef des apôtres. . . . Pierre reçoit du Christ ressuscité l'autorité suprême. De cette façon le prince des apôtres éclipsait tous les témoins intimes de la résurrection" (Léon Vaganay, *L'Évangile de Pierre* [EBib; Paris: Gabalda, 1930], 93–94).

[19]Maria G. Mara, trans., *Évangile de Pierre* (SC 201; Paris: Cerf, 1973). A new critical edition of the *Gospel of Peter* will soon be available from Thomas J. Kraus and Tobias Nicklas, eds., *Griechische Fragmente des sog. "Petrusevangeliums"/Griechische Fragmente des sog. "Offenbarung des Petrus"* (GCS n.s. 7; Berlin: de Gruyter, forthcoming 2003). Their edition is based in part on recent photos of the well known Akhmim codex (P. Cair 10759). The newer photos have enabled them to improve on the Gebhardt edition of 1893, and as a result they can also suggest some revisions of Dieter Lührmann's treatment of the papyrus fragments, which is based on the older photographs. They also dispel the popular myths in the discovery and earlier descriptions of the papyri and parchments (e.g. that the *Gos. Pet.* was found in a monk's tomb). For additional information on this text, including the issue of date, see Éric Junod ("Évangile de Pierre," in *Écrits apocryphes chrétiens* [Paris: Gallimard, 1997], 241–54); Enrico Norelli, "Situation des apocryphes pétriniens," *Apocrypha* 2 (1991): 31–83; Koester, *Ancient Christian Gospels,* 216–40; John Dominic Crossan, *The Cross that Spoke: The Origins of the Passion Narrative* (San Francisco: Harper & Row, 1973); Jünger Denker, *Die theologiegeschichtliche Stellung des Petrusevangeliums: Ein Beitrag zur Frühgeschichte des Doketismus* (Bern: Lang, 1975). Jerry W. McCant ("The Gospel of Peter: Docetism Reconsidered," *NTS* 30 [1984]: 258–73) deals with the question of docetism and argues that there is no good basis for believing that the *Gospel of Peter* is docetic. Raymond Brown ("The *Gospel of Peter* and Canonical Gospel Priority," *NTS* 33 [1987]: 325) suggests, "We are more likely dealing with a work in which ambiguous phraseology could be read in a docetist way."

[20]ἐγὼ δὲ Σίμων Πέτρος καὶ Ἀνδρέας ὁ ἀδελφός μου λαθόντες ἡμῶν τὰ λίνα ἀπήλθαμεν εἰς τὴν θάλασσαν (*Gos. Pet.* 14.60). A new fragment attributed to the *Gospel of Peter* is POxy 4009, which also uses the first person pronoun (μοί) to identify the recipient of Jesus' saying. See Dieter Lührmann, "POx 4009: Ein neues Fragment des Petrusevangelium?" *NovT* 35 (1993): 390–410.

[21]See Junod ("Évangile de Pierre," 242), who dates the text to the first half of the second century. See also Percival Gardner-Smith, "The Date of the Gospel of Peter," *JTS* 27 (1926): 404; Norelli, "Situation des apocryphes pétriniens," 31–83.

of manipulation and compositional development.[22] Helmut Koester, for instance, points out that the redactional elements in this gospel "reveal the hand of the original author of the *Gospel of Peter*, who tries to connect several originally independent resurrection accounts."[23] Three epiphany accounts appear in the text: 1) the guards (and the elders) at the tomb witness Jesus' resurrection; 2) Mary Magdalene and the other women witness the open tomb; and 3) Peter and Andrew and some other disciples witness Jesus' appearance at the lake.[24] It is at the beginning of this last epiphany that the fragment breaks off. This sequence of epiphanies produces a subtle but crucial twist on what appears in Matthew, Mark, and John. The first epiphany account, describing the role of the guards and elders at the tomb as witnesses of Jesus' resurrection, is a new element, appearing in none of the canonical resurrection accounts.[25] The introduction of this first epiphany into the sequence of events significantly changes the role of the women. It effectively functions to remove the women from their role as the first recipients of the resurrection news. This difference is a crucial one because this change moves women into a secondary role in the *Gospel of Peter*; they are no longer the primary witnesses to the resurrection or the mediators of the kerygma—men are.[26]

In the second epiphany account, Mary Magdalene and the other women appear in the text for the first time as they arrive at the tomb.[27] They have come, it seems, to overcome an earlier failing: they had not done "what women are accustomed to do for the dead."[28] Instead of Jesus, the women find a young man in a luminous robe in the middle of the sepulchre who

[22]Arthur J. Dewey, "Time to Murder and Create: Visions and Revisions in the *Gospel of Peter*," *Semeia* 49 (1990): 101–27.

[23]Koester, *Ancient Christian Gospels*, 231 n. 3.

[24]Ibid., 217.

[25]Although the narrative detail of guards stationed at the tomb is found in the Gospel of Matthew, the guards are not eyewitnesses of Jesus' resurrection.

[26]Mentioned in the presentation of Caroline Vander Stichele from the Universiteit van Amsterdam in "A Disciple of the Lord and Her Friends: Women in the *Gospel of Peter*," SBL Annual Meeting 1997.

[27]Koester, "Apocryphal and Canonical Gospels," 129. Koester identifies the incongruency inherent in having the tomb closed again after Jesus' resurrection. The replacement of the stone after the scene with the guards and elders indicates the composite nature of the text. He points out, "Indeed, in this context the appearance of the angel, with all appropriate features of an epiphany, only serves as a courtesy to the women: Jesus had already left the tomb."

[28]ἃ εἰώθεσαν ποιεῖν αἱ γυναῖκες ἐπὶ τοῖς ἀποθνῄσκουσι (12.50).

tells them that Jesus is risen and gone and adds, "if you do not believe, look in and see the place where he lay for he is not there."[29] Without indicating whether the women did or did not comply with his invitation, the text explains that "the women then fled frightened."[30] The significance of this second epiphany is that it contains no commissioning—whether from the resurrected Christ or even from the angelic young man—mandating the women to spread the resurrection news.[31]

Although the ending of the *Gospel of Peter* is lost, the third epiphany account points toward an appearance of Christ to Peter and other disciples. It states that they returned to their homes and took their nets out to sea, thus introducing a narrative whose beginning echoes that of the secondary conclusion of John (21:1–23). This third epiphany in the sequence functions to portray Peter and Andrew, not the women, as the intended recipients of Christ's next resurrection appearance.

If it is the case that some rivalry existed even in the first century between Peter and Mary Magdalene as apostolic witnesses, then the pro-Petrine *Gospel of Peter* should reflect this rivalry by reducing Mary's status, as the pro-Petrine Gospel of Luke does. At first glance, Mary Magdalene's role in the *Gospel of Peter* seems fairly similar to her role in most of the other sepulchre scenes. The author specifically mentions Mary Magdalene, designates her a "disciple of the Lord" (μαθήτρια τοῦ κυρίου [12.50]), and states that she and "friends" (τὰς φίλας [fem. plural; 12.51]) came to the tomb.[32] However, comparison of the *Gospel of Peter* with other texts

---

[29]*Gosp. Pet.* 12.56. Vander Stichele pointed out that the words of the messenger "if you do not believe" suggest the possible unbelief of the women.

[30]τότε αἱ γυναῖκες φοβηθεῖσαι ἔφυγον (13.57).

[31]Crossan (*The Cross That Spoke*, 14) presents the wide range of opinions on this text's independence or dependence by quoting two scholars: "Maurer says that 'although Peter himself is indicated as the author (v. 26f., 60), what lies before us is a further development of the traditional material of the four canonical Gospels' (*NTA* 1:180 [*NTApoc⁴*])." Ron Cameron (*The Other Gospels: Non-Canonical Gospel Texts* [Philadelphia: Westminster, 1982], 78), on the other hand, "concludes that form criticism and redaction criticism indicate that the *Gospel of Peter* was dependent upon a number of sources, but it is quite possible that the document as we have it antedates the four gospels of the New Testament and may have served as a source for their respective authors." See Christian Maurer and Wilhelm Schneemelcher, "The Gospel of Peter," *NTApoc⁵* 1:216–27.

[32]There is a difference of opinion whether μαθήτρια has any special significance. Bovon suggests that the term may have special significance considering that Mary is called a μαθήτρια τοῦ κυρίου (Bovon, "Mary Magdalene's Paschal Privilege," 151).

reveals some critical differences. This story presents numerous standard details of the events of Jesus' crucifixion, such as the scourging, the two criminals crucified on either side of Jesus, and the division of Jesus' garments by the casting of lots, and yet it makes no mention of any women at the crucifixion scene, unlike the four canonical gospels. Terence Smith may be correct in suggesting that the absence of the women lessens the contrast drawn in Mark, Matthew, and John between the faithful women and the male disciples who fled when Jesus was arrested.[33] If this is an intentional omission, it is a logical one for a pro-Petrine text to commit. The Gospel of Luke also mitigates the contrast, but in a different way. It depicts the women at the crucifixion scene, as do the other three canonical gospels, but does not mention that the male disciples fled. Finally, the most significant element for the issue of authority is the fact that in the *Gospel of Peter*, Mary and the other women never receive a commission to deliver the good news as they do in the majority of the resurrection narratives.

Textual comparisons highlight further evidence of the shaping of the tradition in this text. For example, Koester contends that there exist "numerous features in these accounts which are obviously secondary" with respect to earlier traditions and the form of the passion narrative: 1) Jesus is condemned and crucified by Herod, while Pilate is completely exonerated;[34] 2) the anti-Jewish polemic seems intensified; and 3) the story of Jesus' resurrection from the tomb is told elaborately, introducing the feature of the cross that follows Jesus out of the tomb and speaks.[35] I add to this list of secondary elements the diminished role of Mary Magdalene. The *Gospel of Peter* thus resembles the Gospel of Luke in the way it places Mary Magdalene with the other women in a secondary and thus superfluous position as resurrection witnesses.

Marjanen, on the other hand, finds no substantive reason that this term indicates any status (Marjanen, *The Woman Jesus Loved*, 26). The term μαθήτρια appears in the New Testament only in Acts as a description of Tabitha (9:36), whom Peter brings back to life; in this instance no special status is indicated by the term.

[33]Smith, *Petrine Controversies*, 41.

[34]Koester, *Ancient Christian Gospels*, 217–18.

[35]Ibid., 233 n. 2. Koester argues that the appearance of the young man from heaven at the tomb (11.44) is a redactional insertion: "this angelic person is needed in the tomb for the following story of the discovery of the empty tomb (12.50–13.57)."

Summary

As readers of the New Testament, we are accustomed to seeing the agreement of the synoptic gospels (Matthew, Mark, and Luke) over against the exceptional nature of the Gospel of John. However, with respect to the role of Mary Magdalene and her position in the gospels, we find something quite different. The Gospels of Matthew and Mark more closely resemble the Gospel of John, and the Gospel of Luke is in this case the exception.

A comparison of the canonical resurrection narratives presents numerous differences among the accounts, but considering the broad geographic and chronological range in which these narratives circulated, it is amazing that the discrepancies are not greater and even more numerous. It is intriguing that the narratives vary not only on the point of the bestower of the commissioning (Jesus or one or two angelic beings), but also on the point of its intended recipients (brethren or disciples). Despite the variation and narrative fluidity, however, what emerges as especially remarkable is that Mary Magdalene appears at the tomb in each of these canonical gospels, either alone or in the company of others. She is not only always present but is also always listed first at the sepulchre scenes, even in Luke—the text that credits her with the least status overall. She is thus one of the most consistent, stable elements in the New Testament resurrection narratives as a whole. Alone among the canonical gospels, however, Luke omits a commission for Mary Magdalene to tell the other disciples what she has seen. This study explains Luke's diminution of Mary Magdalene as the counterpart of that gospel's clear preference for Peter and correlates Luke's program with a similar program in the *Gospel of Peter*.

The *Gospel of Peter* and the Gospel of Luke challenge the tradition represented in the canonical gospels insofar as they privilege the position of Peter over that of Mary Magdalene. Interestingly, in this alternative strand of tradition, the *Gospel of Peter* and the Gospel of Luke have a number of other elements in common with respect to Mary Magdalene: 1) neither reports an actual appearance of Jesus to Mary Magdalene or other women as do Matthew and John; 2) both record an angelophany to Mary Magdalene as do Matthew, Mark, and John, but in neither the *Gospel of Peter* nor Luke is she commissioned to tell the other disciples the good news, as she is in Matthew, Mark, and John; and 3) both texts portray Peter as authoritative and attribute resurrection appearances by Jesus to

Peter instead of Mary. These commonalities must be more than random occurrences. One can discern in both texts the ways in which material has been manipulated to highlight the role of Peter, while Mary is denied a resurrection appearance and a commissioning. The prominence of Peter in both these texts thus coincides with the corresponding presentation of a nonapostolic role for Mary Magdalene.

CHAPTER FIVE

Competition between Peter and Mary Magdalene in Other Texts

As the discussion of the *Gospel of Peter* in the previous chapter has already shown, exploring noncanonical resurrection narratives sheds additional light on the variations in resurrection witnesses and apostolic authority. The study of a broader base of literature beyond that canonized in the New Testament is proving ever more useful to the field of early Christian studies by adding to our knowledge of the diversity of early Christian groups. We have already seen that even in the earliest resurrection narratives there existed a tension concerning the leadership positions of Mary Magdalene and Peter. Additional documents from the first few centuries of early Christian history can further elucidate the conflicting traditions in existence among the early Christians concerning these two figures.

This chapter, therefore, examines how five other noncanonical early Christian texts represent the roles of Mary Magdalene and Peter, noting the interactions of these characters with others, including Jesus, and especially the frequency with which these two figures are portrayed in competition with each other. Indeed the scripted dialogues of the *Gospel of Thomas*, the *Gospel of Mary*, and *Pistis Sophia* portray more than mere competition; they could even be described as verbal confrontations between Peter and Mary Magdalene or between Peter and Jesus concerning Mary Magdalene. This chapter examines the representations of these two figures in specific passages in each of these three texts, as well as a brief examination of leadership roles in the *Dialogue of the Savior* and *Sophia of Jesus Christ*.

Descriptions of conflict between Peter and Mary Magdalene in early Christian literature invite one to ask what purposes such representations of controversy could serve. Why, moreover, do the *Gospel of Thomas*, the *Gospel of Mary*, and *Pistis Sophia* always specifically name the figure of Peter as the one who attempts to challenge or diminish Mary Magdalene's position? Before exploring these questions and their implications further, let us first examine each of these three texts in more detail. Scholars have already produced an immense amount of research on these controversy narratives.[1] I will offer here only a brief overview of this research for the purpose of setting the foundation for the chapters to come.

Portrayals of Peter and Mary in the *Gospel of Thomas*

The *Gospel of Thomas* is an ancient collection of 114 sayings of Jesus, known as "logia,"[2] representing the genre of wisdom literature. It exists primarily in a Coptic version along with a few Greek fragments found among the papyri discovered in Oxyrhynchus, Egypt (frgs. 1, 654, and 655).[3] While scholars recognize the value of this text in its preservation of certain aspects of the development of sayings attributed to Jesus in early Christian history, they disagree whether this collection stems from the first or the second century. Scholars such as Helmut Koester make a strong argument for situating this gospel in the first century.[4] Some

---

[1]Studies of these explicit confrontations began years ago with Schüssler Fiorenza, *In Memory of Her*, 304–15; Bovon, "Mary Magdalene's Paschal Privilege," 153; Pagels, *Gnostic Gospels*, 33–83; Karen King, "Introduction" [to the *Gospel of Mary* (BG 8502, 1)], in *Nag Hammadi Library in English* (ed. James M. Robinson; San Francisco: Harper and Row, 1988), 523–24.

[2]This division of the gospel into logia is the work of modern editors; it is not found in the original text. Text in *Nag Hammadi Codex II, 2–7* (ed. Bentley Layton; Leiden: Brill, 1989), 38–49. See also Jacques-É. Ménard, *L'Évangile selon Thomas* (NHS 5; Leiden: Brill, 1975).

[3]The papyrus fragment, P. Oxy 654, contains the *Gos. Thom.* prologue and logia 1–7; P. Oxy 1 contains *Gos. Thom.* logia 26–33, 77a, and P. Oxy 655 contains *Gos. Thom.* logia 24, 36–39. They were found near modern Bahnasa, Egypt. See Marvin W. Meyer, trans. and introduction, *The Gospel of Thomas: the Hidden Sayings of Jesus* (interpr. Harold Bloom; New York: HarperSanFrancisco, 1992), 7.

[4]For more on dating the text to the first century, see Helmut Koester, "Introduction [to *The Gospel according to Thomas*]," in *Nag Hammadi Codex II, 2–7* (ed. Bentley Layton; NHS 20; Leiden: Brill, 1989), 38–49. Stevan Davies dates the gospel to the mid-first

of the sayings in this gospel appear to be earlier than their parallels in the New Testament because they are sometimes simpler in form, lacking in allegorization, or missing the kind of interpretive comments that can typically appear at the end of such sayings in the canonical gospels.[5] The Thomas gospel, moreover, is almost totally lacking in such Christological titles as "Christ/Messiah," "Lord," and "Son of Man," the kind of epithets that became much more common after Jesus' death.[6] Scholars also debate the gospel's provenance; many have argued for an origin in Syria, especially in Edessa,[7] although others have suggested Antioch and other sites.[8]

---

century (50–70 c.e.) in *The Gospel of Thomas and Christian Wisdom* (New York: Seabury, 1983), 3. Meyer dates this text to the second century or the latter part of the first century ce, in Meyer, *The Gospel of Thomas*, 10.

[5]Examples of the simpler forms of certain sayings are the *Gos. Thom.* 68 compared to Q/Luke 6:22; *Gos. Thom.* 95 compared to Q/Luke 6:34; and *Gos. Thom.* 47a–b compared to Q/Matt 6:24/Luke 16:13 (Koester, *Ancient Christian Gospels,* 85). See also idem, "Three Thomas Parables," in *The New Testament and Gnosis: Essays in Honor of Robert McL. Wilson* (ed. A. H. B. Logan and A. J. M. Wedderburn; Edinburgh: T&T Clark, 1983), 195–203. In this text, Koester gives more examples, including *Gos. Thom.* 65 compared to Mark 12:1–9, Matt 21:33–41, and Luke 20:9–16. He explains, "the conclusion seems obvious: the Gospel of Thomas indeed preserved a more original and non-allegorical version of this parable" (p. 199).

[6]Koester, *Ancient Christian Gospels,* 86.

[7]Koester, "Introduction [to *The Gospel according to Thomas*]," 38–49. The earliest articles on the topic of provenance include Henri-Charles Puech, "Das Thomas Evangelium," in Hennecke-Schneemelcher, *NTApok³,* including date and provenance, 207, as well as Puech's *En quête de la Gnose: Sur l'Évangile selon Thomas: Esquisse d'une interprétation systématique* (Paris: Gallimard, 1978). As early as 1957, on the basis of the name Judas Thomas, Puech argued for the provenance of this text as Edessa or a neighboring area (Puech, *Évangile selon Thomas,* 42–44), although he does allow for the possibility that the attribution of the text to Judas Thomas in logion 1 is a later addition to the text. Puech wrote that he believed that there were several versions of the *Gospel of Thomas,* with the first version being more orthodox than the version appearing in the Nag Hammadi corpus, although even the earlier version was nevertheless marked by encratism. In his opinion, the text exhibits the kind of Christianity found in Syria and in Egypt in the second century. It was therefore in one of these two countries that the text was written, but Puech leans in favor of Syria or a surrounding region on the basis of the apostle's name (Puech, *Évangile selon Thomas,* 53).

[8]Desjardins discusses the issue of the provenance of the *Gospel of Thomas* in more detail in Michel R. Desjardins, "Where Was the Gospel of Thomas Written?" *TJT* 8 (1992): 121–33. On one side of the argument is Stevan Davies, who wishes to remove the *Gospel of Thomas* from Edessa ("There is no evidence at all for the Edessene composition of all documents approved by the Manicheans" [Davies, *Thomas and Christian Wisdom,* 20]).

In the context of this study, we will focus on the portrayals of the disciples and the particular roles that they hold in the sayings that the *Gospel of Thomas* preserves. This gospel, for example, specifically names only a few contemporaries of Jesus. In the order of their appearance, these figures are: Didymus Judas Thomas (#1 and #13), James the Just (#12), Simon Peter (#13 and #114), Matthew (#13), Mary (#21 and #114), John the Baptist (#46), and Salome (#61). Some debate has occurred concerning the identity of this Mary in the *Gospel of Thomas* and the *Gospel of Mary*; I will be following the majority of scholars in identifying each of them as Mary Magdalene and will respond to the minority position below, in the context of my discussion of the *Gospel of Philip* and *Pistis Sophia*. Of these seven figures, only five possess individual speaking parts in the text: Judas Thomas, Simon Peter, Matthew, Mary, and Salome.

The first of these five, Judas Thomas, is named in the ancient title of the text: "These are the secret words which the Living Jesus spoke and Didymos Judas Thomas wrote."[9] Judas Thomas also appears in logion 13 along with Simon Peter and Matthew. In this saying three disciples offer a response to Jesus' invitation: "Make a comparison to me and tell me whom I am like."[10] Simon Peter answers that Jesus is like "a righteous messenger" (ⲛ̅ⲟⲩⲁⲅⲅⲉⲗⲟⲥ ⲛ̅ⲇⲓⲕⲁⲓⲟⲥ). Matthew responds that Jesus is like "a wise man of understanding" (ⲛ̅ⲟⲩⲣⲱⲙⲉ ⲛ̅ⲫⲓⲗⲟⲥⲟⲫⲟⲥ ⲛ̅ⲣⲙ̅ⲛ̅ϩⲏⲧ). Finally, Judas Thomas states: "Master, my mouth will not at all be capable

---

He places it instead in Antioch, thereby rejecting Helmut Koester's arguments. Along the same lines as Davies is the earlier work of Barbara Ehlers, "Kann das Thomasevangelium aus Edessa stammen?" *NovT* 12 (1970): 70–77. She examines texts believed to have originated in Syria and finds that the Church of Edessa does not fit the *Gospel of Thomas*. In a response to her article, Albertus F. J. Klijn ("Christianity in Edessa and the Gospel of Thomas," *NovT* 14 [1972]: 70–77), defends Puech's original idea. In part the argument hinges on the use of the name Judas Thomas Didymus: Ehlers places the origin of this name "keineswegs in Edessa" while Klijn states "nobody can deny that the earliest traces of this tradition can only be found in Syria" (Klijn, "Christianity in Edessa," 77).

[9]ⲛⲁⲉⲓⲛⲉ ⲛ̅ϣⲁϫⲉ ⲉⲑⲏⲡⲛⲉⲛⲧⲁ ⲓ̅ⲥ̅ ⲉⲧⲟⲛϩ ϫⲟⲟⲩ ⲁⲩⲱ ⲁϥⲥϩⲁⲓ̈ⲥⲟⲩ ⲛ̅ϭⲓ ⲇⲓⲇⲩⲙⲟⲥ ⲓ̈ⲟⲩⲇⲁⲥ ⲑⲱⲙⲁⲥ (*Gos. Thom.* incipit). According to Meyer this incipit (the opening lines of the document) provides what is most likely the earlier version of the title; a second, later title appears at the end of the document: "The Gospel According to Thomas" (Meyer, *Gospel of Thomas*, 67). This incipit also exists in a Greek fragment of the *Gospel of Thomas* (POxy 654).

[10]ⲡⲉϫⲉ ⲓ̅ⲥ̅ ⲛ̅ⲛⲉϥⲙⲁⲑⲏⲧⲏⲥ ϫⲉ ⲧⲛ̅ⲧⲱⲛⲧ ⲛ̅ⲧⲉⲧⲛ̅ϫⲟⲟⲥ ⲛⲁⲉⲓ ϫⲉ ⲉⲉⲓⲛⲉ ⲛ̅ⲛⲓⲙ (*Gos. Thom.* 13). Text from NHS; translation from Thomas O. Lambdin, "The Gospel according to Thomas," in *Nag Hammadi Codex II, 2–7* (ed. Bentley Layton; 2 vols.; Leiden: Brill, 1989), 53–93.

of saying whom you are like."[11] Jesus responds only to the third answer, the one that Judas Thomas offers, and in the process underscores the importance of this figure for the gospel as a whole. He says to Thomas, "I am not your master. Because you have drunk you have become intoxicated from the bubbling spring which I have measured out."[12] Jesus' reaction also indicates a certain nonhierarchical relationship with him as he suggests that Thomas not call him "Master" or "Teacher." These two appearances of Judas Thomas, in the prologue and logion 13, underscore his authority and proximity to Jesus.[13] Perkins rightly argues that logia 12 and 13 deal with degrees of authority and enlightenment among male disciples.[14] The rhetorical result of the dialogue in logion 13 of the *Gospel of Thomas* is a portrayal of Peter as possessing a notion or recognition of Jesus that is somewhat less enlightened than that of Judas Thomas.

It seems noteworthy that a text granting speaking parts to only five of the companions of Jesus attributes two of them to women: Mary (logion 21) and Salome (logion 61). When Mary first appears in the text she inquires about the characteristics of the disciples: "Whom are your disciples like?"[15] Jesus responds: "They are like little children who have settled in a field which does not belong to them."[16] Salome's appearance in this gospel offers an enigmatic dialogue in which she makes an inquiry of Jesus: "Who are you, man, and whose (son)? You took your place upon

---

[11]ⲡⲥⲁϩ ϩⲟⲗⲱⲥ ⲧⲁⲧⲁⲡⲣⲟ ⲛⲁϣⲁⲡϥ ⲁⲛ ⲉⲧⲣⲁⲭⲟⲟⲥ ϫⲉ ⲉⲕⲉⲓⲛⲉ ⲛⲛⲓⲙ (*Gos. Thom.* 13).

[12]ⲁⲛⲟⲕ ⲡⲉⲕⲥⲁϩ ⲁⲛ ⲉⲡⲉⲓ ⲁⲕⲥⲱ ⲁⲕϯϩⲉ ⲉⲃⲟⲗ ϩⲛ ⲧⲡⲏⲅⲏ ⲉⲧⲃⲣⲃⲣⲉ ⲧⲁⲉⲓ ⲁⲛⲟⲕ ⲛⲧⲁⲉⲓϣⲓⲧⲥ̄ (*Gos. Thom.* 13).

[13]This gospel implicitly communicates a preference for Judas Thomas over James the Just in part by the juxtaposition of sayings 12 and 13. Jesus says to them, "Wherever you are, you are to go to James the righteous, for whose sake heaven and earth came into being" (ⲡⲙⲁ ⲛⲧⲁⲧⲉⲧⲛⲉⲓ ⲛⲙⲁⲩ ⲉⲧⲉⲧⲛⲁⲃⲱⲕ ϣⲁ ⲓ̈ⲁⲕⲱⲃⲟⲥ ⲡⲇⲓⲕⲁⲓⲟⲥ ⲡⲁⲉⲓ ⲛⲧⲁ ⲧⲡⲉ ⲙⲛ ⲡⲕⲁϩ ϣⲱⲡⲉ ⲉⲧⲃⲏⲧϥ̄ [*Gos. Thom.* 12]).This text thus acknowledges James the Just, and then immediately thereafter recognizes the insight and position of Judas Thomas. Koester identifies a similar ranking of apostolic authority in John 21, as the text acknowledges the position of Peter. In this case, it does so, however, in a limited way without diminishing the authority of the Beloved Disciple.

[14]Pheme Perkins, "Gospel of Thomas," in *A Feminist Commentary*, vol. 2 of *Searching the Scriptures* (ed. Elisabeth Schüssler Fiorenza; 2 vols.; New York: Crossroad, 1994), 2:558.

[15]ⲡⲉⲝⲉ ⲙⲁⲣⲓϩⲁⲙ ⲛ̅ⲓ̅ⲥ̅ ϫⲉ ⲉⲛⲉⲕⲙⲁⲑⲏⲧⲏⲥ ⲉⲓⲛⲉ ⲛⲛⲓⲙ (*Gos. Thom.* 21).

[16]ⲡⲉⲭⲁϥ ϫⲉ ⲉⲩⲉⲓⲛⲉ ⲛ̄ϩⲛ̄ϣⲏⲣⲉ ϣⲏⲙ ⲉⲩϭⲉⲗⲓⲧ ⲁⲩⲥⲱϣⲉ ⲉⲧⲱⲟⲩ ⲁⲛ ⲧⲉ (*Gos. Thom.* 21).

my bench and ate from my table."[17] Perkins contends that logion 21 and logion 61 indicate that Mary and Salome "are clearly disciples whose insight is similar to that of Thomas."[18] She supports her thesis with respect to Mary by pointing out that the words introducing logion 21 parallel those of Jesus' words at the beginning of logion 13. In logion 13, Jesus tests his disciples by asking them to provide a simile or comparison to express to whom Jesus can be compared, while in logion 21 Mary asks a parallel question concerning to whom the disciples can be compared.[19] Marjanen disagrees with this interpretation because "the parenetic part of Jesus' reply indicates that Mary Magdalene is not testing Jesus' understanding but is seeking to be taught by him."[20] Mary's authoritative position in *Dialogue of the Savior*, in which she makes a definitive statement on the same topic concerning who the disciples are like (*Dial. Sav.* §53; 139,11), supports Perkins's point that Mary has insight similar to that of Thomas, but not, in my opinion, enough to put her on the same authoritative level as Thomas in this text.

The final saying in the *Gospel of Thomas* portrays Peter attempting to expel Mary from the company of the disciples.[21] (It is worth noting that besides the two authority figures for this gospel, Jesus and Judas Thomas, Peter and Mary are the only two names to appear twice in this text.) In this final saying Peter complains: "Let Mary leave us, because women are not worthy of life."[22] Jesus replies: "Look, I myself shall lead her so that I will make her male in order that she too may become a living spirit, resembling you males. For every woman who makes herself male will enter the kingdom of heaven."[23]

Pagels, along with others, suggests that the historical context of this exchange between Jesus and Peter may have been a conflict over the place of women in the community that produced the gospel.[24] Since this

[17]ⲛ̄ⲧⲁⲕ ⲛⲓⲙ ⲡⲣⲱⲙⲉ ϩⲱⲥ ⲉⲃⲟⲗ ϩⲛ̄ ⲟⲩⲁ ⲁⲕⲧⲉⲗⲟ ⲉⲝⲛ̄ ⲡⲁϭⲗⲟϭ ⲁⲩⲱ ⲁⲕⲟⲩⲱⲛ ⲉⲃⲟⲗ ϩⲛ̄ ⲧⲁⲧⲣⲁⲡⲉⲍⲁ (*Gos. Thom.* 61).

[18]Perkins, "Gospel of Thomas," 2:558.

[19]Ibid.

[20]Marjanen, *The Woman Jesus Loved,* 42 n. 32.

[21]Perkins, *Peter,* 157.

[22]ⲡⲉϫⲉ ⲥⲓⲙⲱⲛ ⲡⲉⲧⲣⲟⲥ ⲛⲁⲩ ϫⲉ ⲙⲁⲣⲉ ⲙⲁⲣⲓϩⲁⲙ ⲉⲓ ⲉⲃⲟⲗ ⲛ̄ϩⲏⲧⲛ̄ ϫⲉ ⲛ̄ⲥϩⲓⲟⲙⲉ ⲙ̄ⲡϣⲁ ⲁⲛ ⲙ̄ⲡⲱⲛϩ (*Gos. Thom.* 114).

[23]ⲉⲓⲥϩⲏⲏⲧⲉ ⲁⲛⲟⲕ ϯⲛⲁⲥⲱⲕ ⲙ̄ⲙⲟⲥ ϫⲉⲕⲁⲁⲥ ⲉⲉⲓⲛⲁⲁⲥ ⲛ̄ϩⲟⲟⲩⲧ ϣⲓⲛⲁ ⲉⲥⲛⲁϣⲱⲡⲉ ϩⲱⲱⲥ ⲛ̄ⲟⲩⲡⲛ̄ⲁ̄ ⲉϥⲟⲛϩ ⲉϥⲉⲓⲛⲉ ⲙ̄ⲙⲱⲧⲛ̄ ⲛ̄ϩⲟⲟⲩⲧ ϫⲉ ⲥϩⲓⲙⲉ ⲛⲓⲙ ⲉⲥⲛⲁⲁⲥ ⲛ̄ϩⲟⲟⲩⲧ ⲥⲛⲁⲃⲱⲕ ⲉϩⲟⲩⲛ ⲉⲧⲙⲛ̄ⲧⲉⲣⲟ ⲛ̄ⲙ̄ⲡⲏⲩⲉ (*Gos. Thom.* 114).

[24]Pagels, *Gnostic Gospels,* 58; see also Perkins, "Gospel of Thomas," 2:558.

conflict scene is the concluding logion of the 114 sayings, scholars have questioned whether it in fact belonged to the original collection of sayings.[25] It may in all probability represent a later addition, but whether it became a part of the collection in the first century or the second, its very presence in the text is significant. In this saying Jesus denies Peter's request and promises instead to "make her [Mary] male so that she too can become a living spirit."

The interpretation of the words to "make her male" remains highly disputed in scholarly circles.[26] Part of the dispute turns on a discrepancy between the apparent meaning of the phrase "to make her male" and a seemingly contradictory saying in logion 22 that states: ". . . when you make the male and the female one and the same, so that the male not be male and the female female . . . then you will enter the [the kingdom]."[27] The dialogue in logion 114 has as many interpretations as there are interpreters.

Marvin Meyer explains that logion 22, containing the words "make the male and the female one and the same," and the last logion 114, containing the words to "make her male," are in his opinion "not necessarily dissonant."[28] De Conick also believes that these two sayings are

[25]For example, Davies, *Thomas and Christian Wisdom,* 152.

[26]See April D. De Conick, *Seek to See Him: Ascent and Vision Mysticism in the Gospel of Thomas* (VCSup 33; Leiden: Brill, 1996), 7. She states that Thomas seems to be referring to the Genesis story in logion 114 here: "Since Eve was taken from Adam's side, so she must reenter him and become 'male' in order to return to the prelapsarian state of Adam before the gender division" (p. 18, plus 19–20). See also Paul Schüngel, "Ein Vorschlag, EvTho 114 neu zu übersetzen," *NovT* 36 (1994): 394–401; Sasagu Arai, "'To Make Her Male': An Interpretation of Logion 114 in Gospel of Thomas," in StPatr 24 (ed. Elizabeth A. Livingstone; Leuven: Peeters, 1993), 373–76; Marguerite Lelyfeld, *Les logia de la vie dans l'Évangile selon Thomas: A la recherche d'une tradition et d'une rédaction* (NHS 34; Leiden: Brill, 1987), 138–43.

[27]ϣⲓⲛⲁ ⲉⲧⲉⲧⲛⲁⲉⲓⲣⲉ ⲙ̄ⲫⲟⲟⲩⲧ ⲙⲛ̄ ⲧⲥϩⲓⲙⲉ ⲙ̄ⲡⲓⲟⲩⲁ ⲟⲩⲱⲧ ϫⲉⲕⲁⲁⲥ ⲛⲉϥⲟⲟⲩⲧ ⲣ̄ ϩⲟⲟⲩⲧ ⲛ̄ⲧⲉ ⲧⲥϩⲓⲙⲉ ⲣ̄ ⲥϩⲓⲙⲉ . . . ⲧⲟⲧⲉ ⲧⲉⲧⲛⲁⲃⲱⲕ ⲉϩⲟⲩⲛ ⲉ[ⲧ]ⲙⲛ̄[ⲧⲉⲣ]ⲟ (*Gos. Thom.* 22).

[28]Marvin W. Meyer, "Making Mary Male: The Categories 'Male' and 'Female' in the Gospel of Thomas," *NTS* 31 (1985): 554–70. See also John Dart, "The Two Shall Become One," *ThTo* 35 (1978–1979): 321–25; Wayne A. Meeks, "Image of the Androgyne: Some Uses of a Symbol in Earliest Christianity," *HR* 13 (1973–74): 165–208, esp. 193–97; Karl H. Rengstorf, "Urchristliches Kerygma und 'gnostische' Interpretation in einigen Sprüchen des Thomasevangeliums," *Le Origini dello Gnosticismo: Colloquio di Messina 13–18 Aprile 1966. Testi e Discussioni* (SHR; Numen Sup 12; ed. Ugo Bianchi; Leiden: Brill, 1967): 563–74, esp. 565–66.

not contradictory but for different reasons. She explains saying 114 in terms of theological differences: "This renunciation includes a life of singlehood or celibacy justified on the basis of an encratite exegesis of the Genesis story."[29] Other possibilities along that line include Jorunn Jacobson Buckley's suggestion that the phrase " 'to make her male' may refer to an ascetic rejection of all the marks of gender by the Gnostic solitary ones, or to a return to the androgynous asexuality of Adam with the spiritual Eve before the hostile creator god separated them, or to a ritual through which women passed before they could be members of a Gnostic sect."[30] Elizabeth Castelli similarly relates this text to Christian women's asceticism.[31] Whatever the particular explanation of these words, what is clear is that the exchange includes as part of Jesus' answer a denial of Peter's request and a defense of Mary. Whatever significance this phrase "to make her male" may have had, the text indicates that Peter's attempt to limit the circle of disciples is met with a refusal to acquiesce to Peter's misguided demands that comes directly and authoritatively from Jesus himself.[32]

An intriguing element concerning the interactions in the dialogue lies in the way the 114 sayings almost always stem from either Jesus or the disciples as a group, with four exceptions, in which only a handful of disciples receive an individual speaking part: #13, #21, #61, #114. Thus one has to wonder why Peter's only two speeches in the text include what appears to be his inadequate confession in logion 13 and his objection to Mary in logion 114. Perkins encapsulates well the narrative dynamics when she explains that on the basis of logion 13, which clearly presents Peter's status as inferior to that of Thomas, the reader should therefore anticipate that Peter's proposal to exclude Mary as "not worthy of life" will be a sign of ignorance as well.[33]

---

[29]See De Conick, *Seek to See Him*, 19.

[30]See Jorunn Jacobson Buckley, "An Interpretation of Logion 114 in *The Gospel of Thomas*," *NovT* 27 (1985): 245–72. Jacobson Buckley builds on Rengstorf as well as Philipp Vielhauer, "ΑΝΑΠΑΥΣΙΣ, Zum gnostischen Hintergrund des Thomasevangeliums," *Apophoreta: Festschrift für Ernst Haenchen* (ed. W. Eltester; BZNW 30; Berlin: Töpelmann, 1964), 281–99.

[31]Elizabeth Castelli, "Virginity and its Meaning for Women's Sexuality in Early Christianity," *JFSR* 2 (1986): 61–88.

[32]Perkins, *Peter*, 157.

[33]Perkins, "Gospel of Thomas," 2:558.

Portrayals of Mary and Peter in the *Gospel of Mary*

Even more dramatic than Peter's request to exclude Mary from the group in the *Gospel of Thomas* is the portrayal of a verbal confrontation between Peter and Mary in the *Gospel of Mary*.[34] This text remained unknown until late in the nineteenth century when "a single fragmentary copy in Coptic translation came to light."[35] This Coptic codex, called *Papyrus Berolinensis 8502,1,* written in the Sahidic dialect, preserves the largest portion of the text (though six of the approximately eighteen pages are still missing).[36] Since then, two additional Greek fragments have

---

[34]King, "Introduction" [to *Gospel of Mary*] in *NHL*, 523–24; idem, "The Gospel of Mary," in *The Complete Gospels: Annotated Scholars Version* (ed. Robert J. Miller, rev. and exp. ed.; Sonoma, Calif.: Polebridge, 1994), 357–66; idem, "The Gospel of Mary Magdalene," in *A Feminist Commentary,* vol. 2 of *Searching the Scriptures* (ed. Elisabeth Schüssler Fiorenza; New York: Crossroad, 1994), 601–34; Robert McL. Wilson and George W. MacRae, "BG,1: The Gospel According to Mary," in *Nag Hammadi Codices V, 2–5 and VI with Papyrus Berolinensis 8502, 1 and 4* (ed. Douglas M. Parrott; NHS 11; Leiden: Brill, 1979), 453–71; George W. MacRae and Robert McL. Wilson (trans.), "The Gospel of Mary," in *NHL* (ed. James M. Robinson; 3d ed.; San Francisco: Harper and Row, 1988), 524–27; Marjanen, *The Woman Jesus Loved;* Robert McL. Wilson, "The New Testament in the Gnostic Gospel of Mary," *NTS* 3 (1956/1957): 236–43; Colin H. Roberts, "463: The Gospel of Mary," *Catalogue of the Greek Papyri in the John Rylands Library* III (Manchester: University Press, 1938), 18–23; Henri-Charles Puech and rev. Beate Blatz, "The Gospel of Mary," in *Gospels and Related Writings,* vol. 1 of *New Testament Apocrypha* (ed. Wilhelm Schneemelcher; trans. R. McL. Wilson; Cambridge: James Clark and Co.; Louisville, Ky.: Westminster/John Knox, 1991), 391–95; P. J. Parsons, "3525. Gospel of Mary," in *The Oxyrhynchus Papyri: Volume 50* (Graeco-Roman Memoirs, No. 70; London: Egypt Exploration Society, 1983), 12–14; Michel Tardieu, *Écrits Gnostiques: Codex de Berlin* (Sources gnostiques et manichéennes 1; Paris: Cerf, 1984), 20–25, 75–82, 225–37; Anne Pasquier, "L'eschatologie dans l'Évangile selon Marie: Étude des notions de nature et d'image," in *Colloque International sur les Textes de Nag Hammadi (Québec, 22–25 août 1978)* (ed. B. Barc; Québec-Louvain: Presses de l'Université Laval, 1981), 390–404; idem, *L'Évangile selon Marie* (BCNH; Section "Textes" 10; Québec: Les Presses de l'Université Laval, 1983), discussion of date: 3–4; Pheme Perkins, "Mary, Gospel of," *ABD* 4:583–84.

[35]King, "Gospel of Mary Magdalene," *Searching the Scriptures,* 2:602.

[36]Ibid. The *Coptic Papyrus Berolinensis 8502* is an early-fifth-century Coptic codex. See Hans-Martin Schenke, "Bemerkungen zum koptischen Papyrus Berolinensis 8502," in *Festschrift zum 150 jährigen Bestehen des Berliner Ägyptischen Museums* (Mitteilungen aus der Ägyptischen Sammlung 8; Berlin: Akademie Verlag, 1974), 315–22. See also Walter C. Till, "Die Berliner gnostische Handschrift," *Europäischer Wissenschafts-Dienst* 4 (1944): 19–21; idem, "Εὐαγγέλλιον κατὰ Μαριάμ," *La parola del passato* 1 (1946):

surfaced, but they add no previously unknown text. Papyrus Rylands III 463,[37] a single fragment dated to the early third century, preserves one portion of the original Greek text; Papyrus Oxyrhynchus 3525, also dated to the third century, preserves another.[38]

Scholars generally date the *Gospel of Mary* to the second century; Karen King places it in the first half of the second century, while Anne Pasquier places it in the second half. King makes some strong arguments for dating this text to the first half of the second century based on "its life situation in the early second century debates over women's leadership and the role of the apostles."[39] She contends, for instance, that typically in the latter half of the second century most arguments concerning women's leadership—whether for or against—invoked the authority of Paul. No literary parallels to Pauline arguments appear in the *Gospel of Mary*, as one might expect if the text were later. In fact, the text as a whole lacks any certain literary dependence on the New Testament.[40] King thus maintains that she finds no substantial reasons to place it in the second half of the second century.

This text portrays Mary both as the recipient of an appearance of Christ in a vision and as the recipient of praise from Christ for not "wavering" (*Gos. Mary,* BG 10,14). For this text Mary thus functions as the authority figure and guarantor of the tradition as she comforts the disciples and

---

260–65; idem, "Die Gnosis in Aegypten," *La parola del passato* 4 (1949): 230–49; Walter C. Till and Hans-Martin Schenke, *Die gnostische Handschriften des Koptischen Papyrus Berolinensis 8502* (ed. Hans-Martin Schenke; 2nd ed.; TU 60; Berlin: 1972); Schmid, *Maria Magdalena in gnostischen Schriften.* Also, King, "Gospel of Mary Magdalene," *Searching the Scriptures,* 2:602.

[37]Roberts, "463. The Gospel of Mary," 18–23; Dieter Lührmann, "Die griechischen Fragmente des Mariaevangeliums POx 3525 und PRyl 463," *NovT* 30 (1988): 321–38.

[38]Published also in *Oxyrhynchus Papyri* (vol. 50; London: Egypt Exploration Society, 1983), 12. POxy 3525 corresponds to pages 9,1–10,14 of the Coptic while PRyl III 463 corresponds to 17,5–21 (front) and 18,5–19,5 (back). At this time in early Christian history texts were not protected by any kind of canonical status. Since a complete copy of the *Gospel of Mary* has yet to be found, we can only hypothesize how the original document began.

[39]King, "Gospel of Mary Magdalene," *Searching the Scriptures,* 2:628.

[40]Contra Wilson, "The New Testament in the Gnostic Gospel of Mary," 236–43. He admits, "Since we have to deal in most cases with echoes rather than with full quotations, it is extremely difficult to determine whether at some points the Greek original contained a quotation at all" (p. 238). Nevertheless, he believes there are "clear allusions to all four Gospels, in addition to some that are more doubtful" (p. 242).

shares her vision with them.[41] She then successfully rallies them: "She turned their hearts toward the Good, and they began to discuss the words of the Savior."[42] King's research on the various types of visions and dreams described in early Christian literature explains the importance of such phenomena and interpretations, as Mary functions in the role of "prophetic revealer to the other disciples."[43] Although Judith Hartenstein has recently suggested that this vision predates Jesus' death and resurrection,[44] most scholars place this gospel in a postresurrection setting.[45]

Peter is the one who asks Mary to tell them the words of the Savior that she remembers. When she finishes explaining her vision, however, he and Andrew attack the veracity of her statements. Pagels interprets Peter as someone "who not only fails to receive visions himself, but who also opposes and slanders the person gifted with visions."[46] The figure of Levi, on the other hand, subsequently defends Mary against the attack. In the Greek version Levi accuses Peter of acting "like an adversary," saying, "Peter, your hot temper is always with you and now you are questioning the woman as though an adversary to her?"[47] The Coptic version similarly

---

[41]Although the term "apostle" does not appear here, the ending of the text, "they began to go forth [to] proclaim and to preach," clearly indicates a role of proclamation.

[42]ⲛ̄ⲧⲁⲣⲉⲛⲁ/ⲣⲓ2ⲁⲙ ⲭⲉ ⲛⲁⲓ̈ ⲁⲥⲕ̄ⲧⲉ ⲡⲉⲩ2ⲏⲧ / [ⲉ2]ⲟⲩⲛ ⲉⲡⲁⲅⲁⲑⲟⲛ ⲁⲩⲱ ⲁⲩ̄ⲣⲁ̄ⲣⲭⲉ/[ⲥⲑⲁⲓ] ⲛ̄ⲣ̄ⲅⲩⲙ[ⲛ]ⲁⲍⲉ 2ⲁ ⲡⲣⲁ ⲛ̄ⲡ̄ⲱⲁ/[ⲭ]ⲉ ⲙ̄ⲡ[ⲥⲱ̄ⲣ] (*Gos. Mary,* BG 9,21–24). See Pheme Perkins, *The Gnostic Dialogue: The Early Church and the Crisis of Gnosticism* (Theological Inquiries; New York: Paulist, 1980), 133.

[43]King, "Prophetic Power and Women's Authority," 35 n. 17; see also Silke Petersen, *'Zerstört die Werke der Wieblichkeit!' Maria Magdalena, Salome und andere Jüngerinnen Jesu in christlich-gnostischen Schriften* (NHMS 48; Leiden: Brill, 1999), 163–65.

[44]Judith Hartenstein, *Die Zweite Lehre: Erscheinungen des Auferstandenen als Rahmenerzählungen frühchristlicher Dialoge* (TUGAL 146; Berlin: Akademie, 2000). See King's discussion of Hartenstein's theory in Karen L. King, "Why All the Controversy: Mary in the *Gospel of Mary,*" in *Which Mary?: The Marys of Early Christian Tradition* (ed. F. Stanley Jones; SBLSymS 19; Atlanta: Society of Biblical Literature, 2002), 64–65.

[45]King, "Gospel of Mary Magdalene," *Searching the Scriptures,* 2:602; Pagels, *Gnostic Gospels,* 15.

[46]Elaine Pagels, "Visions, Appearances, and Apostolic Authority: Gnostic and Orthodox Traditions," in *Gnosis: Festschrift für Hans Jonas* (ed. Barbara Aland; Göttingen: Vandenhoeck & Ruprecht, 1978), 424.

[47]Λευε[ì]ς λέγει Πέτρῳ·/ Πέτρε, ἀ[εί] σο[ι] τὸ ὀργίλον παράκει/ται καὶ ἄρτι οὕτως συνζητεῖ[ς] τῇ / γυναικὶ ὡς ἀντικείμενος αὐτῇ (PRyl 463, verso 1–4).

reads: "Peter you have always been hot-tempered. Now I see you contend-
ing against the woman like the adversaries."[48]

Although it is possible that theological or philosophical differences
lay behind Peter's objections to Mary, the consistent way in which the
figure of Peter refers to women or to Mary's gender in each of these
major controversy dialogues strongly suggests that the issue at stake
involves leadership roles for women. Below are four examples: [1] In
the aforementioned passage in the *Gospel of Thomas,* Peter challenges
Mary's role not with the words, "Let Mary leave us for she is not worthy
of life," but rather asserts, "Let Mary leave us for women are not worthy
of life" (*Gos. Thom.* 114). [2] When Peter objects to Mary's vision in the
Gospel of Mary, he does not ask, "Did Jesus really speak with Mary....,"
but asks, "Did he really speak with a woman without our knowledge (and)
not openly? Are we to turn about and all listen to her?" (*Gos. Mary* 17,
6–18,10).[49] [3] In *Pistis Sophia 1-3,* to be discussed shortly, Peter complains about Mary: "My Lord we are not able to suffer this woman who
takes the opportunity from us, and does not allow anyone of us to speak,
but she speaks many times" (*Pis. Soph.* 1.36). [4] Along the same vein,
in *Pistis Sophia 4* Peter says: "My Lord, let the women cease to question,
that we also may question" (*Pis. Soph.* 4.146).

In addition to gender, another issue comes to the fore in two key passages describing Peter's attacks: the concept of being "deemed worthy."
The context of these controversies suggests that references to Mary's
"worthiness" allude to more than a mere character trait, and indeed that
they touch on "worthiness" as a quality necessary to bearers of the apostolic tradition. As we have seen, the issue of "worthiness" also arises
in the *Gospel of Thomas* when Peter claims that Mary "is not worthy
of life."[50] The Greek text of the *Gospel of Mary* presents Peter's negative reactions: "After examining these ma[tt]ers, <Peter said>, 'Has the
Sa[vior] spoken secretly to a woman and <not> openly so that [we] would
all hear? [Surely] he did [not want to show] that [she] is more worthy than

---

[48]ⲡⲉⲧⲣⲉ ⲭⲓⲛ ⲉⲛⲉϩ ⲕϣⲟⲡ ⲛⲣⲉⲩ/ⲛⲟⲩϭⲥ ϯⲛⲁⲩ ⲉⲣⲟⲕ ⲧⲉⲛⲟⲩ ⲉⲕⲣ̄/ⲅⲩⲙⲛⲁⲍⲉ ⲉϩⲛ ⲧⲉⲥ-
ϩⲓⲙⲉ ⲛ̄ⲑⲉ ⲛ̄/ⲛⲓⲁⲛⲧⲓⲕⲉⲓⲙⲉⲛⲟⲥ (*Gos. Mary,* BG 18,7–15).

[49]It is interesting, by contrast, that Andrew's objection in the text does not revolve
around the person of Mary but is based, instead, on theological arguments. He says, "For
certainly these teachings are strange ideas."

[50]The Didache also makes several references to the concept of worthiness with respect
to individuals (*Did.* 13.1 and *Did.* 15.1).

we are?"[51] The Coptic version of the text reads similarly: "Peter answered and spoke concerning these same things. He questioned them about the Savior: 'Did he really speak with a woman without our knowledge [and] not openly? Are we to turn about and all listen to her? Did he prefer her to us?' "[52] Levi responds to Peter's challenge of Mary with the words: "If the Savior made her worthy, who are you indeed to reject her?"[53] The Coptic similarly reflects this question of worthiness: "If the Savior made her worthy, who are you to scorn her?"[54]

This connection between worthiness and apostolic authority becomes especially clear in the words of the Valentinian Ptolemy: "If God permit, you will learn in the future about their origin and generation, when you are accounted worthy of the apostolic tradition which we also have received by succession, because we can prove all our statements from the teaching of the Savior" (*Ptolemy to Flora* #7.9).[55] In this second-century text, Ptolemy confirms the importance of being accounted "worthy of the apostolic tradition" in a letter addressed to Flora, a female leader.

Coincidentally, the group of enigmatic sayings that Mary speaks in the *Dialogue of the Savior,* for which she is so highly praised, involves a reference to being worthy and being like one's teacher.[56] The *First Apocalypse of James* is another text in which Mary Magdalene appears and one that includes a "defense of the women disciples of Jesus who are included in the chain of authoritative witnesses" — a position that the author is clearly

---

[51]<Πέτρος λέγει> περὶ τοιούτ[ω]ν πρα[γμά]/των ἐξεταζόμενος ὁ Σω[τὴρ μήτι]/ λάθρα γυν[α]ικὶ ἐλάλει καὶ <οὐ> φ[α]/νερῶς, ἵνα πάντες ἀκούσω[μεν;]/ [μὴ ἀ]ξιολογωτέραν ἡ[μ]ῶν [αὐτὴν] / [ἀποδεῖξαι ἤθ]ε[λε; . . .] (PRyl 463, recto 11–16).

[52]ⲡⲉⲧⲣⲟⲥ ⲡⲉⲭⲁϥ ϨⲀ ⲡⲣⲁ/ⲛⲛⲉⲉⲓϨⲃⲏⲩⲉ ⲛⲧⲉⲉⲓⲙⲓⲛⲉ ⲁϥ/ⲭⲛⲟⲩⲟⲩ ⲉⲧⲃⲉ ⲡⲤⲰⲢ ⲭⲉ ⲙⲏⲧⲓ/ ⲁϥϢⲀⲭⲉ ⲙⲚ ⲟⲩⲤϨⲓⲙⲉ Ⲛⲭⲓⲟⲩⲉ/ ⲉⲣⲟⲛ ϨⲚ ⲟⲩⲰⲚϨ ⲉⲃⲟⲗ ⲀⲚ ⲉⲛⲚⲀ/ⲕⲧⲟⲛ ϨⲰⲰⲚ ⲚⲦⲚⲤⲰⲦⲚ ⲦⲎⲢⲚ/ ⲚⲤⲰⲤ ⲚⲦⲀⲀϥⲤⲟⲧⲡⲤ ϨⲞⲨⲞⲨ ⲉⲣⲟⲛ (Gos. Mary, BG 17,16–22). See King, "Prophetic Power and Women's Authority," 21–41.

[53]εἰ ὁ σωτὴ[ρ] ἀξίαν αὐτὴν ἡγήσατο,/σὺ τίς εἶ ἐξουθενῶν αὐτήν; (PRyl 463, verso 5–6).

[54]ⲉϢⲭⲉ Ⲁⲡ/ⲤⲰⲦⲎⲢ ⲆⲈ ⲀⲀⲤ ⲚⲀϨⲓⲟⲤ ⲚⲦⲔ Ⲛⲓⲙ/ ⲆⲈ ϨⲰⲰⲔ ⲉⲚⲞⲭⲤ ⲉⲃⲟⲗ (Gos. Mary, BG 18,10–12).

[55]μαθήσῃ γάρ, θεοῦ διδόντος ἑξῆς καὶ τὴν τούτων ἀρχήν τε καὶ γέννησιν, ἀξιουμένη τῆς ἀποστολικῆς παραδόσεως, ἣν ἐκ διαδοχῆς καὶ ἡμεῖς παρειλήφαμεν, μετὰ καὶ τοῦ κανονίσαι πάντας τοὺς λόγους τῇ τοῦ σωτῆρος ἡμῶν διδασκαλίᾳ. See Robert McL. Wilson in *Gnosis: A Selection of Gnostic Texts* (ed. Werner Foerster; 2 vols.; Oxford: Clarendon, 1972–1974), 1:161. See also Koester, *Ancient Christian Gospels,* 32.

[56]ⲀⲨⲰ ⲡⲉⲣ ⲅⲀⲦⲎⲤ ⲚⲦⲠϢⲀ ⲚⲦⲉϥⲦⲣⲟⲫⲎ· ⲀⲨⲰ ⲡⲚⲀⲑⲎⲦⲎⲤ Ⲛϥⲉⲓⲛⲉ ⲚⲡⲉϥⲤⲀϨ (Dial. Sav. §53; 139,11).

needing to defend.[57] From the first centuries of Christianity the concept of "being worthy" became associated with eligibility for the office of bishop.[58] In fact, in the Eastern Orthodox Church even today, the congregational response at a bishop's enthronement is a unanimous cry that the prospective candidate is "worthy." Since these challenges to Mary's status sometimes involve Peter's questioning Mary's "worthiness," it is entirely possible that this leadership controversy involves an evaluation of one's worthiness, especially with respect to gender.

These two explicit confrontations in the *Gospel of Mary* and the *Gospel of Thomas* concerning Mary's worthiness and her leadership are not isolated instances; further conflict concerning Mary's leadership appears in two books of *Pistis Sophia*.

Portrayals of Mary and Peter in *Pistis Sophia 1–3* and *Pistis Sophia 4*

Pistis Sophia portrays one of the greatest leadership roles for Mary, who dominates the revelation dialogue both in the number of questions she asks and interpretations she offers.[59] In these texts, however, her leadership role is met with correspondingly greater resistance from Peter concerning her participation. The text now called *Pistis Sophia* is actually comprised of two earlier works designated as *Pistis Sophia 1–3* and *Pistis Sophia 4*.[60] Scholars frequently date *Pistis Sophia 1–3* to the second half of the third century, and Harnack dates *Pistis Sophia 4* slightly earlier, to the first half of the third century.[61] Both Carl Schmidt and Walter Till agree with Harnack's dating.[62]

---

[57]Pheme Perkins, *Gnosticism and the New Testament* (Minneapolis: Fortress, 1993), 167. She explains that the four names in the list of women are reconstructed according to Manichaean sources (p. 228 n. 14).

[58]Lampe, s.v. "ἄξιος," *Patristic Greek Lexicon,* 167.

[59]Schüssler Fiorenza, *In Memory of Her*, 305.

[60]Carl Schmidt, ed., *Pistis Sophia* (trans. Violet MacDermot; NHS 9; Leiden: Brill, 1978).

[61]Adolf von Harnack, *Untersuchungen über das gnostische Buch* Pistis Sophia (TU 7/2; Leipzig: Hinrichs, 1891), 106–12. See also idem, "Ein jüngst entdeckter Auferstehungsbericht," *ThSt* (Fs. B. Weiss; Göttingen: Vandenhoeck & Ruprecht, 1897), 1.

[62]Marjanen (*The Woman Jesus Loved*, 172 n. 11) discusses the dating of these texts, stating that it is difficult to date the two texts with respect to each other based on the observations of Schmidt. See Carl Schmidt, *Pistis Sophia: Ein gnostisches Originalwerk*

Further examples of a competition for authority in the representations of Peter and Mary Magdalene appear in both *Pistis Sophia 1–3* and *Pistis Sophia 4*. In these two texts Mary holds the most prominent role among the followers as the primary interlocutor with Jesus.[63]

In Peter's first speaking part in *Pistis Sophia 1–3,* he complains to Jesus about Mary: "My Lord, we are not able to suffer this woman who takes the opportunity from us, and does not allow anyone of us to speak, but she speaks many times."[64] Along these same lines, *Pistis Sophia 4* portrays these words from Peter just after Mary speaks: Peter complains, "My Lord, let the women cease to question, that we also may question."[65] In light of the other controversy texts, it is not surprising to find Peter's role again an adversarial one with respect to Mary in *Pistis Sophia.*

Another scene in *Pistis Sophia 1–3* bears evidence of this leadership controversy as Mary complains to Jesus about Peter's intimidation: "My Lord, my mind is understanding at all times that I should come forward at any time and give the interpretation of the words which she [Pistis Sophia] spoke, but I am afraid of Peter, for he threatens me and hates our race."[66] Scholars are divided whether the word ΓΕΝΟC signifies "kind," referring here to gender, or "race," as in "the Jewish race."[67] Whatever

---

des 3. Jahrhunderts aus dem Koptischen übersetzt (Leipzig: Hinrichs, 1925), XL–LXXXI; idem, "Die Urschrift der Pistis Sophia," *ZNW* 24 (1925): 218–40; Carl Schmidt and Walter Till, *Die Pistis Sophia: Die beiden Bücher des Jeû: Unbekanntes altgnostisches Werk* (3d ed.; GCS 45; Berlin, 1954, repr. 1959, 1962). For more information, see Deirdre Good, "Pistis Sophia," in *A Feminist Commentary,* vol. 2 of *Searching the Scriptures* (ed. Elisabeth Schüssler Fiorenza; 2 vols.; New York: Crossroad, 1994), 678–707. See also Michel Tardieu and Jean-Daniel Dubois, *Introduction à la littérature gnostique I* (Paris: Cerf and CNRS, 1986), 80–81.

[63]Pheme Perkins argues, however, that the role of Mary Magdalene in Gnostic texts is not sufficient evidence that the Gnostics upheld community leadership by women (Perkins, *Gnostic Dialogue,* 136 n. 10).

[64]ⲁϥϫⲟⲟϥ ⲉⲃⲟⲗ ⲛ̄ϭⲓ ⲡⲉⲧⲣⲟⲥ ⲡⲉϫⲁϥ ⲛ̄Ⲓ̄Ⲥ̄ ϫⲉ ⲡⲁϫⲟⲉⲓⲥ· Ⲧ̄Ⲛ̄ⲛⲁϣ-ⲁⲛⲉⲭⲉ ⲁⲛ ⲛ̄ⲧⲉⲓ̈ⲥϩⲓⲙⲉ· ⲉⲥⲭⲓ ⲛ̄ⲡⲙⲁ ⲛ̄ⲧⲟⲟⲧⲛ̄· ⲁⲩⲱ ⲛ̄Ⲥ̄ⲕⲁ-ⲟⲩⲟⲛ ⲛ̄ⲙⲟⲛ ⲉϣⲁⲭⲉ· ⲁⲗⲗⲁ ⲉⲥϣⲁⲭⲉ ⲛ̄ϩⲁϩ ⲛ̄ⲥⲟⲡ· (*Pis. Soph.* 1.36).

[65]ⲡⲉϫⲁϥ ⲛ̄ϭⲓ ⲡⲉⲧⲣⲟⲥ ϫⲉ ⲡⲁϫⲟⲓ̄ⲥ ⲙⲁⲣⲉ ⲛⲉϩⲓⲟⲙⲉ ϩⲱ ⲉⲣⲟⲟⲩ ⲉⲩϣⲓⲛⲉ ⲧⲁⲣⲛ̄ϣⲓⲛⲉ ϩⲱⲱⲛ· (*Pis. Soph.* 4.146).

[66]ⲡⲉϫⲁⲥ ϫⲉ ⲡⲁϫⲟⲉⲓⲥ· ⲡⲁⲛⲟⲩⲥ ⲟⲩⲛⲟⲉⲣⲟⲥ ⲡⲉ ⲛ̄ⲟⲩⲟⲉⲓϣ ⲛⲓⲙ ⲉⲧⲣⲁⲉⲓ̈ ⲉⲑⲏ ⲛ̄ⲥⲟⲡ ⲛⲓⲙ· ⲧⲁⲧⲁⲩⲉ-ⲡⲃⲱⲗ ⲛ̄ⲛ̄ϣⲁⲭⲉ ⲉⲛⲧⲁⲥϫⲟⲟⲩ· ⲁⲗⲗⲁ ⲉⲓ̄ⲣ̄ϩⲟⲧⲉ ϩⲏⲧϥ̄ ⲛ̄ⲡⲉⲧⲣⲟⲥ ϫⲉ ϣⲁϥⲁⲡⲓⲗⲉⲓ ⲉⲣⲟⲓ̈ ⲁⲩⲱ ϥⲙⲟⲥⲧⲉ ⲛ̄ⲡⲉⲛⲅⲉⲛⲟⲥ· (*Pis. Soph.* 2.72).

[67]Pagels (*Gnostic Gospels,* 78), for example, translates it: "he hates the female race."

the interpretation, however, Peter definitely displays some aggression, as evidenced by the use of the Coptic verb ⲘⲟⲤⲦⲈ, "to hate."[68]

As alluded to earlier, *Pistis Sophia 4* likewise portrays a controversy scene involving Peter and a figure named Mary or Mariam in which immediately after Mary's speech Peter complains that the women should cease to question so that he and the others could have a turn (4.146). Even though *Pistis Sophia* as a text is frequently accepted as a unity, these controversy scenes should actually be interpreted as two ancient witnesses to verbal confrontations between Peter and Mary rather than just one.[69] Upon further examination *Pistis Sophia 4* differs significantly from *Pistis Sophia 1–3* as it seems to feature only one Mary whose identity is more difficult to discern because there are no specific indicators or additional phrases in *Pistis Sophia 4* to help specify this Mary as either Mary Magdalene or Mary, the mother of Jesus. Interestingly, the most frequent form of the name Mary in *Pistis Sophia 1–3* is Ⲙⲁⲣⲓⲁ ("Maria") which never occurs in *Pistis Sophia 4*. Instead, every reference to the primary figure of *Pistis Sophia 4* employs only the name: ⲘⲁⲣⲓⲋⲁⲘ ("Mariam"), apparently referring to only one character. Although the name Mariam appears proportionately less frequently than in *Pistis Sophia 1–3*, it nevertheless still appears eight times,[70] a ratio significantly higher than all the other disciples. Additionally, at least one more reference to Mary must have existed as the text states after a large lacuna, "Mariam continued again and said . . ." (*Pistis Sophia* 4.144).[71] The use of her name thus exceeds all other disciples (with four references to Thomas, two to Andrew, Bartholomew, Peter, and John, and only one to James, Simon the Canaanite, Philip, and Salome).

One of the issues most relevant to the discussion of Mary Magdalene and both the *Gospel of Thomas* and the *Gospel of Mary* is the identification of the "Mary" in both texts — whether she is Mary Magdalene or Mary, the mother of Jesus. As I noted above, most scholars concur that this figure is Mary Magdalene,[72] although there are a few who have recently called

---

[68]Crum, *Coptic Dictionary, s.v.* "ⲘⲟⲤⲦⲈ."

[69]My thanks to Professor François Bovon for this insight.

[70]She appears in chapters 138, 139, 144, 145, 146, and 148.

[71]A lacuna of 8 pages or 4 leaves exists at this point in the text.

[72]Marjanen, *The Woman Jesus Loved,* 39; Good, "Pistis Sophia," 678–707.

this identification into question.[73] The issue of her identity in the *Gospel of Thomas* and the *Gospel of Mary* is somewhat difficult to determine with so few clues in the text. Part of the justification for believing this figure to be Mary Magdalene draws on parallel controversy dialogues in which the figure in conflict is known to be her, such as the *Gospel of Philip* and *Pistis Sophia*.

Identification of Mary Magdalene in the Gospel of Philip

The *Gospel of Philip* is especially helpful in the identification of Mary because it describes the presence of several Marys in Jesus' life and even differentiates them from each other: "there were three who walked with the Lord at all times: Mary his mother, and her sister, and Magdalene, the one who was called his companion."[74]

---

[73]Lucchesi, for example, in Enzo Lucchesi, "Évangile selon Marie ou Évangile selon Marie-Madeleine?" *AnBoll* 103 (1985): 366. The next section on *Pistis Sophia* provides more information. He suggests Mary the mother because of the tradition that Jesus appeared to his mother in the garden. The earliest that this tradition can be found, however, is Ephrem in his commentary on the Diatessaron, as will be discussed in more detail later in this work. The question whether this tradition could be traced all the way back to Tatian remains unanswered. In the same line, see Stephen J. Shoemaker, "Mary and the Discourse of Orthodoxy: Early Christian Identity and the Ancient Dormition Legends" (Ph.D. diss., Duke University, 1997). For arguments against the interpretation of this figure being Mary the mother, see De Boer, *Mary Magdalene*, 81 and Marjanen, *The Woman Jesus Loved*, 94–95. Marjanen, for example, points out that the only known resurrection conversations of Mary the mother with the Risen One are the *Questions of Bartholomew* and *Pistis Sophia*. The context of the *Questions of Bartholomew* is significantly different from the *Gospel of Mary*, and in *Pistis Sophia* "the mother of Jesus has an insignificant role compared to that of Mary Magdalene" (Marjanen, *The Woman Jesus Loved*, 95 n. 2).

[74]ⲛⲉ ⲟⲩⲛ̄ ϣⲟⲙⲧⲉ ⲛⲟⲟϣⲉ ⲙⲛ̄ ⲡⲭⲟⲉⲓⲥ ⲟⲩⲟⲉⲓϣ ⲛⲓⲙ ⲙⲁⲣⲓⲁ ⲧⲉϥⲙⲁⲁⲩ ⲁⲩⲱ ⲧⲉⲥⲥⲱⲛⲉ ⲁⲩⲱ ⲙⲁⲅⲇⲁⲗⲏⲛⲏ ⲧⲁⲉⲓ ⲉⲧⲟⲩⲙⲟⲩⲧⲉ ⲉⲣⲟⲥ ϫⲉ ⲧⲉϥⲕⲟⲓⲛⲱⲛⲟⲥ (§32, *Gos. Phil.* 107, 6–9). I cite the reconstructed text of Walter C. Till, *Das Evangelium nach Philippos* (PTS 2; Berlin: de Gruyter, 1963). The text continues the clarification with another description: "His sister and his mother and his companion were each a Mary" (ⲙⲁⲣⲓⲁ ⲅⲁⲣ ⲧⲉ ⲧⲉϥⲥⲱⲛⲉ ⲁⲩⲱ ⲧⲉϥⲙⲁⲁⲩ ⲧⲉ ⲁⲩⲱ ⲧⲉϥϩⲱⲧⲣⲉ ⲧⲉ [§32, *Gos. Phil.* 107, 10–11]). Schenke corrects the words "her sister" to "his sister" in line 8, apparently to agree with line 10; but Robert McL. Wilson (*The Gospel of Philip* [New York: Harper & Row, 1962], 97) disagrees on the basis of John 19:25, Matt 27:55, and Mark 15:40. The quotations are followed by two sets of numbers, incorporating two styles of citation used for this text.

This text is therefore useful because it explicitly identifies Mary Magdalene as Jesus' companion and furthermore identifies her as having a special status in the group: "the companion of the [Christ is] Mary Magdalene. [But the Lord loved] her more than [all] the disciples [and used to] kiss her [often] on her [. . .] . . ."[75]

Furthermore, in addition to describing an exceptional position for Mary Magdalene with respect to Jesus, this text conveys how her status causes difficulties for some of the male disciples: "The rest of [the disciples . . .]. They said to him, 'Why do you love her more than all of us?' The Savior answered and said to them, 'Why do I not love you like her?' "[76] This conflict appears to be the result of some sort of jealousy on the part of the other disciples, though it is difficult to determine what political or other factors stand behind this portrayal. This text specifically identifies Mary Magdalene as the figure against whom some of the other disciples are therefore complaining and thus provides some contextual motive for the controversies between them.

When the *Gospel of Mary*, therefore, presents a scene similar to this one in the *Gospel of Philip,* in which Levi points out that the Redeemer loved Mary "more than us," the parallel to Mary Magdalene is difficult to miss. The Coptic text states, "Surely the Savior knows her very well. That is why he loved her more than us."[77] The Greek text tells us: "For surely knowing her, he loved her very well."[78]

At an earlier point in the *Gospel of Mary* the Greek version portrays the dialogue thus: "Peter said to Mary: 'Sister, we know that you have

[75]ⲁⲩⲱ̣ ⲧ̣ⲕⲟ̣ⲓ̣ⲛⲱⲛⲟⲥ ⲙ̄ⲡⲉ̣[ⲭⲥ ⲧⲉ ⲙⲁⲣ]ⲓⲁ ⲧⲙⲁ[ⲅⲇⲁ]ⲗⲏⲛⲏ ⲛⲉⲣⲉⲡ[ϫⲟⲉⲓⲥ ⲙⲉ] ⲙ̣̄ⲙ[ⲁⲣⲓⲁ ⲛ]ϩⲟⲩⲟ ⲁⲙ̄ⲙⲁⲑⲏ[ⲧⲏⲥ ⲧⲏⲣⲟⲩ ⲁⲩⲱ ⲁϥ]ⲁⲥⲡⲁⲍⲉ ⲙ̄ⲙⲟⲥ ⲁⲧⲉⲥ̣[. . .]ⲛ̄ⲥⲟⲡ· (§55, *Gos. Phil.* 111,32–37). For more on Mary in the *Gospel of Philip*, see Jorunn Jacobson Buckley, *Female Fault and Fulfilment in Gnosticism* (*SR*; Chapel Hill: University of North Carolina Press, 1986), 108–11, 114, 118–19, 123–25, 136. Buckley also discusses Mary in the *Gos. Thom.*, 84–87, 91, 102–4, 134, 136.

[76]ⲁⲡⲕⲉⲥⲉⲉⲡⲉ ⲙ̣̄[ⲙⲁⲑⲏⲧⲏⲥ . .] . ⲉⲣⲟ . [.] . [. .]ⲙⲁ ⲡⲉϫⲁⲩ ⲛⲁϥ ϫⲉ ⲉⲧⲃⲉ ⲟⲩ ⲕⲙⲉ ⲙ̄ⲙⲟⲥ ⲡⲁⲣⲁⲣⲟⲛ ⲧⲏⲣⲛ̄ ⲁϥⲟⲩⲱϣⲃ̄ ⲛ̄ϭⲓ ⲡⲥⲱⲧⲏⲣ ⲡⲉϫⲁϥ ⲛⲁⲩ {ⲡⲉϫⲁϥ ⲛⲁⲩ} ϫⲉ ⲉⲧⲃⲉ ⲟⲩ ϯⲙⲉ ⲙ̄ⲙⲱⲧⲛ̄ ⲁⲛ ⲛ̄ⲧⲉⲥϩⲉ (§55; *Gos. Phil.* 111,37–112,5). Here I follow the text and translation of *NHC* II,2–7, pp. 168–69; Till's reconstruction is based on a different reading of the characters surrounding the breaks in 111,37–112,1.

[77]ⲡⲁⲛⲧⲱ‘ⲥ’ ⲉⲣ̣ⲉⲡⲥⲱⲧⲏⲣ ⲥⲟⲟⲩⲛ ⲙ̄ⲙⲟⲥ ⲁⲥⲫⲁⲗⲱⲥ ⲉⲧⲃⲉ ⲡⲁï ⲁϥⲟⲩⲟϣⲥ̄ ⲛ̄ϩⲟⲩⲟ ⲉⲣⲟⲛ (*Gos. Mary,* BG 18,13–15).

[78]πάν/τως γὰρ ἐ̣κεῖνος εἰδὼς αὐτὴν ἀ̣σ̣ /φ[αλ]ῶ̣[ς] ἠγάπησεν·[PRyl 463, verso 6–8]). Greek text from PRyl 463 in Lührmann, "Die griechischen Fragmente," 329. It may be

been loved extensively by the Savior as no other woman.' "[79] In the Coptic version: "Peter said to Mary, "Sister, we know that the Savior loved you more than the rest of women. Tell us the words of the Savior which you remember — which you know (but) we do not, nor have we heard them."[80] In response to this request, Mary then conveys her vision to the disciples and encourages them.

Levi's subsequent description of Mary's position in the group is significantly stronger than Peter's, as he states that Jesus loved her more than all the other disciples, not more than all the other women, as did Peter. Part of the controversy reflected in the text may have revolved around this special status of Mary Magdalene.[81] As in the *Gospel of Philip*, it is therefore also evident that some tension occurs concerning Mary Magdalene because of the portrayal of a close bond between Jesus and Mary Magdalene. Although the *Gospel of Philip* names no specific disciple as the one expressing disapproval of Mary's special status before Jesus, the *Gospel of Mary* does specify the names, with the result that Peter again appears to be involved in the representation of resistance to Mary's position. Marjanen explains, "Peter's problem with Mary Magdalene is that she is spiritually more advanced than his male colleagues and that she is

---

fruitful here to raise the issue concerning the placement of punctuation before or after μᾶλλον to decide whether it should be connected either with the end of this sentence or the beginning of the subsequent one. If μᾶλλον goes with the verb that follows it in the Greek, as Lührmann proposes then, the Greek indicates that Levi said, "Let us *rather* be ashamed." If μᾶλλον is connected instead with the previous sentence, we could conjecture that even the Greek had the meaning that the Savior loved her *more* than the others and that the redundant adverb πάντως should be read as πάντων indicating "more than all," thus making it easier to comprehend why the Coptic indicates that Levi states that the Savior loved Mary more than all the rest. The Greek syntax with such a distance between the words πάντων and μᾶλλον (as well as the absence of ἤ), however, would be somewhat strange.

[79][λέγει Πέτρος πρὸ]ς Μαριάμμην· ἀδελφή, οἴδαμεν ὅτι πολλ[ὰ ἠγαπήθης ὑπὸ τοῦ σωτ]ῆρος ὡς οὐκ ἄλλη γυνή (POxy 3525: lines 15–16).

[80]ⲡⲉϫⲉ ⲡⲉⲧⲣⲟⲥ ⲛ̄ⲙⲁⲣⲓϩⲁⲙ ϫⲉ ⲧⲥⲱⲛⲉ ⲧⲛ̄ⲥⲟⲟⲩⲛ ϫⲉ ⲛⲉⲣⲉⲡⲥⲱ̄ⲣ̄ ⲟⲩⲁϣⲉ ⲛ̄ϩⲟⲩⲟ ⲡⲁⲣⲁ ⲡⲕⲉⲥⲉⲉⲡⲉ ⲛ̄ⲥ̄ϩⲓⲙⲉ ϫⲱ ⲛⲁⲛ ⲛ̄ⲛ̄ϣⲁϫⲉ ⲙ̄ⲡⲥ̄ⲱ̄ⲣ ⲉⲧⲉⲉⲓⲣⲉ ⲙ̄ⲡⲉⲩⲛⲉⲉⲩⲉ ⲛⲁⲓ̈ ⲉⲧⲉ-ⲥⲟⲟⲩⲛ ⲛ̄ⲙⲟⲟⲩ ⲛ̄ⲛⲁⲛⲟⲛ ⲁⲛ ⲟⲩⲇⲉ ⲙ̄ⲡⲛ̄ⲥⲟⲧⲙ·ⲟ·ⲩ (*Gos. Mary*, BG 10,1–6).

[81]Anne Pasquier has an interesting thesis concerning the reaction of Peter. She posits that his reaction originally followed the words Mary shares with the distraught disciples. He objects to her use of "us" in *Gos. Mary*, BG 9,20 ("He made us human beings"), a category to which he believes Mary, a woman, does not belong. Pasquier argues that it is antithetical in the eyes of Peter that Mary, a woman, could claim she has reached the level of "androgynous unity" as the male disciples have (Pasquier, *L'Évangile selon*

a woman."[82] The text shows the importance of Mary as she discloses the
words that the Savior shared with her alone. "Only after the transmission
of these words by Mary, the apostles are able to go forth and proclaim the
gospel."[83] The identification of Mary as Mary Magdalene in the *Gospel
of Mary* is also supported by the evidence of *Pistis Sophia.*

Identification of Mary Magdalene in Pistis Sophia 1–3

Pistis Sophia 1–3, like the *Gospel of Philip*, sometimes provides specific
identifiers of both Mary Magdalene and Mary, the mother of Jesus, with
the result that determining the identity of Mary in certain instances is
sometimes easier than in other texts. In fact, in a number of ways this text
proves helpful in solving some of the identification questions, as these
two women are referenced twelve and eleven times respectively.[84]

   The first Mary to appear in the text is Mary, mother of Jesus. All of
the explicit references to Mary, the mother, appear only in the first book
of *Pistis Sophia.* These few appearances of Mary, the mother, often refer
to her being part of the physical or material sphere, such as: "Maria,
my mother according to the matter to whom I was entrusted,"[85] echoing
the reference to "matter" in her introduction into the text as a "mother
according to the material body" (*Pis. Soph.* 1.8). Likewise, the text re-
iterates the concept of her being "entrusted" in the praise she receives
from Jesus: "Truly, truly, I say that they will bless you from end to end
of the earth for the pledge of the First Mystery was entrusted to you"
(*Pis. Soph.* 1.59). It is not from Jesus that this blessing comes but from
others who will bless her because of what was entrusted to her. This is a
text that philosophically tends to negate the physical realm and therefore

---

Marie [BCNH.T 10; Québec: Les Presses de l'Université Laval, 1981], 98). For a con-
cise summary of the interpretations of Till, Pasquier, and Tardieu, see De Boer, *Mary
Magdalene*, 87–92.

   [82]Marjanen, *The Woman Jesus Loved*, 181.

   [83]Gerard P. Luttikhuizen, "The Evaluation of the Teaching of Jesus in Christian Gnostic
Revelation Dialogues," *NovT* 30 (1988): 163.

   [84]For a detailed breakdown of the statistics, see Ann Graham Brock, "Setting the
Record Straight—The Politics of Identification: Mary Magdalene and Mary the Mother in
Pistis Sophia," in *Which Mary?: The Marys of Early Christian Tradition* (ed. F. Stanley
Jones; SBLSymS 19; Atlanta: Society of Biblical Literature, 2002), 43–52.

   [85]ⲙⲁⲣⲓⲁ ⲧⲁⲙⲁⲁⲩ ⲕⲁⲧⲁ ⲑⲩⲗⲏ ⲧⲉⲛⲧⲁⲓⲥⲟⲓⲗⲉ (*Pis. Soph.* 1.61).

frequently portrays Jesus encouraging renunciation, including "the whole world and all the matter in it" (*Pis. Soph.* 2.95). This theme of renunciation appears throughout the text (see *Pis. Soph.* 1.33–35, 2.100, and 3.104), and includes the command to "renounce the whole world . . . and all its relationships" (*Pis. Soph.* 3.102 and 3.106). Thus the status of Mary, the mother, with its close connection to the material world, does not appear to be an especially high one, especially as Jesus addresses her: "From you has come forth the material body in which I exist, which I have cleaned and purified" (*Pis. Soph.* 1.59). Such an attitude is not unusual in a text that tends to diminish the material world, including numerous exhortations to renounce "the world and all the matter in it." No other explicit references to Mary, the mother, occur outside of the first of the four books of *Pistis Sophia*.

Pistis Sophia 1–3 describes the presence of a second character named Mary, unquestionably distinguished from Mary, the mother, in at least twelve passages that refer to her explicitly as "Mary the Magdalene."[86] These explicit references to "the Magdalene" portray her quite differently from Mary, mother of Jesus. For instance, immediately after ⲙⲁⲣⲓⲁ ⲧⲙⲁⲅⲇⲁⲗⲏⲛⲏ (Mary Magdalene) speaks, the text points out that "the Savior marveled greatly at the answers to the words she gave" (*Pis. Soph.* 2.87). The author portrays Mary Magdalene throughout this text as one who remains strong and intercedes on behalf of the others "who have despaired completely" (*Pis. Soph.* 2.94). In one example, she offers an interpretation for Salome, and the "power of light within Mary Magdalene welled up" (*Pis. Soph.* 3.132). In response to one of Mary Magdalene's questions, Jesus promises, "I will fulfill you in all powers and all pleromas . . . so that you may be called the pleromas, fulfilled with all knowledge" (*Pis. Soph.* 2.85). Statements praising Mary Magdalene add up throughout the text, such as the one in which the Savior announces: "Maria Magdalene (ⲙⲁⲣⲓⲁ ⲧⲙⲁⲅⲇⲁⲗⲏⲛⲏ) and John the Virgin (ⲓⲱⲀⲛⲛⲏⲥ ⲡⲡⲁⲣⲑⲉⲛⲟⲥ) will be superior to all my disciples" (*Pis. Soph.* 2.96).

When one compares these explicit references of Mary Magdalene to Mary, the mother, the ones that express especially high praise inevitably belong to Mary Magdalene. As these passages make clear, Jesus describes ⲙⲁⲣⲓⲁ ⲧⲙⲁⲅⲇⲁⲗⲏⲛⲏ as superior, as filled with the power of light, and as providing explanations that evoke "marvel." The strength and quality of these positive references suggest that Mary Magdalene is the primary

[86]*Pis. Soph.* 2.83, 2.85, 2.87, 2.88, 2.90, 2.94, 2.96, 2.97, 2.98, 2.99, 3.127, 3.132.

interlocutor with Jesus in the text and thus is the Mary spoken of when her identity is unspecified.

Although the explicit references to Mary are enough to convince many scholars that Mary Magdalene is the primary figure of the text, I offer here an additional interpretive tool to strengthen the case. *Pistis Sophia 1–3* provides an unusually high number of appositional phrases immediately following Mary's name that supply additional identifiers concerning the primary Mary. These identifiers include phrases such as "Mary, the other one," or "Mary, the blessed one," as well as "Mary, the pure spiritual one." In one sample description of Mary, the text states:

> ⲘⲀⲢⲒϨⲀⲘ ⲦⲘⲀⲔⲀⲢⲒⲀ· ⲦⲀⲒ ⲈⲒⲚⲀⲬⲞⲔⲤ ⲈⲂⲞⲖ ϨⲚ ⲘⲘⲨⲤⲦⲎⲢⲒⲞⲚ ⲦⲎⲢⲞⲨ ⲚⲦⲈ ⲚⲀⲠⲬⲒⲤⲈ· ϢⲀⲬⲈ ϨⲚ ⲞⲨⲠⲀⲢϨⲎⲤⲒⲀ ⲬⲈ ⲚⲦⲞ ⲦⲈⲦⲈⲢⲈ ⲠⲈⲤϨⲎⲦ ⲤⲞⲨⲦⲰⲚ ⲈϨⲞⲨⲚ ⲈⲦⲘⲚⲦⲈⲢⲞ ⲘⲠⲘⲎⲨⲈ· ⲚϨⲞⲨⲞ ⲈⲚⲞⲨⲤⲚⲎⲨ ⲦⲎⲢⲞⲨ·

> "Mariam, the blessed one, whom I will complete in all the mysteries of the height, speak openly, you are she whose heart is more directed to the kingdom of heaven, than all your brothers." (*Pis. Soph.* 1.17)

Recent scholarly discussion concerning the identity of the primary Mary in these texts has revolved around the way the text refers to Mary as "the blessed one." For example, the text states: "Now it happened when Jesus heard Mariam saying these words, he said to her: 'Excellent, Mariam, *the blessed one*, you pleroma or you all-blessed pleroma, who will be blessed among all generations'" (*Pistis Sophia* 1.34).

Shoemaker contends that the Mary in this last reference should be acknowledged as Mary, the mother of Jesus, because this epithet "would surely prompt an ancient listener familiar with Luke's gospel to associate this Mary with the Virgin rather than the Magdalene."[87] Such a claim, however, constitutes an overgeneralization, because the use of the description "blessed" for a female figure predates Luke's usage (see Judith 13:18 and the *Apocalypse of Baruch* 54:10), and in Christian literature it also

---

[87]Shoemaker, "Mary and the Discourse of Orthodoxy," 186. See Luke 1:42: "In a loud voice she exclaimed: 'Blessed are you among women'" and Luke 1:48 "From now on all generations will call me blessed." See also, Stephen J. Shoemaker, "Rethinking the 'Gnostic Mary': Mary of Nazareth and Mary of Magdala in Early Christian Tradition," *JECS* 9 (2001): 558.

appears in reference to other female figures. Furthermore, in *Pistis Sophia* *1–3*, the epithet ⲦⲘⲁⲕⲁⲣⲓⲁ ("the blessed one") appears at least seventeen times—either in the female or male form—but never in conjunction with explicit references to Mary, the mother. Rather, the reference to Mary, "the blessed one," explicitly refers to the Mary that is not the mother: Jesus spoke to his mother, saying, "you and the other Mary, the blessed one" (ⲛ̄ⲧⲟ ⲙ̄ⲛ ⲧⲕⲉⲘⲁⲣⲓ2ⲁⲙ ⲦⲘⲁⲕⲁⲣⲓⲟⲥ [*Pis. Soph.* 1.59]).

Another juxtaposition of speakers in this text confirms the use of the term ⲦⲘⲁⲕⲁⲣⲓⲁ ("the blessed one") as an identifier for the Mary who is not the mother:

ⲁⲥⲱ̄ⲡⲉ 6ⲉ ⲛ̄ⲧⲉⲣⲉ ⲓ̄ⲥ ⲥⲱ̄ⲧⲘ̄ ⲉⲛⲉⲓ̈ⲱⲁ̄ⲭⲉ· ⲡⲉⲭⲁ4 ⲭⲉ ⲉⲩⲅⲉ
ⲙⲁⲣⲓ2ⲁⲙ ⲦⲘⲁⲕⲁⲣⲓⲁ ⲧⲁⲓ̈ ⲉⲧⲛⲁⲕⲗⲏⲣⲟⲛⲟⲙⲓ ⲛ̄ⲧⲙ̄ⲛ̄ⲧⲉⲣⲟ ⲧⲏⲣ2ⲥ̄
ⲙ̄ⲡⲟⲩⲟⲓ̈ⲛ· ⲙ̄ⲛ̄ⲛ̄ⲥⲁ ⲛⲁⲓ̈ ⲁⲥⲉⲓ· 2ⲱ̄ⲥ ⲉ2ⲏ ⲛ̄6ⲓ ⲙⲁⲣⲓⲁ ⲧⲘⲁⲁⲩ ⲙ̄ⲥ̄
ⲡⲉⲭⲁⲥ ⲭⲉ ⲡⲁⲭⲟⲉⲓⲥ ⲁⲩⲱ ⲡⲁⲥⲱ̄ⲧⲏⲣ ⲕⲉⲗⲉⲩⲉ ⲛⲁⲓ̈ 2ⲱ̄ ⲉⲧⲣⲁⲭⲱ
ⲙ̄ⲡⲉⲓ̈ⲱⲁ̄ⲭⲉ ⲛ̄ⲟⲩⲱ2ⲙ̄·

Now it happened when Jesus heard these words he said: "Excellent, Mariam, the blessed one, who will inherit the whole kingdom of the Light." After these things Mary, the mother of Jesus, also came forward and said, "My Lord and my Savior, command me also that I answer this discourse." (*Pis. Soph.* 1.61)

The text that follows this interchange presents more praise for Mary, the blessed one (who is not the mother), as she is singled out again, this time for a spiritual inheritance: ⲉⲩⲅⲉ ⲙⲁⲣⲓ2ⲁⲙ ⲧⲉⲕⲗⲏⲣⲟⲛⲟⲙⲟⲥ ⲙ̄ⲡⲟⲩⲟⲉⲓⲛ ("Excellent, Mariam, you inheritor of the light" [*Pistis Sophia* 1.62]). The way these examples differentiate this Mary from Mary, the mother of Jesus, suggests that ensuing occurrences of the phrase, "Mary, the blessed one" also refer to the Mary who is not the Mother.[88]

---

[88]In addition to Mary Magdalene a few other disciples receive the term "the blessed one" (ⲧⲘⲁⲕⲁⲣⲓⲁ [fem.]/ⲡⲘⲁⲕⲁⲣⲓⲟⲥ [masc.]). Philip is the first male disciple to speak (*Pis. Soph.* 1.22) and is given the special commission to record (*Pis. Soph.* 1.43). He is subsequently identified as blessed (*Pis. Soph.* 1.42 and 2.82), as are also Andrew (*Pis. Soph.* 1.45), Thomas (*Pis. Soph.* 2.70), Martha (*Pis. Soph.* 2.80), and Peter (*Pis. Soph.* 2.66) included in the plural 2ⲉⲛⲛⲁⲕⲁⲣⲓⲟⲥ (*Pis. Soph.* 1.37). John, interestingly, is called both: ⲡⲘⲁⲕⲁⲣⲓⲟⲥ . . . ⲁⲩⲱ ⲡⲘⲉⲣⲓⲧ ("the blessed . . . and beloved one" [2.90]). James does not receive the epithet ⲙⲁⲕⲁⲣⲓⲟⲥ but is twice referenced as ⲡⲘⲉⲣⲓⲧ (the "beloved" [*Pis. Soph.* 2.68 and 2.78]). Lastly, none of the references specifically referring to Mary, the mother, designates her as ⲧⲘⲁⲕⲁⲣⲓⲁ as the text does for Mary Magdalene.

Thus a scholar cannot convincingly argue that the description "blessed" necessarily refers to Mary, the mother. When the *Gospel of Mary* therefore depicts Jesus' description of Mary with the phrase, "blessed are you that you did not waver," it should likewise not be assumed that such a phrase refers to Mary, the mother. Morard explains that in the case of Mary in the *Gospel of Mary*, she is called "blessed" because of her special inner tranquility—because she demonstrates such an inward peace.[89]

In addition to "Mary, the blessed one," the text of *Pistis Sophia* presents other epithets or appositional phrases that similarly set Mary apart, such as "Mary, the pure spiritual one" (ⲧⲉⲡⲛⲉⲩⲙⲁⲧⲓⲕⲏ ⲛ̄ϩⲓⲗⲓⲕⲣⲓⲛⲉⲥ ⲙⲁⲣⲓⲁ). This phrase occurs for the first time in the section in which Mary Magdalene (ⲙⲁⲣⲓⲁ ⲧⲙⲁⲅⲇⲁⲗⲏⲛⲏ) has just finished speaking and Jesus marvels at her answers (*Pis. Soph.* 2.87). The text then explains the reason for his admiration: "because she had become completely pure Spirit" (ⲉⲃⲟⲗ ϫⲉ ⲛⲉⲁⲥⲣ̄ⲡⲛ̄ⲁ ⲧⲏⲣⲥ̄ ⲛ̄ϩⲓⲗⲓⲕⲣⲓⲛⲉⲥ [*Pis. Soph.* 2.87]). The Savior next praises her according to her spiritual state: "Excellent, Maria, the *pure spiritual one*" (ⲉⲩⲅⲉ ⲧⲉⲡⲛⲉⲩⲙⲁⲧⲓⲕⲏ ⲛ̄ϩⲓⲗⲓⲕⲣⲓⲛⲉⲥ ⲙⲁⲣⲓⲁ [2.87]). In this case, the "pure spiritual" Mary is quite explicitly identified with numerous additional references that immediately follow and name her as Mary "the Magdalene" (in *Pis. Soph.* 2.88, 2.90, 2.94, 2.96, 2.97, 2.98, and 2.99). Following this special designation of being "a pure spiritual one"—specifically linked here to ⲙⲁⲣⲓⲁ ⲧⲙⲁⲅⲇⲁⲗⲏⲛⲏ—are additional references to "Mary, the spiritual one" appearing frequently thereafter (including the "all-blessed Mary, the spiritual one," in 3.114; "Mary, the spiritual one of pure light," in 3.116 and 3.118; "Mary, the spiritual and pure one," in 3.120; and simply "the spiritual one," in 3.121, 3.122, and 3.130). Once the text establishes these links between the "pure spiritual

---

[89]Françoise Morard, "Un Évangile écrit par une femme?" *BCPE* 49.2–3 (May, 1997): 27–34. Morard explains that this inner peace is connected with the essential message of the *Gospel of Mary*—that Mary is the one with true revelation. This revelation includes the need for the unity of soul, spirit, and mind, male and female in a new being. This text is thus an example of a more widespread early Christian criticism of the divided soul and the divided human being. Morard argues that in the *Acts of Andrew* we have a visualization of this teaching in the reunification of both aspects in the figure of Maximilla; that is, a recovery of the unity of Adam and Eve before the fall (*Acts Andr.* 37–46). Morard raises the possibility that since such a message would have been attractive for women in antiquity, these traditions such as the one behind the *Gospel of Mary* might have been preserved by a group of women, perhaps even written down by a woman, but admits that it cannot be proved (p. 33).

one" and Mary Magdalene, it seems logical that subsequent uses of the same phrase also refer to her. Indeed one would be hard-pressed to attribute these references instead to Mary, the mother, since no explicit link between "a pure spiritual one" and Mary, the mother, ever appears in this text. Thus these appositional phrases and additional epithets of Mary Magdalene significantly reduce the ambiguity of Mary's identity and add their weight to an already strong case for Mary Magdalene's prominence in the text.[90]

The previous section presents explicit challenges to the authority of Mary in various texts. It indicates that the two figures of Peter and Mary Magdalene rarely, if ever, enjoy equal status in the same text. In other words, when Mary functions as part of an inner circle of disciples, Peter tends not to be a member of that select group with the exception of appearing as an antagonist. We shall now look at two texts that do portray Mary as part of an elect group.

Portrayal of Mary in the *Dialogue of the Savior*

The *Dialogue of the Savior* (NHC III,5) belongs to codex III of the Nag Hammadi discoveries along with four other texts: the *Apocryphon of John* (NHC III,1), *the Gospel of the Egyptians* (NHC III,2), *Eugnostos the Blessed* (NHC III,3), and *Sophia of Jesus Christ* (NHC III,4). Dated to the early decades of the second century,[91] the text itself is fragmentary and known only in a Sahidic Coptic translation of a Greek original. This text appears to be a compilation of various sources that elaborates and expands upon an older dialogue. This text's final form primarily comprises a revelation dialogue between a figure called the "Lord" and several disciples concerning a variety of subject matters, such as ritual activity (probably baptism), and both realized and future eschatology. Part of the literary value of this compilation is the way it preserves what is considered to be rather early versions of Jesus' say-

---

[90]Although in some texts, especially in the Middle Ages, the figure of Mary sometimes appears to be a composite figure, who is from Magdala, for example, but has a sister named Martha, I would still advise caution not to "universalize" these Marys into a composite figure too quickly. We shall see in chapter 7 why alterations in the identity of Mary may stem from political motivations rather than mere confusion.

[91]Helmut Koester and Elaine Pagels, "Introduction," in *Nag Hammadi Codex, III,5: The Dialogue of the Savior* (ed. Stephen Emmel; NHS 26; Leiden: Brill, 1984), 16.

ings, thus presenting evidence of the ongoing development of sayings traditions. The estimation of some of these sayings as "early" does not necessarily indicate that they are therefore any more authentic or authoritative because they somehow have a closer link to Jesus, but instead underscores their value in tracing the development of such sayings in the life of early Christian communities. This usefulness as a resource prevents readers from dismissing it as merely the product of some "gnostic" group.

Dialogue of the Savior is also valuable in an examination of the early representations of the disciples because it preserves the memory of an elect group of Jesus' followers that includes the female disciple Mary. In fact, one third—fourteen—of the references to individual disciples in the *Dialogue of the Savior* are to this female figure called Mary, presumed to be Mary Magdalene,[92] and thirteen of those references are speaking parts that provide her a prominent voice in the text.

In one section of this sayings source, after Mary speaks three aphorisms, the text describes that "she spoke this word as a woman who understood completely."[93] The content of her three aphorisms appears as follows:

ϫⲉ ϩⲓⲛⲁⲓ ⲉⲧ ⲕⲁⲕⲓⲁ ⲙ̅ⲡⲉϩⲟⲟⲩ ⲡⲉϩⲟⲟⲩ
ⲁⲩⲱ ⲡⲉⲣⲅⲁⲧⲏⲥ ⲙ̅ⲡϣⲁ ⲛ̅ⲧⲉϥⲧⲣⲟⲫⲏ·
ⲁⲩⲱ ⲡⲙⲁⲑⲏⲧⲏⲥ ⲛ̅ϥⲉⲓⲛⲉ ⲙ̅ⲡⲉϥⲥⲁϩ·

Just so the wickedness of each is sufficient, and
The labourer is worthy of his food
The disciple resembles his teacher.

The subsequent description of Mary's three "words"—that she spoke as a woman who understood completely (or who understood everything)—is the most positive depiction of any of the disciples in the text.[94] Another affirmation of Mary in this text is Jesus' declaration

---

[92]Koester and Pagels, "Introduction [*The Dialogue of the Savior*]."

[93]ⲡⲉ ⲉⲓϣⲁϫⲉ ⲁⲥϫⲟⲟϥ ϩⲱⲥ ⲥϩⲓⲙⲉ ⲉⲁⲥⲉⲓ ⲛⲉ ⲉⲡⲧⲏⲣϥ̅· (*Dial. Sav.* §53; 139,12–13).

[94]Marjanen (*The Woman Jesus Loved*, 29) states that one should not make her the most dominant disciple within the circle of Jesus' closest followers before the text is carefully studied in light of those passages where a similar task is entrusted to other disciples as well (*Dial. Sav.* 126,8–10; 126,16–17; 142,21–24). In response it must be said that no other disciple receives this acclamation of having spoken as someone "who understood completely" or "who understood the all."

that Mary has come to the world "to make clear the abundance of the revealer" (*Dial. Sav.* §61; 140,17–19).

Additional evidence of Mary's prominence in this text becomes apparent when one analyzes not only the words attributed to each figure but also the types of speech that each of the three primary disciples contribute. Such analysis brings some intriguing textual dynamics to light. For instance, whereas the other two primary disciples play a role typical of disciples, asking questions of Jesus, the author attributes to Mary a role largely involving explanations or interpretations. Mary's speech, thus, does not follow the usual revelation dialogue pattern, in which a disciple asks a question and a revealer figure responds. Instead, the text portrays Mary as a frequent participant in the dialogue (at least thirteen times), asking questions only five times.

Because this text features a dialogue of the resurrected Jesus with three primary disciples—Mary, Judas (Thomas), and Matthew—it provides a counter-balance to the inner circle of male disciples known from the canon, namely Peter, James, and John, who are selected to witness the transfiguration, for example. In *Sophia of Jesus Christ*, Mary, Thomas, and Matthew are again portrayed as members of a select group of disciples that now includes Philip and Bartholomew.

Portrayal of Mary in *Sophia of Jesus Christ*

Sophia of Jesus Christ, a text that scholars generally date to the second half of the second century c.e., focuses primarily upon five disciples, namely: Mary, Matthew, Thomas, Philip, and Bartholomew.[95] This text presents a postresurrection appearance story in which Mary participates along with the others in a dialogue with the Savior. All five disciples appear to receive approximately the same status in the text: each of them asks two questions apiece, except for Bartholomew, who asks only one.

The choice of these five as the primary actors in *Sophia of Jesus Christ* appears to have been deliberate on the part of the author. Douglas Parrott suggests that the author rejected an alternative inner circle (namely Peter,

---

[95]Douglas M. Parrott, trans., "Sophia of Jesus Christ (III,4 and BG 8502,3)," in *NHL*, 220–43; Henri-Charles Puech, "Gnostische Evangelien und verwandte Dokumente," in *Evangelien*, vol. 1 of *Neutestamentliche Apokryphen in deutscher Übersetzung* (ed. Edgar Hennecke and Wilhelm Schneemelcher; 3d ed.; Tübingen: Mohr [Siebeck], 1959–1964), 158–271.

Andrew, James, and John) sometimes singled out in canonical narratives, such as those of the disciples' calls (Luke 5:1–11), the transfiguration (Mark 9:2), or the vigil in the Garden of Gethsemane (Mark 14:33).[96] Parrott states that "the reason for the choosing of Philip, Thomas, Matthew, Bartholomew, and Mary to be named in the *Sophia of Jesus Christ* is that the more obvious disciples, Peter, Andrew, James, and John, were already identified with a particular way of understanding Christ that the writer of *Sophia of Jesus Christ* knew would have a negative impact upon his intended audience, presumably because it had negative overtones to him."

I concur with Parrott's conclusion that this "inner group" of *Sophia of Jesus Christ* represents an alternative constellation of disciples, and I also agree that this circle most probably reflects a deliberate choice on the part of the author. I take issue, however, with his underlying assumption that suggests that the author chose this "alternative" list of names over against others who were already well known or easily identified because it implies that the "alternative" group were not also well known or identified with certain theologies or concepts. One need only review a list of early Christian apocryphal gospels and acts to see that this grouping of names, including Mary, Philip, and Thomas, had already acquired prominence and authority in their own right from the earliest stages of Christianity. Thus the author may have deliberately chosen this group not because they were unknown but because they represent a recognized alternative inner circle.

A similar preferential circle, including Mary and three other women, appears also in the *First Apocalypse of James*: "When you speak these words of this [perception], encourage these [four]: Salome and Mariam [and Martha and Arsinoe . . .]."[97] It may not be a coincidence that shortly after the words on behalf of these four women, including Mary, there follows a rebuke of the "twelve": "And he went at that time [immediately]

---

[96]Douglas M. Parrott, "Gnostic and Orthodox Disciples in the Second and Third Centuries," in *Nag Hammadi, Gnosticism, & Early Christianity* (ed. Charles W. Hedrick and Robert Hodgson, Jr.; Peabody, Mass.: Hendrickson, 1986), 202.

[97]ⲉⲱⲱⲡⲉ ⲉⲕ[ⲱⲁ]ⲏⲭⲉ ⲛⲉⲓ̈ⲱⲁⲭⲉ ⲛ̅ⲧⲉ ⲧⲉⲓ̈[ⲉⲥⲑ]ⲏⲥⲓⲥ ⲧⲱⲧ ⲛ̅ϩⲏⲧ ⲛ̅ⲡⲉⲉⲓ [ϥⲧⲟⲟⲩ] ⲥⲁⲗⲱⲙⲏ ⲙⲛ̅ ⲙⲁⲣⲓⲁⲙ [ⲙⲛ̅ ⲙⲁⲣⲑⲁ ⲙⲛ̅ ⲁⲣⲥ]ⲓⲛⲟⲏ (*The [First] Apocalypse of James* [NHC V,3] 40. 22–26). As Böhlig mentions, the four names are reconstructed from the four names in the *Manichaean Psalm-Book*, 192,21–24; 194,19–22.

and rebuked the Twelve, and cast [out] of them contentment [concerning the] way of knowledge [. . .]."[98] In chapter 8, I will explore further the development of a strong link between the "twelve" and Peter, who appears so frequently as their spokesperson.[99]

Summary

The texts in this examination are only a sampling of the numerous early Christian texts in which Mary Magdalene appears as a primary character or authority figure.[100] Yet this sample suggests that when an author chooses a select, inner group of disciples, Mary Magdalene and Peter do not function side by side as witnesses of equal status, as Mary and the other disciples do in the texts examined above.[101] In fact, in the numerous examples offered here in which both Mary and Peter do

---

[98]ⲁⲩⲱ ⲁϥⲃⲱⲕ ⲛ̄ⲡⲓⲟⲩⲟⲉⲓⲱ ⲛ̄ [ⲥⲁ]ⲧ[ⲟ]ⲟⲧϥ̄ ⲁϥⲥⲟ2ⲉ ⲛ̄ⲡⲓⲙⲛ̄ⲧ [ⲥⲛⲟ]ⲟⲩϭ· ⲁⲩⲱ ⲁϥ-ⲛⲟⲩⲭⲉ [ⲉⲃⲟⲗ] ⲛ̄2[ⲏ]ⲧⲟⲩ ⲛ̄ⲟⲩⲧⲱⲧ ⲛ̄2ⲏⲧ [ⲉⲧⲃⲉ †ⲡ]ⲟⲣⲟⲓ̈ⲁ ⲛ̄ⲧⲉ [ⲟ]ⲩⲅⲛⲱⲥⲓⲥ *(The [First] Apocalypse of James* [NHC V,3] 42.20–26).

[99]Regarding the authority issue, Perkins draws parallels between the *Gospel of Mary* and the *Letter of Peter to Philip* (NHC 8,2) because they display similar leadership patterns, except that in the *Gospel of Mary,* it is Mary who is the leader. She is the one who must encourage the fearful disciples to embark on the preaching mission commanded by the risen Lord. Like Peter in *PetPhil,* she must warn them that they are destined to suffer as Jesus did (9,5–24). See introduction by Marvin W. Meyer, "Letter of Peter to Philip (VIII,2)," in *Nag Hammadi Library in English* (trans. Frederik Wisse; 3d ed.; San Francisco: Harper & Row, 1988), 431–37. Marvin Meyer likewise points out that in the *Letter of Peter to Philip,* "The letter itself was added at the beginning of this narrative in order to stress the authoritative place of Peter" (p. 433). Meyer explains, "The only other apostle mentioned by name is Philip, who is submissive to the authority of Peter and whose place in the tractate seems intended to highlight the pre-eminent authority of Peter" (p. 431).

[100]Other texts include, for example, the *Great Questions of Mary,* cited and summarized by Epiphanius (*Panarion* 26.8.1–20), and the Manichaean Psalms. See Ute E. Eisen, *Amtsträgerinnen im frühen Christentum: Epigraphische und literarische Studien* (Forschungen zur Kirchen-Dogmengeschichte 61; Göttingen: Vandenhoeck & Ruprecht, 1996) or the English translation, *Women Officeholders in Early Christianity: Epigraphical and Literary Studies* (trans. Linda M. Maloney; Collegeville, Minn.: Liturgical Press, 2000).

[101]This chapter argues that Mary and Peter rarely appear as part of a select group of disciples in the same text. The *Ecclesiastical Canons of the Apostles* appears to be an exception to this tendency. However, this document does not fit into the same category of texts as *Sophia of Jesus Christ* because although the chosen authority figures include the unusual grouping of Peter, Andrew, John, James, and Mary Magdalene, these figures

appear together, just the opposite is true. This and previous chapters
have presented evidence that: 1) although both figures, according to
tradition, receive special appearances from the risen Jesus, Mary and
Peter never both receive individual resurrection appearances from Jesus in the same text; and 2) when Mary and Peter are both present in
the text, Peter consistently challenges her authority or diminishes her
status, often in overt and blatant ways. On the other hand, I know of
no ancient Christian text that portrays Mary, the mother, and Peter in
controversy with one another. In fact, in chapter 7, I will show evidence
that in texts that present Mary, the mother, in company with Peter, Mary
rather consistently acknowledges or defers to Peter's authority, and to
male authority in general.[102]

The crisis of authority depicted in the competition between Peter and
Mary Magdalene in the texts above is directly relevant to the contradictory
traditions concerning who had apostolic authority and who received the
first resurrection appearance. Against the argument that the controversy
in texts such as the *Gospel of Mary* and the others in this chapter are connected to the first-century controversy over the original resurrection witness, Gerd Lüdemann contends that the sources cited above are relatively
late and the controversy they depict "cannot directly be projected back"
into the time of the New Testament texts.[103] Opinions such as Lüdemann's
require reconsideration for several reasons. First, these writings are not

---

do not function on an equal status. Instead this text, like the other texts featuring Peter
and Mary treated in this chapter, presents a challenge to Mary's leadership role. In this
case, however, rather than placing the diminishing words in Peter's mouth, the author has
Mary Magdalene herself speak against women's eucharistic ministry, saying: "The weak
shall be saved through the strong." The Greek version appears in Adolf von Harnack, *Die
Lehre der zwölf Apostel* (TU 2, 5; Leipzig, 1884), 225–37, §24–28. The Syriac edition
is found in John P. Arendzen, "An Entire Syriac Text of Apostolic Church Order," *JTS*
3 (1902): 59–80, esp. 71, §19–20. See Pagels, *Gnostic Gospels,* 78. Elisabeth Schüssler
Fiorenza (*In Memory of Her,* 307) explains the rhetorical dynamic functioning in this
text, by which "a woman herself is used here to provide the theological argument against
women's ministry."

[102]For example, texts such as the *Questions of Bartholomew* and numerous Syriac
works portray a particularly close tie between Peter and Mary the mother.

[103]Gerd Lüdemann (*The Resurrection of Jesus: History, Experience, Theology* [Min-
neapolis: Fortress, 1994], 143) specifically mentions the Gospel of Luke because of
Elisabeth Schüssler Fiorenza's argument that the differences in resurrection portrayals
are related to texts such as these that contain confrontations.

equally or indisputably late.[104] As mentioned previously, many scholars date the *Gospel of Thomas* to the first century. Second, even a later text, such as *Pistis Sophia*, may preserve traces of an earlier historical conflict. Wilckens argues, "It is therefore possible, from the point of *method,* that some parts in writings which are, in *literary* terms, of a later date, are nevertheless, in terms of their place in *tradition,* of great antiquity."[105] Third, and most importantly, this study argues that the explicit portrayal of tensions between Peter and Mary Magdalene in the texts in this chapter has its antecedent in the implicit portrayal of such tensions in the conflicting resurrection traditions of the first century. One is therefore not projecting this controversy back into the first century; the tension is already implicitly present in the discrepancies regarding the identity of the first resurrection witness.

Gathering the texts that describe controversies between these two leadership figures along with texts that portray the gradual elimination of one of these authority figures is but a first step in the study of these controversies. The next step is to suggest a reconstruction of the historical context of these narratives in which such controversy took place. Even though numerous texts, such as the Acts of the Apostles, attempt to portray Christian communities rather idealistically, thus going to great lengths either to eradicate or to diminish differences among them, evidence from the apostolic fathers exists that describes the sociological controversies between groups. Remnants of the debates about the nature of women's leadership roles appear, for example, in the contrast between the words of Hippolytus quoted in the first chapter and Tertullian, who states: "it is not permitted for a woman to speak in the church, nor is it permitted for her to teach, nor to baptize, nor to offer [the Eucharist], nor to claim for herself a share in any masculine function—least of all, in priestly office."[106]

Therefore, when numerous texts, such as the *Gospel of Mary* and the *Gospel of Thomas,* do portray a controversy between leading figures, it is probable that such dialogue points not merely to literary tropes but to historical confrontation involving issues similar to the ones the early church fathers discussed. It is possible to make the sociological link between

---

[104]The writing of the *Gospel of Thomas* may even have occurred close to the time of Luke. As mentioned earlier, scholars such as Helmut Koester date the *Gospel of Thomas* to the first century. Koester, "Introduction [to *The Gospel according to Thomas*]," 38–49.

[105]Wilckens, *Resurrection,* 3.

[106]Tertullian, *De virginibus velandis,* 9.

text and historical context. We can see from the literary evidence that a dialogue was indeed occurring, but the wider sociological/cultural settings are difficult to establish and to a certain extent beyond the scope of this study. Clearly these controversy-containing texts existed within a historical *Sitz im Leben*, but before the discovery of the Nag Hammadi texts, we were left to glean much of this context from records that reflected a more "orthodox" standpoint, including third- and fourth-century church orders. What this study can point to is that the controversy passages contained in the *Gospel of Thomas*, the *Gospel of Mary*, and *Pistis Sophia* show no direct literary dependence upon each other. These texts portraying tensions between the early Christian figures of Peter and Mary Magdalene derived from independent traditions and survived in widespread locations. This breadth in chronology and geography indicates that controversy between the figures of Mary and Peter does not represent a local conflict of short duration nor one that is dependent upon a single literary trajectory, but rather reflects an issue faced in many literarily unrelated texts from widely dispersed locations.

The previous chapter presented commonalities between the *Gospel of Peter* and the pro-Petrine tendencies in the Gospel of Luke. The next chapter examines another text that invokes the authority of Peter: the *Acts of Peter*. It analyzes the portrayals of women in this text and compares the authoritative roles in it to those depicted in the *Acts of Paul*, a text from approximately the same time period. Peter's adversarial role in these controversy texts suggests that he is the figure of choice for voicing objections to women's leadership status. The next chapter presents a case study, so to speak, of how a text that draws on the authority of Peter simultaneously portrays women's roles and potential for leadership. It seeks to see if the representation of women's leadership in the *Acts of Peter* follows the pattern apparent in the Gospel of Luke and the *Gospel of Peter*.

CHAPTER SIX

Advocacy of Authority and Women's Leadership: The *Acts of Paul* versus the *Acts of Peter*

L ooking at Mary Magdalene's portrayal as an apostle in early Christian literature is part of the larger work of constructing a picture
of women's leadership in the early Christian church as a whole. The
Acts of Paul and the *Acts of Peter* embody two contrasting views on
women's leadership in the early church. The *Acts of Paul* and the *Acts
of Peter* rank among the most well-known apocryphal accounts of the
early Christian missionary movement. Both texts are Christian religious
works that, in addition to providing instruction and entertainment,[1] also
enrich our knowledge of early Christian evangelism and narrative strategies.[2] These two texts have an amazing amount of material in common.
Written in the second century, they are so chronologically close to each
other that scholars debate which of them came first.[3]

Similarities between the two accounts include sea journeys by both
apostles, dialogues between the apostles and ship captains, conversions
of Nero's servants by the apostles, and martyrdoms for both Peter and

---

[1]For more information on this thesis, see Richard Pervo, *Profit With Delight: The
Literary Genre of the Acts of the Apostles* (Philadelphia: Fortress, 1987).

[2]For a slightly more detailed version of the following research, see Ann Graham Brock,
"Political Authority and Cultural Accommodation: Social Diversity in the *Acts of Paul* and
the *Acts of Peter*," in *The Apocryphal Acts of the Apostles: Harvard Divinity School Studies*
(ed. François Bovon, Ann Graham Brock, and Christopher R. Matthews; Cambridge: Harvard
University Center for the Study of World Religions, 1999), 145–69.

[3]For a detailed examination see the paper by Dennis R. MacDonald, "*The Acts of Paul*
and *The Acts of Peter*: Which Came First?" *Society of Biblical Literature 1992 Seminar
Papers* (ed. Eugene H. Lovering, Jr.; Atlanta: Scholars Press, 1992), 214–24, and, in the
same volume, the responses by Robert F. Stoops, "Peter, Paul and Priority in the Apocryphal

Paul. Especially prominent among these commonalities is the well-known *Quo vadis* scene in which Jesus personally appears to Peter and to Paul respectively and has a strikingly similar encounter with each of them. While some of these similarities, such as the dialogues with ship captains and the martyrdoms, could simply be attributable to the similarity of elements that are typical of the oral legends behind the genre of the apocryphal acts,[4] other elements in the two acts are so close in detail as to make an interrelationship between the two texts practically a foregone conclusion.

The similarities between these two apocryphal Christian documents from the second century are thus generally undeniable, especially with respect to narrative details and parallel events. The presence of so many commonalities in the narrative might lead one to surmise that these texts are the products of authors or redactors who share similar worldviews. By comparing how the figures of Peter and Paul interact with their followers in each of the texts, however, I will show the ways in which these two accounts advocate different social attitudes. This chapter includes an analysis of the portrayals of both the apostles and secondary characters, both male and female, in the narrative. Despite the fact that the manuscript witnesses of both the *Acts of Peter* and the *Acts of Paul* are fragmentary at some points, scholars have nevertheless reconstructed major portions of each text.[5] The specific areas of focus are the positions of women in leadership roles, and Christian

---

Acts," 225–33, and Richard Valantasis, "Narrative Strategies and Synoptic Quandaries: A Response to Dennis MacDonald's Reading of *Acts of Paul* and *Acts of Peter*," 238.

[4]Valantasis, "Narrative Strategies and Synoptic Quandaries," 234–39.

[5]An analysis of both of these texts is complicated by the lack of an "original" manuscript for either act as a whole. Comments on the *Acts of Peter* will primarily draw from observations on the *Actus Vercellenses*, the Latin version of the *Acts of Peter*, which preserves the bulk of the *Acts of Peter*. Latin and Greek quotations from the *Acts of Peter* are drawn from Léon Vouaux, *Les Actes de Pierre: Introduction, textes, traduction et commentaire* (Les apocryphes du Nouveau Testament; Paris: Letouzey et Ané, 1922). Although the text that Richard Lipsius published closely parallels the manuscript from which he worked, even including errors, Vouaux has improved upon the text whenever he saw the need. Greek quotations from the *Acts of Paul* are taken from Léon Vouaux, *Les Actes de Paul et ses lettres apocryphes* (Les apocryphes du Nouveau Testament; Paris: Letouzey et Ané, 1913), or from Carl Schmidt, ΠΡΑΞΕΙΣ ΠΑΥΛΟΥ: *Acta Pauli nach dem Papyrus der Hamburger Staats- und Universitäts-Bibliothek* (Glückstadt/Hamburg: Augustin, 1936). The Coptic quotations from the *Acts of Paul* are taken from Carl Schmidt, *Acta Pauli aus der Heidelberger koptischen Papyrushandschrift Nr. 1* (Leipzig: Hinrichs, 1904). English quotations of text from these two apocryphal acts are either the author's own translation or are taken from the "Acts of Peter" and the "Acts of Paul," *NTApoc*[5] 2:276–322, 352–87. Critical editions of the *Acts*

accountability to familial, social, and ecclesiastical responsibilities. In this chapter I will argue that although similarities clearly exist between the two texts in terms of the narrative elements they employ, these texts differ significantly on the level of the ideologies they espouse, especially with respect to the proper role of women. In fact, one could describe these perspectives concerning the role of women in the church as diametrically opposed. These two texts, therefore, are particularly helpful in representing attitudes towards women's leadership in the second century. The tendencies they exhibit help to explain how the memories and traditions of the first female leaders, such as Mary Magdalene, were kept alive or lost.

Interactions with Characters in the *Acts of Paul*

The *Acts of Paul* incorporates numerous models of strong female leadership. Most prominent among the female figures is Thecla, who experiences an abundance of miraculous events and thus serves as a witness to many nonbelievers. Similarly, two other characters, Eubula and Artemilla, also desire to be baptized and subsequently resist familial and societal pressure in order to follow Paul. Significant roles are also played by other female figures such as Queen Tryphaena, Myrta, and Theocleia.

Since speeches composed by the authors are one of the primary means by which they convey their messages, this section examines the speeches and dialogues that the authors place upon the lips of the apostles and their accompanying characters. Interestingly, when the apostle Paul is portrayed as speaking to women, his messages differ in the *Acts of Paul* and in the *Acts of Peter*. The *Acts of Paul* does not, for example, transmit any speeches by Paul in which he chastises women or refuses them Eucharist as he does in the *Acts of Peter*, but rather depicts Paul strengthening and commissioning them. He tells Thecla, for example: "Go and teach the word of God!" (ὕπαγε καὶ δίδασκε τὸν λόγον τοῦ θεοῦ [41]).

Whereas, on the one hand, the *Acts of Peter* contains three variations on the theme of women who either die or become paralyzed when faced with sexual temptation,[6] women in the *Acts of Paul* respond differently to

---

of Paul by Willy Rordorf and of the *Acts of Peter* by Gérard Poupon are forthcoming in CCSA.

[6] I.e., Peter's daughter, the gardener's daughter, and Rufina.

their would-be seducers. For example, when a Syrian named Alexander falls in love with Thecla and forces his embrace upon her, Thecla takes hold of him, rips his cloak, takes the crown from his head, and makes him "a laughing-stock" (καὶ ἔστησεν αὐτὸν θρίαμβον [26]). Such active resistance is a far cry from paralysis and passivity.

Although an examination of the dialogue shows that almost all of the speaking parts for women in the *Acts of Paul* lie in a subsection called either the *Acts of Paul and Thecla*, or just the *Acts of Thecla*, the speaking parts are not strictly limited to Thecla. In addition to Tryphaena and Theocleia in the *Acts of Thecla*, other figures such as Nympha, Eubula, and Artemilla are depicted with small portions of dialogue, as well as Myrta, whose speech provides a good case study.[7] In the *Acts of Paul*, the Spirit descends upon Myrta in order that she may prophesy and encourage the brethren. She comforts them with the words:

Παῦλος ὁ τοῦ κυρίου δοῦλος πολλ[ο]ὺς εἰς τὴν ['Ρώμην σώ-
σει κ]αὶ πολλοὺς θρέψει τῷ λόγῳ, ὡς μὴ εἶναι ἀριθμὸν κα[ὶ
φα][νερὸν γενέσθαι ὑπὲρ πάντας τοὺς πιστούς, καὶ μεγάλως ἡ
δόξ[α τοῦ] [κυρίου Χριστοῦ Ιησοῦ] ἐπ᾽ αὐτὸν ὡς μεγάλην χάριν
ἔσεσθε ἐν 'Ρώμην. (PHam 7)

Paul the servant of the Lord will save many in Rome, and will nourish many with the word, so that there is no number (to count them), and he will become manifest above all the faithful, and greatly with the glory [of the Lord Jesus Christ] <. . . come> upon him, so that there will be great grace in Rome.

Although some could interpret that here as elsewhere in the *Acts of Paul*, women's actions are frequently portrayed as uplifting the prestige of the apostle Paul rather than their own positions, nevertheless the women play a significant part in the narrative. In this case Myrta is functioning as a character witness for Paul. Thus Myrta's encouragement of her brethren represents a very different dynamic than that communicated by the complete lack of leadership contributions by any female figures in the *Acts of Peter*, where no women give speeches of encouragement to anyone.

---

[7]For a more detailed examination of the dialogue, see Ann Graham Brock, "Genre of the *Acts of Paul*: One Tradition Enhancing Another," *Apocrypha* 5 (1994): 119–36.

Peter's Interactions with Characters in the *Acts of Peter*

In contrast to the *Acts of Paul*, the *Acts of Peter* exhibits a significant lack of autonomous actions on the part of women. Whereas strong female characters such as Thecla and the other women leave their households, husbands, or fiancés to follow Paul throughout the *Acts of Paul*, it is only in the last section of the *Acts of Peter*, the account of the apostle's martyrdom, that women leave everything behind to follow Peter.[8]

The leading roles in the *Acts of Peter* are instead dominated by male figures such as Peter, Marcellus, and Simon, while roles elucidating women's leadership and contributions are scarce. One of the first women to appear in this narrative (in the Coptic fragment of the *Acts of Peter*) is Peter's daughter, whose side is paralyzed and wasted.[9] Because of her state, the crowd questions why Peter, who is so successful in healing others, does not heal his own daughter. He explains that her paralyzed physical condition "is profitable" both for her and for himself in that it prevented her from being married at an early age to Ptolemaeus. The text even portrays the Lord himself as claiming that the girl had been a temptation to many already at the age of ten years old. Peter and his wife therefore praise the Lord for preserving their daughter from uncleanness and shame (*Papyrus Berlin Coptic 8502*, 135). Apparently, in this text the preferred response to suitors is not to fight them off actively but to become paralyzed in their presence. Predictably, in the *Acts of Peter* the blame for the attraction is placed directly upon the young girl. In fact, Peter even quotes the Lord as having said, "for this (daughter) will do harm to many souls if her body remains healthy" (ⲧⲁⲓ ⲅⲁⲣ ⲥⲛⲁϣⲱⲱϭⲉ ⲛ2ⲁ2 ⲛ̄ ϯⲯⲭⲏ ⲉϣⲱⲡⲉ ⲡⲉⲥⲥⲱⲙⲁ ⲛⲁϣⲱⲡⲉ ⲉϥⲙⲟⲧⲛ̄ ⲉⲣⲟⲥ [*Papyrus Berlin Coptic 8502*, 132]). On the other hand, in the *Acts of Paul*, it is Alexander who seems to be more at fault for inappropriate attraction, since he is described as a "powerful man" who "embraced her [Thecla]

---

[8]In this last section Xanthippe, wife of Albinus, and Nicaria, Agrippina, Euphemia, and Doris, the concubines of Agrippa, all convert to the doctrine of purity.

[9]The story of Peter's daughter is preserved in the Coptic papyrus Berlin 8502. Carl Schmidt first claimed that it belonged to the *Acts of Peter* and Schneemelcher agrees with his evaluation: "The reasons adduced by Schmidt are of varying cogency, but are so convincing as a whole that it can no longer be doubted that we have here a fragment of the first part of the APt, which is otherwise lost." Wilhelm Schneemelcher, "The Acts of Peter," in *NTApoc*[5] 2:278.

on the open street" (αὐτὸς αὐτῇ περιεπλάκη εἰς τὸ ἄμφοδον [26]). In fact, the Syriac version of this text implicates Alexander further by specifically identifying him as "one who wished to do uncleanness with her" (ܪܕܗܐܪܟܐܠ ܡܬܐ ܟܐܩ ܪܠܕܐ ܐܡ).[10] Curiously, in all the versions of the *Acts of Paul*, it is nevertheless Alexander who brings Thecla up on charges before the governor. Alexander's actions make Thecla's being brought before the governor seem all the more unjust, except that in three of the four Syriac manuscripts, an important explanatory detail has either been preserved or added, namely, that when Thecla fights off Alexander, the crown she knocks from his head is identified as the "crown of Caesar." The accusation brought against her is the following:

ܐܗܩ ܐܬ܊ܬ܊ ܠܠ܊ܡ ܪܟܡܠܪ ܐܠܣ ܐܓ̰ܠܣܡ ܡܗܪܟܡ ܠܐ ܪܠܗܕܬ
ܐܡܬܬܒܐܠܪܬ ܡܬܬ ܡ ܬܐܗܬ ܪܠܠܡ

Thecla they have called a violator of the temples because she cast down the crown of Caesar from the head of Alexander.[11]

In another episode believed to have derived from the original *Acts of Peter*, a peasant has a virgin daughter for whom he asks Peter to pray.[12] Ironically, after Peter prays that the daughter receive what is expedient, "the girl immediately fell down dead" (*statim puella iacuit mortua*). The text explains that this happened so that she would be able to "escape the shamelessness of the flesh and to break the pride of the blood" (*effugire*

---

[10]Dennis R. MacDonald discovered a similar dynamic in the Armenian version of the Thecla text, where the accusation against Thecla is not assault but sacrilege—her actions are interpreted as an affront against the imperial cult because of her defilement of the headgear associated with imperial power (*The Legend and the Apostle: The Battle for Paul in Story and Canon* [Philadelphia: Westminster, 1983], 41).

[11]William Wright, *Apocryphal Acts of the Apostles: Syriac and English*. 2 vols. (Amsterdam: Philo, 1968). Syriac text, 1:ܩܠܡ; English translation, 2:132–33.

[12]This narrative is preserved in the Pseudo-Titus Epistle (*De dispositione sanctimonii*, lines 83–93), on p. 50 of the text edited by Donatien De Bruyne, "*Epistula Titi, discipuli Pauli, De dispositione sanctimonii*," *RBén* 37 (1925): 47–72. As a storehouse of quotations from apocryphal works, Pseudo-Titus frequently provides supplementary material to the apocryphal acts. Augustine's reference to the gardener's daughter side by side with Peter's daughter (in *Contra Adimantum Manichaei discipulum* 17) indicates that this narrative from Pseudo-Titus most likely stemmed from the *Acts of Peter*; see Schneemelcher, *NTApoc*⁵ 2:57, 276, 279.

carnis audatiam ac mortificare sanguinis gloriam). After the old man begs Peter to raise her from the dead, she then falls prey to someone who passes himself off as a believer and seduces her, and according to the narrative neither ever appear to anyone again. Although this episode may represent merely a multiform or duplicate narrative paralleling the one concerning Peter's daughter, it nevertheless reinforces the same message as the previously mentioned episode that it is preferable for women to be paralyzed or even dead rather than undergoing struggles with the physical body.

The next major female character in the *Acts of Peter* is Eubula (AVer 17), whose interaction with Peter's primary antagonist places her in a negative light. Simon, whose confrontation with Peter in Rome provides the climax of the narrative, and who is also known as "the angel of the devil" (*Mart. Pet.* 3), is the same antagonist whom Peter had previously driven out of Judaea.[13] While Simon had been in Judaea, "where he did much harm," he had stayed with Eubula, "a woman of some distinction in this world," whom Simon repaid with theft before fleeing the city. Following the theft, Eubula, in a state of dishevelment, receives instructions from Peter to rise from bed, put up her hair, and pray to the Lord Jesus Christ who judges every soul. He tells her, "In him you must be saved, if indeed you repent with all your heart of your former sins" (*in quem te necesse est saluari, si tamen ex toto corde penitueris a prioribus tuis peccatis* [AVer 17]). The narrative continues with Peter advising Eubula to place some of her people by the gate that leads towards Neapolis to keep watch for Simon. In her response to Peter, Eubula throws herself at his feet, acquiesces to his instructions, and because she is greatly distressed even goes to the magistrate, although "she had never (before) come out in public" (*quae numquam in publicum processerat*). As a result, Eubula recovers her property and, after renouncing the world, she gives alms both to the widows and the orphans as well as clothing to the poor.[14] This woman who had never before been out in public thus receives the most significant role in the *Acts of Peter*, a role consisting primarily of repentance and almsgiving.

[13]Many equate this Simon with Simon Magus of Acts 8:9-24, who had tried to obtain spiritual power in exchange for money.

[14]In a sense this story foreshadows that of Marcellus, who similarly housed Simon and who is also portrayed as asking for Peter's forgiveness. Marcellus, however, becomes more of the model of proper repentance in the narrative, with his transformed status being affirmed positively both by his reception of a vision and his ability to perform a miracle.

The next major female figure in the narrative is a blind widow whom Peter heals at Marcellus' house (AVer 20). Subsequently, the other old blind widows say, "We beg you, sir Peter, share also with us his compassion and kindness" (*praecamur, domine Petre, misericordiam et pietatem illius tribuas et nobis* [AVer 21]). They ask for mercy and as a result see the Lord in a variety of forms: as an old man, as a growing youth, and as a boy who gently touched their eyes (AVer 21). Closely following this incident is another story about a widow who in this case cries out to Peter that her only son is dead (AVer 25). After Peter raises him from the dead, the mother of a senator throws herself at Peter's feet and begs him to bring her son back to life. Peter asks that she distribute to the widows the money that she would have laid out for her son's funeral. After the revival of her son, the senator's mother offers her house to Peter, but when Peter refuses, she brings two thousand pieces of silver.[15]

Although the *Acts of Peter* portrays women involved in numerous situations, the speaking parts for women in the *Acts of Peter* are few. The woman suckling the seven-month-old child at her breast, for example, carries out Peter's instructions, but it is her child and not she who delivers Peter's message to Simon. The young child's speech contains approximately fifteen lines of dialogue, which is more than the dialogue of all the women characters combined (AVer 15). The speaking parts for women occur in only five short passages and consist mainly of entreaties. In the *Acts of Peter* the only women with speaking parts tend to be widows and the mother of a senator (possibly also a widow). One widow, for example, begs Peter to revive her dead son because she is concerned that no one will take care of her. She asks, "Now he is dead, who will offer me a hand?" (*Hoc mortuo, qui mihi manum porriget?* [AVer 25]). In this way the actions and dialogue of the women serve primarily as opportunities for Peter to demonstrate his abilities to perform miracles. Only two women speak to communicate something other than a request for a miracle from Peter. The mother of the senator, for example, receives one line of dialogue when she brings two thousand pieces of silver and says, "Divide these among the virgins of Christ who serve him" (*Haec diuide uirginibus Christi qui ei deseruiunt* [AVer 29]). The other instance is Chryse, the woman "notorious all over Rome for fornication" (διαβέβληται γὰρ ἐν ὅλῃ τῇ Ῥώμῃ ἐπὶ

---

[15]For more information on patronage, see Robert F. Stoops, Jr., "Patronage in the *Acts of Peter*," *Semeia* 38 (1986): 91–100.

πορνείᾳ), who receives a few lines of dialogue when she brings 10,000 pieces of gold (AVer 30).

In summary, in both texts women serve as facilitators to highlight the authority and power of Peter and Paul; however, they do so in significantly different ways. In the *Acts of Peter* women's participation or interactions with Peter are acceptable whenever they donate from their wealth or ask for help, but otherwise, opportunities for women's leadership are almost nonexistent. Not only are there no primary female roles, but even merely positive examples are scarce. The unmarried women in the *Acts of Peter* clearly do not fare well in the narrative, as they are in turn either paralyzed, seduced, deceived, notorious, speechless, or dead.[16] The widows who receive various visions are the best models the text has to offer, but the Latin text, preserving the bulk of the *Acts of Peter,* leaves them unnamed and generally grouped together.

Paul's Interactions with Characters in the *Acts of Peter*

Not only do the actions of Peter, the primary character, in the *Acts of Peter*, make an interesting subject for the study of the interrelationships between characters, but the text's portrayal of the interactions of the secondary apostle Paul with other characters—especially in Rome—is also informative.[17] Among those who respond to Paul is a woman named Candida, the wife of the prison officer Quartus. Because of Paul's words, she instructs her husband and he, too, believes. If this event were to follow the typical pattern of the conversion of women in the *Acts of Paul*, one would expect that on hearing Paul's preaching and converting, Candida would leave or reject her husband. In this text, however, she is depicted as converting her spouse.

The most detailed description of interaction between Paul and a female character occurs in the scene with Rufina, who is introduced specifically as a woman who wished that "even she should receive the eucharist at Paul's hands" (*ipsa eucharistiam de manibus Pauli percipere* [AVer 2]). After she approaches Paul, he replies not by granting her request but by immediately chastising her. Paul, "filled with the Spirit of God" (*spiritu*

---

[16]Virgins are mentioned as the intended recipients of some financial support (AVer 29), but as characters they never make it into the narrative.

[17]Poupon's hypothesis that the figure of Paul appears to be grafted onto this text is examined later in this chapter; see n. 29, below.

Dei repletus [AVer 2]), declares that she is not coming to the altar like a true worshipper. Instead he accuses her of rising from beside one who is not her husband but an adulterer, and he declares to her harshly, "behold Satan shall break your body and cast you down in the sight of all who believe in the Lord" (*Ecce . . . Satanas contribulato corde tuo proiiciet te ante oculos omnium credentium in domino* [AVer 2]). Interestingly, as is customary among the women with whom Peter interacts, Rufina subsequently falls down, becoming paralyzed on her left side from head to toe and unable to speak.

Only a few other female characters interact with Paul in the text. These women pay homage to Paul in this way: "And a great crowd of women knelt down and fervently entreated the blessed Paul, and they kissed his feet and escorted him to the harbor" (AVer 3). Two women are specifically named, Berenice and Philostrate, the two matrons who conducted Paul to the harbor (AVer 3). Although this kind of adulation toward Paul, especially from a crowd of women kissing Paul's feet, portrays an initially adoring position toward him, the significant dynamic with respect to Paul follows shortly thereafter, where it is pivotal for the narrative that almost all of the disciples of Paul subsequently fall away. The unfolding of the plot next describes Simon arriving and making such an impact that "out of so great a number that were established in the faith, they all fell away except for the presbyter Narcissus and two women in the lodging-house of the Bithynians and four who could no longer go out of their house" (AVer 4). Therefore, even though Paul made "so great a number" (*tam magnae multitudinis* [AVer 4]) of converts, including the explicit reference in the text to a "great crowd of women" (*plurima turba mulierum* [AVer 3]), nevertheless, only seven Christians remained steadfast as a result of his efforts, with as few as two of them being women. Thus, with Paul's departure the narrative stage is set for Peter to become the primary focus and to save the Christian community in Rome by reconverting them.

This inventory of Paul's interactions with individual women characters in the *Acts of Peter* contains little that is encouraging to women in Christian leadership roles. Two matrons are indeed mentioned in passing but none of the women with whom Paul has any contact has a speaking part in the *Acts of Peter*. In fact, Rufina, whom Paul refuses Eucharist, becomes speechless. Paul's interactions with women in the *Acts of Peter* thus mirror Peter's interactions with women in this text. The resulting portrayal is therefore quite distinct from Paul's treatment of women in the *Acts of Paul*. In fact, in their interactions with both apostles in the *Acts of*

Peter, women are visible and indeed useful to the narrative, but they are definitely not affirmed in leadership roles. When compared to the interactions between Paul and women in the *Acts of Paul*, the refusal of the *Acts of Peter* to endorse women as leaders becomes more evident.

Conformity to Familial and Social Responsibilities

Another major difference between the *Acts of Paul* and the *Acts of Peter* lies in their respective portrayals of familial and societal accountability, a factor closely connected with each text's depiction of women's capacity for leadership. For example, since the *Acts of Paul* tends to portray women positively, Thecla's resistance to social and familial pressures ultimately makes her the heroine of the story and wins Paul's confirmation of her right to teach. In the *Acts of Paul* the usual biological family ties are replaced by the kinship of the Christian family, such as in the figure of Tryphaena. The entire *Acts of Paul* characterizes only one female in less than positive terms: Theocleia, Thecla's mother. This unaffirming portrayal is not the result of Theocleia's failings as the subject or object of sexual passion—the typical female failings in the *Acts of Peter;* rather, this sole dissenting female expresses the position that women must fulfill their familial obligations. When Thecla does not follow through with her betrothal to Thamyris, the narrative portrays Thecla's mother as condemning her own daughter to death with the words, "Burn the lawless one!" (κατάκαιε τὴν ἄνομον [*Acts Thec.* 20]). In the Syriac version of this text, Theocleia goes even further in her denouncement of her daughter, saying:

ܐܘܩܕܘܗܝ ܠܗܕܐ ܫܛܝܬܐ ܒܡܨܥܬܐ ܕܐܬܪܘܢ ܕܢܟ ܕܟܠ ܢܫܐ ܕܚܙܝܢ ܠܗ
ܐܝܠܝܢ ܕܗܢܐ ܝܘܠܦܢܗܝܢ ܢܕܚܠܢ.

Burn the fool in the midst of the theater, that all the women who see her, those whose doctrine this is, may be afraid.[18]

---

[18]See Wright, *Apocryphal Acts of the Apostles*. Syriac text, 1:ܩܡܒ; English trans., 2:127. In the Syriac text an even greater tension between mother and daughter is portrayed. I am grateful to Dr. J. F. Coakley at Harvard University for checking the accuracy of the Syriac.

Thecla's mother, whose own status is at risk because of Thecla's actions, thus is the strongest proponent of culture-conforming behavior in the *Acts of Paul*; her position is directly antithetical to that of the heroine of the story.[19]

Among the other more prominent female figures in the *Acts of Paul* is Tryphaena. The text describes her as significantly more concerned for Thecla's welfare than Thecla's biological mother, with the result that she ultimately becomes Thecla's surrogate Christian mother. In the narrative she embraces Thecla, advocates on her behalf, and even invites her into her home both before and after Thecla's fight with the beasts. She appears to have some stature as a kinswoman of Caesar but perhaps not much political power, as she has less influence with the governor concerning Thecla than Alexander does.[20] Nevertheless, as Tryphaena steadfastly accompanies Thecla to the battle with the beasts, her character represents the way in which newly adopted Christian families supported one another in times of persecution and functioned in the place of the original family ties.

The last section of the *Acts of Peter*, the martyrdom, is the only section that includes the chastity/persecution motif for women.[21] In this respect, therefore, this section seems to resonate more with the *Acts of Paul* than with the rest of the *Acts of Peter*. However, the chastity/persecution motif in this case has a slightly different tenor to it, in that it is the primary means by which the culpability of the authorities is somewhat mitigated and shifted away from the political arena.

In contrast to the *Acts of Paul*, in which new converts are usually women (including members of the upper class, whose husbands then become upset), the Latin text of the *Acts of Peter* portrays significantly more positive responses from upper-class male figures, including the senators Marcellus and Demetrius; the prefect Agrippa even delivers a statement of faith. Thus in the bulk of the *Acts of Peter* the threat to familial unity is lessened by the depiction of greater responses and conversions by

---

[19]The text portrays Thecla as returning to her mother at the end of her narrative (43) in order to attempt to reassure her or reconcile with her, but no outcome is recorded.

[20]Both Alexander and the governor take it seriously, however, when Tryphaena faints and is thought to be dead (35).

[21]For more information on the chastity/persecution motif see François Bovon, "The Life of the Apostles," in idem, *New Testament Traditions and Apocryphal Narratives* (trans. Jane Haapiseva-Hunter; Allison Park, Penn.: Pickwick, 1995), 161; and Virginia Burrus, *Chastity as Autonomy: Women in the Stories of the Apocryphal Acts* (Studies in Women and Religion 23; Lewiston, N.Y.: Mellen Press, 1987).

primary male characters. In numerous ways, therefore, the *Acts of Peter* demonstrates a commitment to social and familial ties. Peter himself sets the example in the portrayal of his own married status and his concern for his daughter, with the result that this is one of the few apocryphal narratives that makes mention of any of the children of the apostles. Peter's advocacy for a primary accountability to familial ties is especially clear in his speech to the widow's son whom he brings back to life. He commands him, "Young man, arise and walk with your mother, so long as you are useful to her" (*iuuenis, surge et ambula cum matre tua usque dum ei prode es* [AVer 27]). Peter then makes a point to instruct the young man that only later, after he has fulfilled his obligations to his mother, should he come forward to service (AVer 27).

In a similar manner, the senator Demetrius is portrayed as bowing to previous societal responsibilities as he regretfully informs Paul that he cannot join him on his missionary journey. Demetrius tells him, "Paul, I could wish to leave the city, if I were not a magistrate, so as not to leave you" (*Paulo, uellem fugere ab urbe, si non essem magistratus, ut a te non discederem* [AVer 3]). Also depicted as honoring a previous commitment is Candida who, when she converts, remains in her marriage and instructs her husband, with the result that he, too, converts. Elsewhere the text states, "So Peter went in and saw one of the old people, a widow that was blind, and her daughter giving her a hand and leading her to Marcellus' house" (AVer 20). The inclusion here of such a small detail as the daughter giving her a hand underlines the importance of familial support in this text.

Thus, while the *Acts of Peter* seeks to establish and define loyalty to family ties as a normative and foundational component of the Christian life, the *Acts of Paul* redefines the notion of family. It portrays family in terms of one's Christian community. With respect to the issue of conformity or resistance to familial obligations, therefore, the *Acts of Paul* and the *Acts of Peter* stand on opposite sides of the fence.

Ecclesiastical Organization

One last significant characteristic of the *Acts of Peter* and the *Acts of Paul* that bears investigation is the difference in how they portray ecclesiastical organization. With respect to church offices, the *Acts of Peter*, for instance, contains a significant number of references to ecclesiastical designations and titles. First among the numerous indications of ecclesiastical organization are three references to an "elder" (*praesbyter*) named Narcissus, who escorts Paul to the harbor (AVer 3). This presbyter is also one of the few Pauline converts who does not fall away (AVer 4) and thus reappears when Ariston brings Peter and Theon to his house (AVer 6). Later in the narrative, the healing of the widow's son includes two more significant ecclesiastical terms: "deacon" (*diaconus*) and "bishop" (*episcopus*). Peter commands the widow's son to stay with his mother as long as he can be useful to her, and then explicitly explains to the young man, "Afterwards, however, you will be free to offer yourself to me in a higher service, in the office of deacon and bishop" (*Postea autem mihi uacabis altius ministrans, diaconi episcopi sorte* [AVer 27]).

The *Acts of Paul* contains so few ecclesiastical designations that even references to the term "apostle" are rare or nonexistent.[22] In contrast, the *Acts of Peter* frequently employs the designation "apostle" (*apostolus*), as well as two uses of the title "co-apostle" (*coapostolus* [AVer 10]). Moreover, Peter receives numerous additional titles including "apostle of Christ" (*apostolus Christi* [AVer 22]) and "apostle of the Lord" (*domini apostolus* [AVer 7]), as well as the distinction conveyed by the statement that God had chosen Peter among all the apostles (AVer 5). By contrast, the extant *Acts of Paul* mirrors the authentic letters of Paul in its scarcity or lack of references to bishops,[23] as well as its omission of references to presbyters or any other hierarchical church titles.[24] Thus, unlike the *Acts of*

---

[22]The only exception occurs in the Corinthian correspondence, which may be an accretion to the *Acts of Paul*. The use of the term in the colophon is probably also secondary. Thomas MacKay presents reasons why "we cannot be certain that the epistle was originally or typically associated with the API" in his article, "Response," *Semeia* 38 (1986): 148. He also refers to his earlier detailed examination in "Observations on P. Bodmer X (Apocryphal Correspondence between Paul and the Corinthian Saints)," in *Actes du XVe Congrès International de Papyrologie* (vol. 3 of Papyrologica Bruxellensia *18*; Bruxelles: Fondation Égyptologique Reine Élisabeth, 1979), 119–28.

[23]Phil 1:1 is the only site in the authentically Pauline letters where the word ἐπίσκοπος appears, and even then it not only appears in the plural but exhibits more of the word's original meaning of "one who oversees," rather than the more technical meaning of "bishop" that appears later (Rengstorf, ἐπίσκοπος, *TDNT* 2:610). Moreover, MacDonald points out that the placement of ἐπίσκοποι in 1:1 may be the work of an assembler, since it is the introductory verse situated at the beginning of what appears to be three Pauline fragments. For further discussion, see MacDonald, *Legend and the Apostle*, 99.

[24]Again, the exception in the *Acts of Paul* lies in the contested "Letter of the Corinthians to Paul." In this epistle the terms "deacon" and "presbyter" are each used once.

Peter, the *Acts of Paul* exhibits a noticeable scarcity of references to any ecclesiastical positions or designations.

While the absence of ecclesiastical titles could indicate an earlier date of composition for the legends of the *Acts of Paul*, it is safer to say that differences concerning the lack of such titles at least opens up the possibility of a more democratic and decentralized perspective toward leadership and hierarchy underlying the *Acts of Paul*. One cannot help but wonder if the presence of a significantly greater number of ecclesiastical titles in the *Acts of Peter* bears any correspondence to the portrayal of women's leadership roles as restricted or nonexistent.

The different positions that these two texts advocate reflect attitudes toward social, familial, and ecclesiastical responsibilities displayed by other early Christian texts. In fact, the differences described here between the *Acts of Paul* and the *Acts of Peter* bear a striking resemblance to a similar disparity between the *Acts of Paul* and the Pastoral Epistles described by Dennis R. MacDonald in his book, *The Legend and the Apostle*. MacDonald cogently argues that leaders in the early church, both those who would grant authority to women and those who would deny it, produced literature that claimed Pauline authority for their respective, and antithetical, positions. The Pastoral Epistles and the *Acts of Paul* reflect the efforts of these two groups to attribute their own views to Paul.[25]

MacDonald points out that in the legends of the *Acts of Paul*, Paul commissions a woman to teach, while in 1 Tim 2:11–15, he is portrayed as forbidding it. In a similar contrast, in the legends behind the *Acts of Paul*, Paul encourages women to practice celibacy in order to be saved, while in the Pastoral Epistles he is portrayed as telling women they shall be saved by bearing children. MacDonald points out that "instead of luring Thecla away from her lover and encouraging her to teach the word of God, the author of the Pastorals indicates that Paul would have her marry, be submissive to her husband, raise lots of children, and live happily — in silent domestication — ever after."[26] Thus the issue of women's leadership

---

[25]Compare the article written by Peter Dunn, "Women's Liberation: The *Acts of Paul*, and Other Apocryphal Acts of the Apostles," *Apocrypha* 4 (1993): 245–61. Dunn argues that the *Acts of Paul* and the pastoral epistles are not to be polarized so strongly. He is right to observe that both are heirs to the Pauline tradition; however, attempts to harmonize these two groups are unsuccessful. While the similarities cannot be denied, the differences between the two branches are much more significant.

[26]MacDonald, *Legend and the Apostle*, 59.

is one of the chief points of contention between the Pastoral Epistles and the legends of the *Acts of Paul.*

Second, not only do the Pastoral Epistles prescribe the restriction of women's leadership in the church, they also tend to discourage critical political sentiments. To demonstrate this tendency toward social conformity and respectability MacDonald cites a number of texts, including Titus 3:1 ("Remind them to be submissive to rulers and authorities, to be obedient") as well as 2 Timothy's overall lack of political hostility toward Rome.[27]

Third, the Pastoral Epistles are rife with the presence of ecclesiastical titles, as well as support for familial and household traditions. The Pastoral Epistles contain descriptions of the qualifications necessary for the offices of bishop, presbyter, and deacon that even include being married and holding a position as the head of a household. MacDonald rightly points out, "Whereas the legends pit the household and the church against each other as competing social institutions, the Pastorals identify the strength of the church with that of the household."[28] His historical examination convincingly describes the competing claims for Paul's authority advanced by the Pastoral Epistles and the *Acts of Paul.*

In a number of significant ways the *Acts of Peter* resonates rather closely with the agenda of the Pastoral Epistles and exhibits a similar kind of claim not only on Peter's but also Paul's apostolic support for its version of Christianity. Gérard Poupon convincingly argues that the material featuring the apostle Paul appears to have been grafted onto the narrative of the *Acts of Peter*, as his appearances are concentrated in the first three chapters of the *Acts*, from which Peter is completely absent.[29] Thus, it seems that the text appropriates Paul's authority by naming him at least thirty times and portraying him as an advocate of social conformity and submission to political authorities—but not, however, as an

---

[27]Ibid., 66–67.

[28]Ibid., 72.

[29]Gérard Poupon, "Les 'Actes de Pierre' et leur remaniement," *ANRW* 2:25/6 (1988): 4372–74. Vouaux also speaks of interpolations in *Les Actes de Pierre*, 26–35. For a summary of the arguments, see Christine M. Thomas, "The Acts of Peter," in *The Apocryphal Acts of the Apostles: Harvard Divinity School Studies* (ed. François Bovon, Ann Graham Brock, and Christopher R. Matthews; Cambridge: Harvard University Center for the Study of World Religions, 1999), 39–62, esp. 44–45. See also her forthcoming book, *The Acts of Peter, Gospel Literature, and the Ancient Novel: Rewriting the Past* (Oxford: Oxford University Press, forthcoming 2003).

advocate of women's freedom to participate in church leadership. In the *Acts of Paul*, for example, when Thecla finds Paul again and tells him everything, the text states that "Paul marveled greatly" (ὥστε ἐπὶ πολὺ θαυμάσαι τὸν Παῦλον [41]), but in the *Acts of Peter* Paul, in his most prominent encounter with a female follower, exhibits behavior that is both threatening and moralistic: he tells Rufina, "behold Satan shall break your body and cast you down in the sight of all that believe in the Lord" (*Ecce. . .Satanas contribulato corde tuo proiiciet te ante oculos omnium credentium in domino* [AVer 2]).

In summary, just as the Pastoral Epistles claim the authority of Paul for both the restriction of women's leadership in the church and the establishment of an ecclesiastical hierarchy, so does the *Acts of Peter* appeal to the authority of the apostles by having both Peter and Paul demonstrate these attitudes in word and deed. Thus these portrayals indicate ways in which the authors advocate significantly different social roles for their constituents, roles that are not endorsed by the *Acts of Paul*.

Summary

Despite numerous similarities between the two apocryphal accounts of the *Acts of Peter* and the *Acts of Paul*, the analysis above indicates ways in which the two texts differ in several critical, meaningful ways. In fact, in a number of places the *Acts of Paul* and the *Acts of Peter* are ideologically incompatible. The two texts are especially disparate with respect to the portrayal of female leadership in early Christianity.

Part of the agenda of the authors of these texts is to fortify the authority of each apostle and, in doing so, the authors frequently attempt to increase the status of that apostle in various ways.[30] Thus Tertullian, in his homily on baptism, relates that the Asian presbyter who wrote the *Acts of Paul* did so because he wished to enhance the prominence of Paul as an apostle. In Tertullian's words, he was "adding something of

---

[30]To fortify the authority of an apostle in such texts is not an argument for an episcopal type of authority in the *Acts of Paul*, but can be interpreted as an effort to give greater depth and weight to the early Christian message of the apostle. For an examination of the position of the *Acts of Thecla* within the larger *Acts of Paul*, see Brock, "Genre of the *Acts of Paul*," 119–36. By means of literary and ideological fissures in the text, the essay argues that Paul did not "abandon" Thecla at keys points of her persecution as some scholars have maintained, but was only grafted onto the independent Thecla legend at a later point.

his own to the prestige of Paul" (*titulo Pauli de suo cumulans*).[31] I find that the dynamic of adding to the prestige of the apostle is operating not only within the *Acts of Paul*, but is also the underlying strategy within the *Acts of Peter*. Tertullian also records that the presbyter who compiled the *Acts of Paul* stepped down from his office because the example of Thecla that he depicted in his writing was being used to claim the right for women to teach and to baptize.[32] From the analysis presented in this chapter, one can confidently surmise that had the final author or redactor of the *Acts of Peter* been in a similar situation he would have faced no such threat to his position. Thus, when one compares the way in which women ultimately fare, the resulting contrast between the *Acts of Paul* and the *Acts of Peter* is a dramatic one.

In the context of this study, a crucial difference between these two texts is that whereas in the *Acts of Paul,* Pauline apostleship is closely associated with strong female leadership, in the *Acts of Peter*, no such apostolic endorsement appears. In addition to the strategies examined here of limiting women's leadership by silencing or subduing them, another strategy for dealing with a woman of prominence, such as Mary Magdalene, is to replace her character with another authority figure, a figure more congenial to texts with pro-Petrine tendencies. The next chapter will examine texts such as the *Acts of Philip,* the *Book of the Resurrection of Jesus Christ,* certain Syriac texts by Ephrem, and the *Questions of Bartholomew*. These documents will offer further support for the thesis that the greater Peter's authority in a text, the more Mary Magdalene's role is altered or compromised.

---

[31]Tertullian, *De baptismo* 17.5 in *Q. Septimii Florentis Tertulliani De Baptismo Liber* (ed. Ernest Evans; London: SPCK, 1964), 37. Poupon does not translate *titulo* as "prestige," but instead interprets that the presbyter is crowning this writing at his own expense with an inscription in the name of Paul. See Gérard Poupon, "Encore une fois: Tertullien, *De baptismo* 17, 5," in *Nomen Latinum* (Fs. André Schneider; Neuchâtel: Faculté de Lettres, 1997), 202–3.

[32]Tertullian, *De baptismo* 17.5.

CHAPTER SEVEN

The Replacement of Mary Magdalene: A Strategy for Eliminating the Competition

Thus far we have seen how early Christian authors chose individual figures from the narratives of Jesus' companions and attributed authority to them and their messages. The usage of the name of a particular disciple or apostle operated as a useful tool of persuasion in the polemics, apologetics, and self-description of early Christian groups. Earlier chapters of this study have demonstrated this in the ways in which the names of Mary Magdalene, Peter, and Paul were thus employed in various works of early Christian literature. This chapter argues further that the replacement of a text's leading figure by another character when that text is translated or otherwise adapted, does not represent an arbitrary choice, but rather provides clues to the politics of the original and adapted texts.

I will first examine the *Acts of Philip*, in which the identity of a primary figure in the narrative changes significantly between the Greek original and its later Coptic version. Namely, the role occupied by Mary Magdalene in the Greek text is occupied by Peter in the Coptic version. Then I will survey other texts, including the *Acta Thaddaei,* the *Book of the Resurrection of Jesus Christ by Bartholomew the Apostle*, some fragmentary Coptic texts, and certain Syriac texts of Ephrem, in each of which the figure of Mary Magdalene has been replaced by the figure of Mary, the mother of Jesus. I am particularly interested in exploring whether the prominence of Peter in these texts has influenced their treatment of Mary Magdalene.

The Greek *Acts of Philip:* The Role of Mary

The Greek version of the *Acts of Philip* (*Acts Phil.*) is a fourth-century text that features three apostles: Philip, Bartholomew, and Mariamne.[1] In this text, Mariamne, or Mary, appears as a primary figure in the second half of the book (*Acts Phil.* 8–15, plus the *Martyrdom*). Several scholars have identified this figure as Mary Magdalene especially because the text's portrayal of Mariamne accords well with the figure of Mary Magdalene as she appears in other sources.[2] For instance, Mariamne (called Mary hereafter for the sake of convenience) plays the role of a comforter, as she does in the Manichaean psalms[3] and in the *Gospel of Mary*; also, Mary shows strength when the disciples have scattered, and she teaches the disciples. Moreover, the Greek version includes Mary numerous times throughout the text in its use of the plural form of apostles (ἀπόστολοι).[4]

---

[1]François Bovon, "Les Actes de Philippe," *ANRW* 2:25/6 (1988): 4432–525.

[2]Bovon, "Mary Magdalene's Paschal Privilege," 156. He states that the use of Μαριάμνη in the *Acts of Philip* is one of the common names for Mary Magdalene used by patristic witnesses and other Greek texts that speak of her with the forms Μαριάμμη, Μαριάμνη, Μαρία, or Μαρία ἡ Μαγδαληνή. In another article ("Les Actes de Philippe," 4460–64), Bovon provides parallels between this text and others that feature Mary Magdalene, thus identifying this Mary with Mary Magdalene. Likewise, Frédéric Amsler in his notes on the *Acts of Philip* states, "Marianne, la sœur de Philippe, n'est autre que la Marie-Madeleine des Évangiles. Elle est une figure estimée des gnostiques en tant que témoin privilégié de la résurrection de Jésus (cf. *Matt* 28, 1.9–10; *Mc* 16, 9–11; *John* 20, 11–18; *Ev Thomas* 21.114; *Pistis Sophia passim; Ev Marie* codex de Berlin) et des encratites, au point d'éclipser même Philippe jusqu'en *Ac Ph* VIII,7." See François Bovon, Bertrand Bouvier, and Frédéric Amsler, trans., *Actes de l'apôtre Philippe* (with introduction and notes by Frédéric Amsler; Apocryphes 8; Turnhout: Brepols, 1996), 176 n. 339.

[3]C. R. C. Allberry, *A Manichaean Psalm-Book, Part II* (Manichaean Manuscripts in the Chester Beatty Collection 2; Stuttgart: Kohlhammer, 1938). In several passages Mary gathers the disciples to comfort them, such as in the section called "Psalms of Heracleides," 187 and 192. The identity of this primary Mary requires further discussion. See Coyle, "Mary Magdalene in Manichaeism?" 54; Marjanen, *The Disciple Jesus Loved*, 206–8; Shoemaker, "Mary and the Discourse of Orthodoxy," 281–82; and Mohri, *Maria Magdalena*, 173–87.

[4]See *Acts Phil.* 8,16 [96]. Likewise *Acts Phil.* 8,21 [101] explicitly includes Mary in the reverential treatment. In this text the construct of the "twelve apostles" does not seem to be operative. The three manuscripts of *Acts Phil.* 8 that depict the division of the lands for mission have no mention of "the twelve" nor do these manuscripts list twelve names. The Coptic text, on the other hand, along with its introduction of the figure of Peter, also introduces the construct of the twelve apostles.

The role that Mary plays in the Greek text of the *Acts of Philip* is quite prominent. For example, "she is present at the side of Christ when he allocates missions to the apostles" (*Acts Phil.* 8,1–2 [94]).[5] She is the one who holds the register (ἡ ἀναγραφή) of the countries, and it is she who prepares the bread and salt, and the breaking of the bread.[6] In this text Mary is also the figure that Christ chooses to console Philip and to encourage him to leave on his mission (*Acts Phil.* 8,3–4 [95]). Furthermore, the Savior addresses her with the words: "I know that you are good and courageous and blessed among women."[7]

In addition to bestowing upon her this praise, Christ also commissions her: "go therefore with him [Philip] to every place where he is going and do not stop encouraging him with love and great compassion" (*Acts Phil.* 8,3 [95]). The wording of the text frequently represents her as the stronger of the two apostles, and Christ even acknowledges that Philip's character flaws require the accompaniment of Mary on his mission: "For I see that he is a very impetuous man, and if we let him go alone he will have many opportunities to return evil for evil."[8]

In *Acts of Philip* 9 (104) Mary continues to play a significant role in the text as she participates in the fight against a dragon by executing an exorcism ritual. Bartholomew and Mary stand holding a chalice in the air and sprinkling the demon while making the sign of the cross. In *Acts of Philip* 11 a new dragon appears as well as a second exorcism in which Mary is less active than in the previous version.

---

[5]Bovon, "Mary Magdalene's Paschal Privilege," 156. References to the recently discovered *Acts Phil.* 8 are from the manuscript Athens, National Library, *346*, published in *Acta Philippi: Textus* (ed. François Bovon, Bertrand Bouvier, and Frédéric Amsler; CCSA 11; Turnhout: Brepols, 1999). See also Frédéric Amsler, *Acta Philippi: Commentarius* (CCSA 12; Turnhout: Brepols, 1999). For a history of the traditions that focused upon the apostle Philip, see Christopher R. Matthews, *Philip: Apostle and Evangelist* (NovTSup 105; Leiden: Brill, 2002).

[6]καὶ αὕτη ἐστὶν ἡ ἑτοιμάζουσα τὸν ἄρτον καὶ τὸ ἄλας, καὶ τὴν κλάσιν τοῦ ἄρτου (*Acts Phil.* 8,2 [94]).

[7]οἶδα ὅτι καλὴ εἶ καὶ ἀνδρεία τῇ ψυχῇ καὶ εὐλογημένη ἐν γυναιξίν (*Acts Phil.* 8,3 [95]). Parallels are in Jdt 13:18 and Luke 1:42. The epithet the angel Gabriel gives to Mary the mother in Luke 1:28 is similar to the one Philip gives to Ireos in *Acts Phil.* 5,7 [48].

[8]ὁρῶ γὰρ αὐτὸν ὅτι ἄνθρωπος τολμηρός ἐστιν σφόδρα, καὶ ἐὰν ἀφῶμεν αὐτὸν μόνον, ἀνταποδοῦναι ἔχει πολλὰς ἀνταποδόσεις εἰς ὃν παρέρχεται τόπον (*Acts Phil.* 8,3 [95]).

Acts of Philip 14 describes the healing of Stachys, in which Philip "after drawing him [Stachys] to himself, extended his hand and dipped his finger into the mouth of Mariamne and anointed. . . ." (*Acts Phil.* 14,7). At this point the text breaks off, and, unfortunately, a large lacuna, one folio in length, follows. It is possible that the lacuna's appearance at precisely this point in the narrative signals the deliberate censorship of the text because of its content. The description of the healing of Stachys by means of Mary's saliva may very well have been offensive to some readers.[9] After reporting the healing and the subsequent praising of the apostles, the text notes that Philip baptized the men and Mary baptized the women (*Acts Phil.* 14,9).

The reference to the baptismal activity of Philip and Mary occurs again in the *Martyrdom of Philip* (*Acts Phil. Mart.*) in chapter 2 of *Xenophontos 32.* The Martyrdom is preserved in three recensions plus one manuscript, *Vaticanus graecus 808,* that merged several recensions. The three recensions (Γ, Θ, and Δ) tell basically the same story, but Δ starts later in the narrative than the others.[10]

The *Martyrdom of Philip* depicts Mary sitting at the entrance of the house of Stachys devoting herself to those who were coming to the house and trying to persuade them to listen to what they were being told by the apostles (*Acts Phil. Mart.* 3 [109] only in Γ). The meeting between Mary and Nicanora, the wife of the Roman governor, is an important one in the text (*Acts Phil. Mart.* 9 [115] in Γ and Θ). Because Nicanora is of Syrian origin and speaks a Semitic language, Mary is the one who communicates

---

[9]See Bovon, Bouvier, and Amsler, *Actes de l'apôtre Philippe*, 213 n. 501. Mary's role in this miracle is just one of many that highlight her contribution to the narrative. She is also present in other sections not mentioned above, such as when a leopard and kid are converted. The text specifically names all three figures—Philip, Mary, and Bartholomew— mentioning that the leopard and kid fell down at the feet of all three of them and worshiped them, at which point they all set out together, praising God (*Acts Phil.* 8,21 [101]). Although the names of a few other disciples such as Peter and John appear in the text, they are noted only cursorily and not as primary actors in the narrative. One of the few references to Peter in the Greek version of the *Acts of Philip* represents him as fleeing from every place which housed a woman (*Acts Phil. Mart.* 36 [142] only in Θ and Δ). Peter's role in this and other texts is examined by Smith in *Petrine Controversies*, 107–8.

[10]The Δ recension begins in *Acts Phil. Mart.* 17 (123). See François Bovon, "The Synoptic Gospels and the Noncanonical Acts of the Apostles," *HTR* 81 (1988): 19–36. The recensions Γ and Δ are fairly close, although Δ is more archaic than Γ, and both Γ and Δ are more archaic than Θ.

with her in Hebrew in the presence of Philip and Bartholomew. Mary tells her, "You have been given as a pledge to the snake but Jesus our redeemer came to redeem you through us [including Mary] to break your bonds and to cut them and to pluck them out of you from their root because you are my sister; one mother gave birth to us as twins."[11] Here Mary is the active agent of liberation; it is through her words that Nicanora is converted to Christianity. Nicanora then speaks to Mary in Hebrew, thankful for the healing and for the proclamation she received, saying, "We received his gnosis through you" (*Acts Phil. Mart.* 10 [116] only in Γ). The pronoun "you" referring to the source of this proclamation is in a plural form (ὑμῶν) that includes Mary along with Philip and Bartholemew.

The Coptic Version of the *Acts of Philip:* The Role of Peter

The *Acts of Philip* exists also in a Coptic text in Fayyumic,[12] and in Achmimic, Sahidic, and Bohairic (dialects of Coptic), as well as Arabic, and Ethiopic versions (the Ethiopic and Arabic texts are fairly close to the Coptic).[13] In these versions it is Philip and Peter, not Mary, who travel together preaching and healing people. They perform signs to overcome the unbelief of people, as well as exorcisms and baptisms. Although the plot of the Coptic version of the *Acts of Philip* differs from the Greek version, nevertheless, a clear relationship exists between the

[11]*Acts Phil. Mart.* 9 (115); this translation is of the Γ recension; the version in *ANF* 8: 497–510 is also a translation of the *Acts of Philip* based on this recension.

[12]This Fayyumic text is preserved in the codex published in Oscar von Lemm, "Koptische Apokryphe Apostelakten," *Mélanges Asiatiques* 10 (1890–92): 110–47. The references here to the Coptic version are to this codex, which is fairly complete in six fragments.

[13]The Achmimic fragment has been edited by Walter E. Crum, *Catalogue of the Coptic Manuscripts in the British Museum* (London: British Museum, 1905), no. 292, ms Or 3581 B (7). The Sahidic version exists in several fragments and codices, one of which is from Codex Borgianus CXXVI, which has been edited by Ignazio Guidi, "Frammenti Copti, nota II^a," *Rendiconti della R. Academia dei Lincei* 3/2 (1887): 20–23. The Bohairic has been edited by Hugh Evelyn-White, *The Monasteries of the Wadi 'n Natrûn* 1/2, Cairo mss. no. 5–6 (Metropolitan Museum of Art Egyptian Expedition; New York: n.p., 1926, 38–43. The Ethiopic version is edited by Solomon C. Malan, *The Conflicts of the Holy Apostles, an Apocryphal Book of the Early Eastern Church Translated from an Ethiopic Manuscript* (London: 1871), and E. A. W. Budge, *The Contendings of the Apostles* (2 vols.: Amsterdam: Philo, 1976), 2:122–36. The Arabic text may be found in Agnes Smith Lewis, *The Mythological Acts of the Apostles* (HSem 4; London: Clay, 1904), xxv, 60–68.

two texts. Both texts portray the apostles being accused of deceiving the people through magic and both texts depict the apostles' subsequent victory over the pagan cult. In both texts, when the apostles arrive at the gates of the allotted city, they are initially refused entrance (*Acts Phil.* 13,1–3 and frg. 2). In both narratives two miracles are necessary: in the Greek, the victories over the snakes as well as the dragons at the gate (*Acts Phil.* 13,1–3); in the Coptic, the exorcism of the unclean spirit and the lowering and raising of the pillar at the gate (frg. 2–3). Both texts include the motifs of a cloud of fire [*Acts Phil. Mart.* 20 (126) only in Γ; frg. 4) and earthquakes,[14] and both depict the building of a church structure as a sign of the people's belief (*Acts Phil.* 41 [147], frg. 5).

The replacement of Mary by Peter as Philip's companion in the Coptic version of the *Acts of Philip* eliminates the authoritative position she held in the original Greek text. It is intriguing that when the *Acts of Philip* appears in the Coptic language, it appears not as a direct translation featuring the same three primary figures, but instead as a retelling of the story, in which Mary Magdalene is no longer the disciple who strengthens Philip. This Coptic text provides one of the most interesting examples of the elimination or replacement of her figure.[15] Both the Greek and Coptic versions contain an allocation of missionary territories, but in the Coptic *Acts of Philip* Peter rather than Mary stands at the side of Christ when these commissions are granted. In both cases Christ makes a resurrection appearance and gives words of encouragement. It is no longer Mary, however, but Peter who fulfills the role of comforting Philip, and then Peter who accompanies Philip on his missionary journey as Mary does in the Greek version. In each version the author portrays Philip with some initial weakness or character flaw, which is alleviated by Mary in the Greek version but by Peter in the Coptic.

Conflict between Mary Magdalene and Peter

The Coptic version of the *Acts of Philip* is but one of several translations or adaptations of texts that omit Mary Magdalene from the original

---

[14]Several parallels exist in *Acts Phil. Mart.* 32 (138) only in Θ and Δ; *Acts Phil. Mart.* 33 (139) only in Θ; see also *Acts Phil. Mart.* 27 (133) only in Θ; and the Coptic frg. 2–3.

[15]Bovon, "Les Actes de Philippe," 4439. He finds that "la rivalité entre les deux, selon diverses traditions gnostiques, a dû favoriser la substitution."

story and replace her with another key figure in early Christian history. The frequency of these substitutions in a number of texts widely distributed in space and time make it unlikely that these substitutions are the result of mere accident or arbitrary decisions. These substitutions or replacements occur in certain Greek and Syriac texts as well as in Coptic fragments. In the majority of the texts that replace Mary Magdalene with another character—especially those texts that substitute Mary, the mother of Jesus, as the first resurrection witness—the apostle Peter is present and prominent.

It is likely that these multiple examples of Mary Magdalene's elimination from the narrative reflect arguments over the relative authority of Peter and Mary Magdalene similar to those described earlier in this study. Mary Magdalene's prominence in early Christian history no doubt stems from the tradition that she was present at the sepulchre for the first resurrection appearance from Jesus and, therefore, for many early Christians, she was the first apostolic witness. Her exalted status was subsequently resisted by other segments of the early church: this is the best explanation for her systematic diminution in or outright erasure from a wide range of texts and traditions. One such reason offered for the devaluation of Mary Magdalene in those other segments of the church is her reported importance for "heretics," such as certain Gnostic circles as well as the Manichaeans. We have seen how the Coptic *Acts of Philip* replaces Mary Magdalene with a man, namely Peter. Another strategy, I submit, for curtailing the prominence of Mary Magdalene was to replace her character with another less threatening figure, such as Mary of Nazareth, the mother of Jesus.

Replacement of Mary Magdalene in *Acta Thaddaei* and in Syriac Texts

The Greek *Acta Thaddaei* (*BHG* 1702–1703) provides an alternative version of the scene at the sepulchre portraying Mary the Mother speaking with Jesus.[16] The text reads: "and he appeared first to his mother and

---

[16]The Greek *Acta Thaddaei,* ed. Richard Adelbert Lipsius, is found in Richard A. Lipsius and Maximilian Bonnet, *Acta Apostolorum Apocrypha* (3 vols.; Leipzig: Mendelssohn, 1891–1903; repr. Darmstadt: Wissenschaftliche Buchgesellschaft, 1959), 1:273–78. See also Aurelio de Santos Otero, "Later Acts of Apostles" in *NTApoc*[5] 2:481; Richard A. Lipsius, *Die apokryphen Apostelgeschichten und Apostellegenden* (2 vols. in 3 and supplement; 1883–1890; repr.; Amsterdam: Philo, 1976), 2/2:178–200; Mario Erbetta, *Atti*

to the other women, and to Peter and John the first of my co-disciples,
then also to us the twelve, who ate and drank with him for many days
after his resurrection from the dead."[17] It is intriguing and probably not
surprising that this text which places Mary, the mother, in the position
of Mary Magdalene also privileges Peter among the disciples, calling
him and John "the first among my co-disciples" (τοῖς πρώτοις τῶν
συμμαθητῶν μου).

A similar dynamic of substituting Mary, the mother of Jesus, for Mary
Magdalene occurs in certain Syriac texts; most frequently in those of
Ephrem.[18] The most common explanation up until now for the replacement
of Mary Magdalene by Mary, the mother, in these texts has been that the
similarity in the names of Mary (of Magdala) and Mary (of Nazareth) has
led to confusion. Annotating a passage in Ephrem's commentary on the
Diatessaron, for instance, Carmel McCarthy states, "Ephrem appears to
confuse Mary, the Mother of Jesus, with Mary Magdalene here."[19] If this
were an isolated case one might accept the hypothesis of sheer confusion.
However, by establishing the frequency of such "confusions" of the two
Marys across a range of early Christian texts, this chapter argues that
the changes in the identity of the primary figures in these texts should
be ascribed to one or more motives, and should not be written off as the
reflections of authorial or scribal confusion. A study of the Greek and,
especially, the Syriac exegetical traditions, for example, reveals a tradition

---

e Leggende (Gli Apocrifi del Nuovo Testamento; 2 vols. Turin: Marietti, 1966), 2:575–76
for the introduction to the Italian translation of the Greek Acts of Thaddaei, and 2:577–78
for the translation; Michel van Esbroeck, "Le roi Sanatrouk et l'apôtre Thaddée," Revue
des Études Arméniennes 9 (1973): 141–283.

[17]καὶ ὤφθη πρῶτον τῇ μητρὶ αὐτοῦ καὶ ἄλλαις γυναιξίν, καὶ Πέτρῳ καὶ Ἰωάννῃ τοῖς
πρώτοις τῶν συμμαθητῶν μου, ἔπειτα καὶ ἡμῖν τοῖς δώδεκα, οἵτινες συνεφάγομεν καὶ
συνεπίομεν αὐτῷ μετὰ τὸ ἀναστῆναι ἐκ νεκρῶν ἐπὶ ἡμέρας πολλάς [§6]). Note the close
parallel in Acts 10:41b.

[18]Louis Leloir, Éphrem de Nisibe, Commentaire de l'évangile concordant ou Diatessaron: Traduit du Syriaque et de l'Arménien (SC 121; Paris: Cerf, 1966). This subject
is treated extensively in Murray, Symbols of Church and Kingdom, 329–30. See also
Shoemaker, "Mary and the Discourse of Orthodoxy."

[19]Carmel McCarthy, Saint Ephrem's Commentary on Tatian's Diatessaron: An English
Translation of Chester Beatty Syriac MS 709 with Introduction and Notes (JSSSup 2;
Oxford: Oxford University Press, 1993), 96. This author notes several sites in which there
a "confusion" or "fusion," such as II, §17; V, §5; and XXI, §27.

that understands this woman at the tomb to be Mary, the mother of Jesus.[20] My research concurs with that of Robert Murray, who finds that in the Syriac tradition those texts that conflate the figure of Mary, the mother, with that of Mary Magdalene appear to be achieving a deliberate and systematic "superimposition" of the Marys.[21] Ephrem, for instance, represents Jesus' mother as taking the place of Mary Magdalene in the garden four times in his commentary on the Diatessaron and in his hymns.[22]

Replacement of Mary Magdalene in Theodoret

In addition to Ephrem, this tendency to replace Mary Magdalene with Mary of Nazareth is also represented by Theodoret in his *Quaestiones et responsiones ad Orthodoxos*.[23] At least two of the three principal manuscripts contain, not the usual text, "Why did the Lord say to Mary, 'Do not touch me?' " but rather, "Why did the Lord say to his mother Mary (πρὸς τὴν μητέρα Μαρίαν), 'Do not touch me?' "[24] Over the centuries a few editors of the printed editions have corrected the manuscripts to omit μητέρα, some without telling the readers what they had done.[25]

---

[20]William L. Petersen, *Tatian's Diatessaron: Its Creation, Dissemination, Significance, and History in Scholarship* (Leiden: Brill, 1994), 398. He refers also to the literature of Tjitze Baarda, "Jesus and Mary (John 20, 16f) in the Second Epistle on Virginity Ascribed to Clement," in *Studien zum Text und zur Ethik des Neuen Testaments* (Fs. Heinrich Greeven; BZNW 47; ed. W. Schrage; Berlin: de Gruyter, 1986), 18–19. See also Shoemaker, "Mary and the Discourse of Orthodoxy."

[21]Murray, *Symbols of Church and Kingdom*, 329–30. See also Haskins, *Mary Magdalen*, 92.

[22]The references in his commentary on the Diatessaron are: II, §17; V, §5 (Arm.) and XXI, §27 (Syr.) and in hymn 5, 70–73 of *Hymnes de Saint Éphrem conservées en version arménienne*, 5, 70–73, text and Latin trans. by Louis Mariès and Charles Mercier (PO 30; Paris: Firmin-Didot, 1961), 54–55; cited also in Murray, *Symbols of Church and Kingdom*, 329–30.

[23]Theodoret in the *Quaestiones et responsiones ad Orthodoxos, 48.*

[24]Johann Carl Theodor von Otto, *Corpus Apologetarum Christianorum* (Jena: Prostat in Libraria H. Duff, 1847–72), V, 70; this edition was collated with a tenth-century codex in Jerusalem by A. Papadopoulos-Kerameus (St. Petersburg, 1895), 63, as cited in Murray, *Symbols of Church and Kingdom*, 331.

[25]Murray points out that some editors such as Robert Étienne (Stephanus) (in [*Works of*] *Justin Martyr* [Lyon, 1551]) and Otto "corrected" the manuscripts by omitting μητέρα, but

The research that scholars such as Murray have done on the Syriac texts reveals several lines of tradition concerning the Marys at the tomb; two of these traditions portray the mother of Jesus as present at the sepulchre. One of these two lines of tradition, represented by Ephrem, substitutes her for Mary Magdalene. Murray believes that this line of tradition, which takes the "Mary" of John 20:11–17 as Christ's mother, is a reaction against the closeness of Mary Magdalene to Christ; indeed she is portrayed as his partner or companion in the *Gospel of Philip* (32). Another tradition, the Antiochene, is represented by such texts as the *Didascalia* and those of Chrysostom. Murray explains that the Antiochene tradition does not replace Mary Magdalene with Mary, the mother, in John 20; rather, this tradition capitalizes on the mention of a second Mary in Matt 28:1 to portray Mary, the mother, on the scene.[26] Indeed, since tradition places Mary, mother of Jesus, at the crucifixion, it is not unlikely that she may have also visited the tomb. An especially interesting aspect of this tradition, however, is the way it gives precedence to Mary, the mother, by naming a second Mary as "the other Mary" and identifying her as the Magdalene. This kind of reordering, naming Mary Magdalene after Mary, the mother, occurs in homilies by Chrysostom[27] as well as in the Syriac *Didascalia Apostolorum*, which asserts: "But in the Gospel of Matthew it is thus written: 'In the evening of the Sabbath, when the first day of the week dawned, came Mary and the other Mary, Magdalene, to see the tomb.' "[28] Some scholars have regarded this reordering as only an error in the text.[29]Arthur Vööbus, however, in his commentary on this text states that in his opinion, "the matter . . . is far more complicated. . . . The Syrian Christians were prompted by the desire to secure an appearance of Christ

---

noted the change. In another case an index reference made one unnoted editorial change evident. Papadopoulos-Kerameus, cited above, omits μητέρα in the manuscript, but his index betrays the omission, directing the reader to find a reference to Mary "the mother" where the word has in fact been excised.

[26]Murray, *Symbols of Church and Kingdom*, 334.

[27]*Hom. Matt.* 88, 2–3 (PG 88, 777–78). See also Leloir, *Éphrem de Nisibe,* 75.

[28]*Didascalia Apostolorum* XXI (p. 207). Arthur Vööbus, ed., *The Didascalia Apostolorum in Syriac: Chapter XI–XXVI* (CSCO Scriptores Syri 180; Louvain: Secrétariat du CSCO, 1979), 2:190.

[29]Richard Hugh Connolly, *Didascalia Apostolorum: The Syriac Version Translated and Accompanied by the Verona Latin Fragments* (Oxford: Clarendon, 1929), 182, cited by Vööbus, *Didascalia Apostolorum in Syriac,* 2:190.

to Mary his mother."[30] In fact, the possibility exists that the substitution of the Marys originates with Tatian himself, especially considering the strength of the tradition in Syriac literature.[31]

Replacement of Mary in Coptic Texts

The substitutions for Mary Magdalene are not limited merely to Syriac examples, but include numerous citations from Coptic texts as well. Just as in the case of the Syriac texts cited above, commentators have often not taken the replacement of names seriously nor acknowledged the possibility that the ancient authors may have been making purposeful changes. M. R. James, for example, explains the replacement of Mary Magdalene in the text as "the reckless identification of the Virgin Mary with all the other Maries of the Gospels."[32] He goes on to note, however, that this carelessness is "characteristic of these Egyptian rhapsodies."[33]

If the following selection of Coptic texts portrays a frequent identification of Mary, the mother, with Mary Magdalene similar to the Syrian tradition's deliberate and systematic "superimposition" of the Marys,[34]

[30]Vööbus, *Didascalia Apostolorum in Syriac,* 2:190. He cites evidence from three categories: exegetical traditions (Saint Ephrem, *Commentaire l'Évangile concordant* [ed. Louis Leloir, CSCO Scr. Arm. II; Louvain: Durbecq, 1954] 61); hymnodic traditions (*Sancti Romani Melodi Cantica* [ed. Paul Maas and C. A. Trypanis; Oxford: Clarendon, 1963], 146); and homiletical traditions (*Les Homiliae cathédrales de Sévère d'Antioche* (suite): Homélie 77 [ed. Marc-Antoine Kugener and E. Triffaux; PO 16:5; Paris, 1922; repr. Turnhout: Brepols, 1976] 810–11). Along with the Greek text and the French translation, this edition includes two Syriac versions by Paul of Callinice and James of Edessa.

[31]From Bauer's point of view, for example, the tradition reaches back to Tatian: "Schon im zweiten Jahrhundert hat man sein Befremden geteilt. Tatian bereits läßt die Mutter Jesu sich beim Grabe einfinden und dem auferstandenen Sohne begegnen." See Walter Bauer, *Das Leben Jesu im Zeitalter der Neutestamentlichen Apokryphen* (Tübingen: Mohr, 1909), 448, and 263; also Tjitze Baarda, *The Gospel Quotations of Aphrahat the Persian Sage,* vol. 1, *Aphrahat's Text of the Fourth Gospel* (Amsterdam: Vrije Universiteit Amsterdam, 1975), 254–57, cited also in the discussion by Shoemaker, "Mary and the Discourse of Orthodoxy," 192–97.

[32]M. R. James, *The Apocryphal New Testament* (Oxford: Clarendon, 1924), 88.

[33]Ibid., 88. He provides several examples, including what he calls the *Book of Bartholomew,* where the appearance of Christ to Mary Magdalene after the resurrection is turned into an appearance to his mother, as well as another Coptic fragment on the Passion to be described in this chapter. See also references in Haskins, *Mary Magdalen,* 418 n. 90.

[34]Murray, *Symbols of Church and Kingdom,* 329–30.

then one can surmise that more than occasional accidental confusion is at the heart of this issue.

Revillout Fragment 14

Fragment 14 in a collection of Coptic fragments edited by Eugène Revillout[35] includes yet another example of the substitution of Mary of Nazareth, the mother of Jesus, for the figure of Mary Magdalene as a resurrection witness. This fragment describes an encounter between Jesus and his mother at the sepulchre that is parallel to the scene in the Gospel of John where Jesus appears to Mary Magdalene and speaks to her in the garden. Since this text is not easily available to many readers, I will quote the majority of the fragment here (though numerous lacunae exist in the text):

ΠΕΧΑϹ ΝΑϤ ϨΝ ΟΥΡΑϢΕ ΧΕ ϨΡΑΒΒΕΙ ΠϹΑϨ ΠΑΧΟΕΙϹ· ΑΥⲰ
ΠΑΝΟΥΤΕ· ΑΥⲰ ΠΑϢΗΡΕ· ΑΚΤⲰΟΥΝ· ΚΑΛⲰϹ ΑΚΤⲰΟΥΝ· ΕΝ-
ΕϹΟΥⲰϢ ΧΕ ΕΝΕϹΟΥⲰϢ ΔΕ ΠΕ ΕΑΜΑϨΤΕ ΜΜΑϤ ΕϮΠΕΙ
ΕΡⲰϤ ϨΑ ΠΡΑϢΕ ΝΤΟϤ ΔΕ ΑϤΚⲰΛΥ ΜΜΟϹ ΑϤΤⲰΒϨ ΜΜΟϹ
ΧΕ Ⲱ ΤΑΜΑΑΥ ΜΠΡ ΧⲰϨ ΕΡΟΙ . . . ΟΥΚΟΥΙ Ⲱ ΤΑΜΑΑΥ· . . .
ΧΕ ΘΒϹⲰ ΝΤΑ ΠΑΕΙⲰΤ ΤΑΑϹ ϨΙⲰⲰΤ ΝΤΕΡΕϤΤΟΥΝΟϹΤ· [. . .]
ΠΕΝΤΑΙΡ ϮϹ ΝΕΒΟΤ ϨΝ ΤΟΥΚΑΛΑϨΗ . . . ϹΟΥⲰΝΤ ΝΗ Ⲱ ΜΑ-
ΡΙΑ ΤΑΜΑΑΥ ΧΕ [ΤΑΙ]ϹΑΡϮ ΝΤΑΙΧΙΤϹ ΝϨΗΤΕ ΝΤΟϹ ΤΝΤΑϹΕΝ-
ΚΟΤΚ ϨΜ ΠΤΑϤΟϹ ΝΤΟϹ ΟΝ ΤΕΝΟΥ ΤΕΝΤΑϹΤⲰΟΥΝ ΜΠΟΟΥ
ΕϹΑϨΕΡΑΤϹ ΕΡΟ —ΜΕϨ ΕΙΛΑΤΕ ΝΝΑϬΙΧ ΜΝ ΝΑΟΥΕΡΗΤΕ· Ⲱ
ΜΑΡΙΑ ΤΑΜΑΑΥ ϹΟΥⲰΝΤ ΧΕ ΑΝΟΚ ΠΕΝΤΑΡϹΑΝΟΥⲰΤ —ΜΠΡϮ
. . . Ⲱ ΤΑΜΑΑΥ ΧΕ ΑΝΟΚ ΠΟΥϢΗΡΕ —ΑΝΟΚ ΠΕΝΤΑΙΚΑΑΤΕ
ΕΤΟΟΤϤ ΝΙⲰϨΑΝΝΗϹ ΜΠΝΑΥ ΝΑΛΕ ΕΠΕϹϮΟϹ —ΤΕΝΟΥ ϬΕ
. . . Ⲱ ΤΑΜΑΑΥ ϬΕΠΗ ΤΑΜⲰ . . . ΝΑϹΝΗΥ . . . ΚΑΤΑ ΝϢΑΧΕ
ΝΤΑΙΧΟΟΥ ΝΗΤΝ ΑΜΗΙΤΝ ΕΤΓΑΛΙΛΑΙΑ ΤΕΤΝΝΑΝΑΥ ΕΡΟΙ

She said to him with joy: "Rabbi, teacher, my lord, and my God, and my son, you have risen, you have really risen." She wanted to take hold of him in order to kiss him in greeting. But he stopped her and requested her, "My mother, do not touch me. . . . [Wait?] a little, oh my mother, for the garment that my Father put upon me when he raised me up. . . . the one in which I remained nine months in your womb. . . . Know these things, oh Mary my mother, this flesh is that which I received from you. This is the one that rested in the tomb. It

---

[35]See also Mario Erbetta, *Vangeli* (Gli Apocrifi del Nuovo Testamento; vol. 1/2; Turin: Marietti, 1981), 329. Fragment 14 is a single manuscript leaf from Paris, Bibliothèque

is the one that also now has risen today, that which is standing before you. Look intently at my hands and my feet. Oh
Mary, my mother, know that it is I whom you nourished. Do
not . . . [doubt?] oh my mother that I am your son. It is I
who entrusted you into the hands of John at the hour of going
up on the cross. Now then, . . . oh my mother, hurry tell my
brothers, . . . according to the words that I have told you, 'Go
into Galilee, you will see me.' "

This sepulchre scene is closely assimilated to the appearance of Jesus to
Mary Magdalene described in John 20:15–17. The similarities between
the Mary Magdalene version in John and this one are striking because
Jesus not only appears and speaks to Mary, his mother, in the same garden setting but also warns her not to touch him. Although the dramatic
situation is essentially identical to the one in John, the alteration of
names effectively functions to make the Mary, the mother, *the* resurrection witness. In fact, Mary, the mother, herself receives the commission
to tell the disciples the resurrection message: "Now then, . . . oh my
mother, hurry tell my brothers, . . . according to the words that I have
told you, 'Go into Galilee, you will see me.' " As James points out, such
substitution occurs here "as elsewhere in Coptic writings."[36] Clearly,
the choice of the person to whom Jesus makes the first resurrection
appearance has serious implications with respect to authority.

Book of the Resurrection of Jesus Christ by Bartholomew the Apostle

A manuscript now in the British Museum preserves another Coptic text
that substitutes Mary, the mother, for Mary Magdalene in the sepulchre
scene:

---

nationale, copte 129/17 fol. 20ʳ–20ᵛ. Coptic fragment no. 14, ed. Eugène Revillout, *Les
apocryphes coptes, I. Les Évangiles des douze apôtres et de Saint Barthélemy* (PO 2.2; ed.
R. Graffin and F. Nau; Paris: Firmin-Didot, 1904; repr. 1946), 169–70. Without sufficient
substantiation, Revillout attributes this fragment to a lost text known only from the title, *The
Gospel of the Twelve Apostles*. In J. Keith Elliott's reference to this fragment (*Apocryphal
New Testament,* 163), he too indicates that this assimilation occurs elsewhere in Coptic
writings.

[36]James, *Apocryphal New Testament,* 151 and 87. On the latter page, among other texts,
James cites the Twentieth Discourse of Cyril of Jerusalem in which Mary, the mother, says
to Cyril that her mother is Anna and states, "I am Mary Magdalene because the name of the
village wherein I was born was Magdalia."

> And Mary said unto Philogenes, "If you are indeed he [I know
> you]." Philogenes said unto her, "You are Mary the mother of
> Thalkamarimath, the interpretation of which is "the joy, the bless-
> ing, and [the gladness]." Mary said unto him, "[If it be you who
> has taken away the body of my Lord, tell] me where you have
> laid it, and I myself will carry it away." Philogenes said unto her,
> "Oh my sister, what is [the meaning of] these words which you
> speak, O you holy virgin, the mother of Christ?"[37]

In the narrative Philogenes tells how the Jews sought a safe sepulchre
for Jesus that the body might not be secretly taken away, and he offered
to place it in a tomb in his own garden and watch over it. They sealed
the tomb and departed. He describes that in the middle of the night he
rose and went to the tomb and saw thousands of angels in four rows,
including Cherubim, Seraphim, Powers, and Virgins. He saw the seven
heavens open, and the Father raised Jesus from the dead.[38] Philogenes
continues his description to Mary:

> Moreover, I saw Peter there, the great interpreter of Jesus, [and
> had he not] laid hold upon me, and helped me, I must have
> fallen into despair and died by reason of [these great] mysteries,
> and this great glory which I saw. . . . And the Savior appeared
> in their presence mounted upon the chariot of the Father of the
> Universe, and he cried out in the language of his Godhead, say-
> ing, "Mari Khar Mariath," whereof the interpretation is, "Mary,
> the Mother of the Son of God." Then Mary who knew the in-
> terpretation of the words, said, "Hramboune Kathiathari Mioth,"

---

[37]This text is taken from the British Museum Ms. Oriental, No. 6804 in E. A. W. Budge,
Coptic Apocrypha in the Dialect of Upper Egypt (London: British Museum, 1913), 10–11
(Coptic), 188 (English). For extensive work on the *Book of the Resurrection of Jesus
Christ by Bartholomew the Apostle,* see Jean-Daniel Kaestli and Pierre Cherix, "Livre de
la résurrection de Jésus-Christ par l'apôtre Barthélemy," in *Écrits apocryphes chrétiens*
(La Pléiade, ed. François Bovon and Pierre Geoltrain; Paris: Gallimard, 1997), 299–356,
esp. 302–4. Kaestli and Cherix have reconstructed two additional manuscripts of this text,
and a critical edition is being prepared for CCSA. They also refer (p. 323) to the homilies
of Pseudo-Cyril of Jerusalem (Annarosa Campagnano, ed., *Ps. Cirillo di Gerusalemme:
Omelie copte sulla Passione, sulla Croce e sulla Vergine* [Milan: Cisalpino-Goliardica,
1980], 158–59) where additional transpositions of Mary take place.

[38]This section is a summary of fol. 6a and 6b in Budge, *Coptic Apocrypha in the Dialect
of Upper Egypt,* 11–12 (Coptic) and 188–89 (English).

whereof the interpretation is, "The Son of the Almighty, and the Master, and my Son."[39]

A long address to Mary from Jesus follows, in the course of which he asks her to go and tell the others the news. Additional Coptic fragments of the *Book of the Resurrection* in the Bibliothèque nationale in Paris[40] supply more details of the conversation between Mary the mother and Jesus. Mary, for instance, says: "If indeed I am not permitted to touch you, at least bless my body in which you did deign to dwell." Jesus blesses the body of Mary. She departs and gives the message to the apostles, and then Peter blesses her.[41] This fragment is very specific in portraying the special position that Peter holds: "Then the Father (with the Son, and with the Holy Spirit) stretched out His hand over the head of Peter, and consecrated him Archbishop (ⲁⲣϫⲏⲡⲓⲥⲕⲟⲡⲟⲥ) of the whole world."[42]

In this text, interesting implications for ecclesial authority become quite clear: the text not only honors Mary, the mother, instead of Mary Magdalene but also at the same time frequently highlights the presence and prominence of Peter. For instance, Peter is singled out as being at the site when the resurrection took place. The owner of the garden, Philogenes, calls Peter "the great interpreter of Jesus" and credits his own survival of the resurrection ordeal to Peter's presence. Finally, when Mary arrives and gives the message to the disciples, Peter or the "great bishop" (depending upon which manuscript one follows) blesses her. The final consecration of Peter as the "Archbishop of the whole world" is followed by the blessing the Father gives to him: "You shall be the chief and head in my kingdom, and you shall be the chief and head over the whole world." Such a statement must have had strong political implications for the readers of this text.

[39]Fol. 6b in Budge, *Coptic Apocrypha in the Dialect of Upper Egypt,* 12 (Coptic) and 189 (English).

[40]Available in Pierre Lacau, *Fragments d'apocryphes coptes* (Cairo: Institut français d'archéologie orientale, 1904), 43–66.

[41]The translation and summary in this latter section is adapted from the English versions provided by James, *Apocryphal New Testament,* 183–84 and the "Appendix" in Budge, *Coptic Apocrypha in the Dialect of Upper Egypt,* 219–26.

[42]Budge, *Coptic Apocrypha in the Dialect of Upper Egypt,* 228.

Moreover, a reexamination of some of the Syriac texts discussed earlier in this chapter reveals that these texts also feature Peter in a prominent role. Such is indeed the case, for example, in Ephrem's exegesis and commentary. Ephrem's fourth *memra* contains the following rather explicit description of Peter's primacy:

> You, Simon, my disciple, have I set as the foundation of the holy Church. I called you *Kepha* [stone] from of old, that you might bear all buildings. . . . You are the fountainhead out of which my doctrine is drawn, and you are the head of my disciples.[43]

In another of Ephrem's texts that fuses Mary, the mother, and Mary Magdalene, another reference to Peter employs *Kepha* as a functional title:

> Again, Mary is like the Church,
> the Virgin, who has borne the first fruits by the Gospel. . . .
> For to Simon, the Foundation,
> Mary was first to run,
> Fittingly did she come to Simon
> and bring him the good news that the Son was risen,
> For he was the Rock (*Kepha*) and Foundation
> of the Church of the Gentiles, the elect.[44]

These documents raise the question of the impact that an author's esteem for Peter's authority may have had on the author's representation of Mary Magdalene's role as diminished or compromised. If a competition between communities honoring these two figures did exist, it follows that pro-Petrine authors would produce texts for their communities that selected alternative authority figures to highlight. Ideally, a pro-Petrine author would substitute Peter himself for Mary; if constrained by features of the tradition to replace Mary Magdalene with a woman, a pro-Petrine author could introduce Mary, the mother of Jesus, into a text. An examination of the way in which ancient authors selected only certain disciples as the primary figures in a chosen text reveals that the groupings of disciples and

---

[43]Thomas J. Lamy, ed., *Sancti Ephraem Hymni et Sermones* (4 vols.; Mecheln: H. Dessain, 1882–1902), 1:411–12 in *Sermo* 4, §1; cited also in Murray, *Symbols of Church and Kingdom*, 217–18.

[44]Lamy, ed., *Sancti Ephraem Hymni et Sermones*, 1:533–34 in *Sermo* 7, §2, translation quoted from Murray, *Symbols of Church and Kingdom*, 147, 218.

the use of their names are significant. It is not uncommon, for instance, for Mary, the mother, to appear in texts that highlight the apostolic authority of Peter, as the following examination of the *Questions of Bartholomew* will show.

The Cooptation of Mary the Mother in the *Questions of Bartholomew*

The *Questions of Bartholomew*[45] portrays well the way in which a text can feature a select grouping of disciples to fulfill specific roles. This Greek text, composed between the second and the sixth century, features Peter, Andrew, Bartholomew, John, and Mary, mother of Jesus.[46] A rhetorical analysis of the text reveals that the primary role that Mary plays is that of spokesperson for the authority of Peter over women. One need only examine some of the dialogue the author attributes to the character of Mary of Nazareth to discern that some polemical or political discourse is being placed upon her lips. Among her first words in the narrative, for instance, is an acknowledgement of Peter's position in the group of the disciples: "She [Mary, the mother] said to Peter, 'Peter, you chief, you great pillar, do you stand behind us? Did our Lord not say, "The head of the man is Christ [Slav. and Lat. 2 add: but the head of the woman is the man]"? Now therefore stand before me and pray'" (II,7). In another section Mary. the mother, declines the chance to speak to the Lord and asks Peter to go instead of her, addressing him with the words, "O stone hewn out of the rock, did not the Lord build his church upon you? Go first and ask him" (IV,3). The author not only portrays Mary, the mother, as deferring to Peter but doing so, in her own words, because he is a male (IV,5). Douglas Parrott, among others, has intuited from the rhetoric of the text that the author may be using Mary, the mother, as a "counterpoint"[47] or as a "foil" to Mary Magdalene.[48]

---

[45]Kaestli, "Questions de Barthélemy," 267–95; Elliott, *Apocryphal New Testament,* 652–72.

[46]Elliott, *Apocryphal New Testament,* 652. The English translation here is taken from his text for convenience. Another modern translation of this text, based on newer textual evidence, is available in Kaestli, "Questions de Barthélemy," 267–95.

[47]Parrott, "Gnostic and Orthodox Disciples," 210.

[48]Ibid., 211.

The attitude attributed to Peter toward Mary, the mother, in this text is significantly different from his interactions with Mary Magdalene as portrayed in the texts previously quoted in this chapter. For instance, Peter honors Mary, the mother, with the words, "You who are highly favoured, entreat the Lord to reveal to us the things that are in the heavens." When she humbly declines, Peter tries again, "O tabernacle who are spread abroad, it behooves you to ask" (IV,4). Mary's response to Peter accords women a secondary position: "You are the image of Adam; was not he first formed and then Eve?" (IV,5). She goes on to describe the contrast between men and women: "Look upon the sun; according to the likeness of Adam it is bright, and upon the moon; because of the transgression of Eve it is full of clay" (IV,5). Despite the fact that Mary. the mother, is accorded an authoritative role in this text, the narrative, whether intentionally or not, actually produces in Mary, the mother, an authority figure who is muted, forbidden to speak by her own son: "But Jesus appeared quickly [Lat. 2 adds: and laid his hand upon her mouth] and said to Mary, 'Utter not this mystery, or this day my whole creation will come to an end' [Lat. 2 adds: and the flame from her mouth ceased]. And the apostles were taken with fear lest the Lord should be angry with them" (II,22).

This text effectively silences the figure of Mary, the mother, while portraying Jesus only three sentences later in the narrative requesting his disciples to "ask me what you will that I should teach you, and I will show it to you" (III,3). Mary's role in this text is thus ambiguous because although the text presents her as a primary figure, her role is a submissive one in which she acknowledges the authority of Peter and repeatedly defers to him. As Elisabeth Schüssler Fiorenza points out, however, the author may be employing Mary's words prescriptively rather than descriptively since "ideological prescription and actual social reality do not always correspond."[49]

Summary

In the earliest Christian gospels only two individuals are singled out as recipients of an individual resurrection appearance from the Lord: Mary Magdalene (John 20:14–17) and Simon Peter (Luke 24:34). As evidenced

[49]Schüssler Fiorenza, *In Memory of Her*, 310.

in early Christian texts, receiving an appearance from the resurrected Lord had profound significance for one's status as an "apostle." As Elaine Pagels has written, "From Luke through Irenaeus, respect for the apostles as eyewitnesses of Jesus and the resurrection translates into respect for the bishops and presbyters, whom ecclesiastical Christians consider the apostles' only legitimate heirs."[50] In texts such as 1 Cor 15 and the Acts of the Apostles, however, Mary Magdalene was not granted the status of apostle in spite of her position as an early witness to the resurrection. An examination of early Christian texts reveals that Mary Magdalene's prominence had to be dealt with: her position either as an apostle or as an eyewitness of the resurrection is often altered, weakened, or eradicated from the narrative altogether.

In this chapter we have seen how Mary Magdalene exercised apostolic leadership in the Greek *Acts of Philip*. In a Coptic rewriting of the *Acts of Philip*, however, her character disappears and Peter appears in her stead, fulfilling her function of supporting Philip in his missionary work. The manipulation of the primary apostolic figures in this case appears to have been quite deliberate. We have likewise seen how other texts replace Mary Magdalene with a female character, specifically Mary the mother. I contend that the replacement of Mary Magdalene by other figures such as Mary the mother occurs with such frequency and in such a range of languages, locations, and centuries that one must in each case ask whether her replacement could not have been a deliberate one, and, if so, why?

One cannot determine all the reasons that motivated such replacements, but a few factors seem to be contributory. As seen before in the texts that replace Mary Magdalene, it may not be coincidental that the figure of Peter often appears to be particularly prominent. If there were tensions between those who respected either the authority of Peter or Mary Magdalene, then a logical pro-Petrine substitution for Mary Magdalene—especially in the sepulchre scene—is Mary, the mother, a figure who, far from challenging the authority of Peter, vocally supports his position and submits herself to his authority. When certain Syriac hymns and commentaries introduce Mary, the mother, in the resurrection accounts, this introduction no doubt reflects the growth of the veneration of Mary the mother, but in this context I wish especially to highlight the significance of the presence of both Peter and Mary, the mother, in texts that manipulate the

[50]Pagels, "Visions, Appearances, and Apostolic Authority," 417.

significance of Mary Magdalene by replacement. Not only does Mary, the mother, grow in stature, but it is in resurrection scenes specifically associated with Mary Magdalene, in particular the garden scene in which Jesus asks not to be touched (John 20:15–18), that the figure of Mary, the mother, often appears.

The fluidity with which early Christian figures such as Mary Magdalene, Mary, the mother, and Peter appear in—and disappear from—different textual traditions suggests that the presence or absence of these figures may very well have had political or theological significance. The displacement of a figure, either in texts or translations, is unlikely to be an arbitrary, confused, or unmotivated act, but is in all probability intentional and deliberate. This chapter contends that the substitutions of names in early Christian texts and translations deserve not only our vigilant attention now but more careful future analysis as well, with an aim towards understanding these substitutions in historical and sociological context. These substitutions have significant implications for apostolic authority.

CHAPTER EIGHT

Apostolic Contradictions and the Crisis of Authority

Claims to the title of "resurrection witness" and "apostle" remained
an important feature of debates over ecclesiastical authority long
after the first generation of Christians. The writings of the church fathers
help to clarify why such claims continued to be so important.[1] Irenaeus,
for example, identifies himself as a successor to the apostles when he
claims that he is "the one and only survivor of his generation who
received from the apostles the truth which is passed on by the church
(and not by the 'sects')."[2] From this statement as well as those of other
early church fathers, it is clear that many believed that the establishment
of apostleship as an intermediary office between Christ and the church
was the required foundational stage in the legitimization of the true
tradition against those who would proffer some other teaching.

Thus for many early Christian leaders, the maintenance of an apostolic
link to Jesus provided them with a vital means of establishing their credibility and eligibility to preach and teach the gospel message.[3] The oldest

---

[1] Numerous early Christian texts employ the concept of apostolicity though there
is not enough space here to examine them all. See for example: *Did.* 11.3, 11.4, 11.6;
2 Clem. 14.2; Ign. *Eph.* 11.2; Ign. *Magn.* 6.1; 7.1; 13.1 and 13.2, Ign. *Trall.* 2.2; 3.1;
3.3; 7.1 and 12.2; Ign. *Rom.* 4.3, Ign. *Phld.* 5.1; 9.1; Ign. *Smyrn.* 8.1; Pol. *Phil.* 6.3 and
9.1; *Herm.* 13.1, (*Vis.* 3.5); 92.4 (*Sim.* 9.15), 93.5 (*Sim.* 9.16), and 94.1 (*Sim.* 9.17) and
102.2 (*Sim.* 9.25).

[2] Irenaeus *Adv. haer.* III, 3, 4 (= Eusebius *Hist. eccl.* IV, 14, 5); Campenhausen, *Ecclesiastical Authority and Spiritual Power*, 163; Koester, *Ancient Christian Gospels*, 16.

[3] The *Epistle of Barnabas,* for example, makes clear that it was Jesus who chose
the apostles in order that they should proclaim his "message" or "gospel": ὅτε δε τοὺς
ἰδίους ἀποστόλους τοὺς μέλλοντας κηρύσσειν τὸ εὐαγγέλιον αὐτοῦ ἐξελέξατο ("When
he [Jesus] chose out his own apostles who were to preach his gospel . . ."; *Barn* 5.9).
See also *Barn.* 8.3. More in Koester, *Ancient Christian Gospels*, 16.

writing of the so-called "Apostolic Fathers," the *First Epistle of Clement,* asserts the importance of the role that the apostles played: "The apostles received the Gospel for us from the Lord Jesus Christ; Jesus Christ was sent forth from God. So then Christ is from God, and the apostles are from Christ" (*1 Clem* 42:1–3).[4] Early Christian authors, as they competed for authority and struggled to establish "true" traditions, selected prominent individual figures from the first generation to serve as the apostolic guarantors of their message.[5] Apostles' names became attached to writings and traditions as direct links to Jesus. Thomas' name in the *Gospel of Thomas,* for instance, functions "not because an apostolic name was needed to confirm the authority of Jesus, the author of the sayings, but in order to safeguard the special form of the tradition of churches which looked back to Thomas as their founder or as the guarantor of their faith."[6]

We have seen how traditions in the early church portrayed the resurrection witness narratives differently depending upon whose traditions they had heard or to whom they held allegiance. In the discussion of Luke and John we have seen how such allegiance to certain figures and their traditions also helped to shape the portrayal of women's leadership capacities. As seen in the previous chapter with the *Acts of Peter* versus the *Acts of Paul* these traditions and allegiances tended to perpetuate themselves. Let us now return to the question of apostleship begun in the first chapter. The same attitudes that would portray or not portray women as the recipients of a divine mandate to spread the good news, would no doubt also be at work in how one presented the qualifications for being an apostle, especially considering how important an apostle was in the role of mediator. This chapter, therefore, presents some of the differences in the definitions and interpretations of apostleship even as they appear in

---

[4] *1 Clement* 42 does not explicitly use the word "succession" (*1 Clem.* 5:3; 42:1–2; 44.1; 47.1; 47.4). "The idea of 'succession' acquires a new, specifically catholic form only when it is linked with the succession of monarchical bishops" (Campenhausen, *Ecclesiastical Authority and Spiritual Power,* 163). Campenhausen identifies one name—Hegesippus—when attempting to determine the first reference to this new pattern of succession.

[5] Helmut Koester, "La tradition apostolique et les origines du gnosticisme," *RTP* 119 (1987): 1–16.

[6] Koester, "Introduction [to *The Gospel according to Thomas*]," 41. The reference to Matthew as the authority for the "sayings" in Papias of Hierapolis is likewise most likely very old. See idem, *Ancient Christian Gospels,* 32–33.

the New Testament itself. It examines the impact of the term the "twelve apostles" upon the concept of apostolic status and focuses in part on the exclusivity inherent within Luke's emphasis on it. And in the end it agrees with Campenhausen's position that with respect to the "twelve," it was "only at a later stage that they were made first into apostles and then finally into the only apostles."[7]

Apostles in the New Testament

The generations after the first apostles clearly upheld the significance of the claim to be an ἀπόστολος. The post-Pauline epistles, written later and in Paul's name, for example, continue the tradition of claiming for Paul an apostolic status and a divine commissioning: "Paul, an apostle of Christ Jesus by the command of God our Savior and of Christ Jesus our hope" (1 Tim 1:1).[8] Likewise, the pseudepigraphical Petrine epistles refer to Peter as an apostle of Jesus Christ, beginning with these words: "Peter, an apostle of Jesus Christ" (1 Pet 1:1), and "Simon Peter, a servant and apostle of Jesus Christ" (2 Pet 1:1).

Although Paul frequently employed the term with respect to his own position, he did not apply the term liberally with respect to others; thus he never actually uses the appellation ἀπόστολος in conjunction with Barnabas, his companion (Gal 2:1–10, 13; 1 Cor 9:6), nor with Titus (2 Cor 8).[9] Paul's use of ἀπόστολος is, however, gender inclusive, as his reference to Junia as an apostle in Rom 16:7 indicates. Some translators in the past have failed

---

[7]Campenhausen, *Ecclesiastical Authority and Spiritual Power*, 14.

[8]It appears that Paul distinguishes his own role from that of others whom he calls ἀπόστολοι ἐκκλησιῶν, "apostles of the churches" meaning envoys or missionaries sent by congregations (2 Cor 8:23; Phil 2:25). See Hans Dieter Betz, *2 Corinthians 8 and 9: A Commentary on Paul's Letters of the Apostle Paul* (ed. George W. MacRae; Hermenia; Philadelphia: Fortress, 1985), 73, 81, 86.

[9]Although two unnamed brothers are called apostles of the church in 2 Cor 8, Titus, another companion of Paul, is not named as an apostle. Betz suggests that Paul purposely keeps the two brothers unnamed: "Paul avoided giving them more status than was due, so as not to diminish the authority of Titus in any way" (Betz, *2 Corinthians 8 and 9*, 73). Paul also employs the term negatively when he calls his opponents ψευδαπόστολοι ("false apostles"; 2 Cor 11:13) and ὑπερλίαν ἀπόστολοι ("super apostles"; 2 Cor 11: 5; 12:11). For more on "false apostles," see Charles K. Barrett, "ΨΕΥΔΑΠΟΣΤΟΛΟΙ (2 Cor 11.13)," in *Mélanges Bibliques* (Fs. B. Rigaux; ed. A. Descamps and A. de Halleux; Gembloux: Duculot, 1970), 377–90; Furnish, *II Corinthians*, 494.

to recognize Paul's inclusivity in this particular occurrence of ἀπόστολος and have assumed instead that any reference to an apostle must be male. This error occurs in part because the name appears in Romans in the accusative case as IOYNIAN, from which one may infer either a feminine nominative form—Ἰουνία ("Junia"), and thus a female apostle—or a masculine nominative form— Ἰουνιᾶς or Ἰουνίας ("Junias"), and thus a male apostle. The problem with the assumption that Paul refers to a male apostle, however, is that no one has ever found the masculine form of this name in any Greek or Latin inscription. As Bernadette Brooten explains, "To date not a single Latin or Greek inscription, not a single reference in ancient literature has been cited by any of the proponents of the 'Junias' hypothesis—there is not a single shred of evidence that the [male version of the] name ever existed."[10] The epigraphical evidence alone establishes for many scholars that Paul refers here to a female apostle.

Additional confirmation of the female gender of this apostle comes from leading theologians in the early church, including Origen of Alexandria (ca. 185–253), the earliest commentator on Rom 16:7, Jerome (340/50–419/20), and Chrysostom (344/54–407), all of whom understood this apostle to be female.[11] In fact, Chrysostom wrote of her, "Oh, how great is the devotion of this woman that she should be counted worthy of the appellation of apostle."[12] To these names Brooten adds those of other theologians and exegetes who believed Junia to be female, thereby making a cumulatively strong argument that Paul refers to a female apostle.[13]

---

[10]Bernadette Brooten, " 'Junia . . . Outstanding among the Apostles' (Romans 16: 7)," in *Women Priests: A Catholic Commentary on the Vatican Declaration* (ed. Leonard Swidler and Arlene Swidler; New York: Paulist, 1977), 142. Some scholars have tried to explain *Junias* as possibly a shortened form of *Junianus, Junianius, Junilius*, or *Junius*. This attempt fails, however, because, as Brooten points out, no attestation for *Junias* as an abbreviation for a male name exists either, and it is thus actually far more philologically cautious to understand Junia as a female apostle.

[11]On Junia, see Schüssler Fiorenza, *In Memory of Her,* 172; Brooten, "Junia," 141.

[12]In *Epistolam ad Romanos,* Homilia 31, 2 (PG 60, 669–70). English translation from *The Homilies of St. John Chrysostom*, The Epistle to the Romans, Homily XXXI (NPNF[1]; ed. Philip Schaff; Peabody, Mass.: Hendrickson, 1994), 11:555. See Arthur Frederick Ide, *Woman as Priest, Bishop & Laity in the Early Catholic Church to 440 A.D.: With a critical commentary on Romans 16 and other relevant Scripture and patrological writings on women in the early Christian Church* (Mesquite, Tex.: Ide House, 1984), 39 (quote), as well as 26 n. 10, 59 n. 33.

[13]Brooten refers to other biblical scholars who over the centuries have understood the name to be a reference to a female apostle, including Hatto of Vercelli (924–961),

Thus Junia becomes another example of a woman who was called an "apostle" in early Christian history but whose status has since been mitigated or challenged. Paul's generally sparing use of the term ἀπόστολος indicates his recognition of the term's significance for claiming authority, and therefore his bestowal of the term upon a woman is in turn strong evidence that the category of "apostle" in the early church was not only of considerable importance but also gender inclusive.

A comparison of Paul's use of ἀπόστολος with its use in the canonical gospels and Acts, however, reveals some significant disparities with respect to this term. These texts present not only a broad range of meanings for the word but also a wide variation in the frequency of its appearance. In the texts that eventually became the New Testament, the term ἀπόστολος appears a total of seventy-nine times;[14] and is absent from or rare in some texts, although in others it occurs with a frequency denoting a foundational concept. It occurs only once, for instance, in Mark (6:30), only once in Matthew (10:2–5, which is a shorter version of the choosing

Theophylact (ca. 1050–ca. 1108), and Peter Abelard (1079–1142). Also Jerome (Romans 7, 763) and Ambrosiaster (*Commentary on the Pauline Epistles*) confirm indirectly that Junia was considered to be a woman, as their Latin translations present the name Julia. This variant reading is taken seriously only insofar as it affirms that they too construed this apostle to be female. See Brooten, "Junia," 141–43. See "Iounias," BAGD, 380. Ute Eisen points out that Junia's active mission and consequent imprisonment, brought her into captivity as well. Thus, "Paul, by recalling Junia's imprisonment, places her *expressis verbis* in the tradition of the apostolic discipleship of the cross, which he posits especially in 2 Corinthians in counterdistinction to the ψευδαπόστολοι (2 Cor 11:13; cf. 2 Cor 6:4–10; 12:9–13)." Eisen, *Women Officeholders in Early Christianity*, 49.

[14]Moulton and Geden, s.v. "ἀπόστολος," *A Concordance to the Greek Testament*, 101–2. Secondary readings also occur (such as Mark 3:14), causing the numbers to vary. Although some take 3:14 to be original (see Wolfgang A. Bienert, "The Picture of the Apostle in Early Christian Tradition," in *NTApoc*[5] [ed. W. Schneemelcher; 2 vols.; Louisville, Ky.: Westminster/John Knox, 1991–92], 6, and Dieter Lührmann, *Das Markusevangelium* [HNT 3; Tübingen: Mohr, 1987], 70), many scholars regard this occurrence as the result of a scribal harmonization of some Markan manuscripts with Luke 6:13. *The Computer-Konkordanz zum Novum Testamentum Graece* (Berlin/New York: De Gruyter, 1980), 207–8, for instance, lists the occurrences of ἀπόστολος as eighty times. Matt 1x; Mark 2x; Luke 6x; John 1x; Acts 28x; Rom 3x; 1 Cor 10x; 2 Cor 6x; Gal 3x; Eph 4x; Phil 1x; Col 1x; 1 Thess 1x; 1 Tm 2x; 2 Tim 2x; Titus 1x; Heb 1x; 1 Pet 1x; 2 Pet 2x; Jude 1x; and Rev. 3x.

of the "twelve" in Mark),[15] and appears only once in the Gospel of John (13:16).[16] On the other hand, in sharp contrast to the other gospels, the Luke–Acts complex contains thirty-four occurrences of ἀπόστολος—almost half of all the occurrences of the term in the New Testament: the word appears six times in Luke (6:13; 9:10; 11:49; 17:5; 22:14; 24:10) and twenty-eight times in Acts (1:2, 26; 2:37, 42, 43; 4:33, 35, 36, 37; 5: 2, 12, 18, 29, 40; 6:6; 8:1, 14, 18; 9:27; 11:1; 14:4, 14; 15:2, 4, 6, 22, 23; 16:4).[17] The rare appearance of ἀπόστολος in the other three canonical gospels compared to the preponderance of the term in the Lukan accounts strongly suggests that this word has special significance for the author. Because of the frequency of this word and its greater emphasis in Luke–Acts, it is fair to assume that the author of Luke–Acts attributes some special role to this term, perhaps to underscore the authority of those who receive its designation.[18]

Within the New Testament, thus, the greatest degree of discernible difference with respect to the definition of the term ἀπόστολος appears in two groups of texts: the Pauline epistles, on the one hand, and Luke–Acts, on the other. Moreover, these are the very texts in which ἀπόστολος appears so frequently that they contain eighty percent of the total number of occurrences of the word in the New Testament.[19] These particular groups of texts, however, so strongly disagree on the meaning and applicability of the term ἀπόστολος that their differences are conceptually irreconcilable. The following examination explicates their differences.[20]

[15]Kirsopp Lake, "The Twelve and the Apostles," in *The Beginnings of Christianity* (ed. F. J. Foakes-Jackson and K. Lake; 5 vols.; London: Macmillan, 1933; repr., Darmstadt: Wissenschaftliche Buchgesellschaft, 1963), 5:47. The rare phrase "the twelve apostles" occurs only in Matt 10:2 and Rev 21:14. The description that "Jesus chose twelve of them whom he also designated as apostles," appears in Mark 3:14 and Luke 6:13.

[16]According to Brown, John uses ἀπόστολος in a nontechnical sense; see Brown, *John*, 2:569; Barrett, *John*, 444. Since John uses this term specifically in a dialogue with Peter, however, this is not entirely certain.

[17]Fitzmyer, *Luke*, 1:254.

[18]Compare the Lukan usage in Luke 22:14 with Matt 26:20 and Mark 14:17.

[19]These are also the only two bodies of documents in which the abstract ἀποστολή occurs (Gal 2:8; 1 Cor 9:2; Rom 1:5; and Acts 1:25). See Bienert, "The Picture of the Apostle" in *NTApoc⁵*, 6.

[20]Kirk, "Apostleship Since Rengstorf," 252; on differences between Paul and Luke, see Heinz Schürmann, *Das Lukasevangelium* (HTKNT 3/1; Freiburg: Herder, 1969), 314–15; Charles K. Barrett, "The Apostles in and after the New Testament," *SEÅ* 21 (1957): 30–49.

Differences in Apostolic Authority between Pauline Texts and the Acts of the Apostles

The author of Luke–Acts, writing at least several decades after Paul, presents a narrower, more restrictive definition for apostleship than does Paul. The first chapter of Acts adds some new elements to the requirements for being an apostle, and, as we shall see, these stipulations contain profound ramifications for early church leadership:

δεῖ οὖν τῶν συνελθόντων ἡμῖν ἀνδρῶν ἐν παντὶ χρόνῳ ᾧ εἰσῆλθεν καὶ ἐξῆλθεν ἐφ᾽ ἡμᾶς ὁ κύριος Ἰησοῦς, ἀρξάμενος ἀπὸ τοῦ βαπτίσματος Ἰωάννου ἕως τῆς ἡμέρας ἧς ἀνελήμφθη ἀφ᾽ ἡμῶν, μάρτυρα τῆς ἀναστάσεως αὐτοῦ σὺν ἡμῖν γενέσθαι ἕνα τούτων.

Therefore it is necessary to choose one of the men who accompanied us the whole time the Lord Jesus went in and out among us, beginning from the baptism of John to the time when Jesus was taken up from us. For one of these must become a witness with us of his resurrection. (Acts 1:21–22)

This text in Acts tightly circumscribes who may be an ἀπόστολος by adding three exclusionary restrictions. First, a unique additional requirement appears: according to Acts, to be an apostle, a person had to be there "from the beginning"—one who accompanied Jesus from the baptism of John until the day when he was taken up to heaven (1: 22). Klein calls this requirement in Acts 1:21–22 the "Magna Carta" of the conception of the "twelve" apostles.[21] In these two verses, Luke thus specifies that "only those who witnessed Jesus' earthly life 'from his baptism' can serve as authoritative witnesses of the resurrection as 'apostles.' "[22] This exclusionary move restricts legitimate witness to the "authority of the first 'apostolic' generation, and can be neither continued nor renewed once this has ended."[23] Moreover, because the selection of a new apostle is portrayed as a process by which the lost

[21]Klein, *Zwölf Apostel*, 204.
[22]Pagels, "Visions, Appearances, and Apostolic Authority," 416.
[23]Campenhausen, *Ecclesiastical Authority and Spiritual Power*, 22; Pagels, "Visions, Appearances, and Apostolic Authority," 416.

apostle shall be replaced, Acts underscores that apostleship is limited to a certain number of recipients—specifically twelve—within this first generation.

The author of Luke–Acts applies another stringent requirement by limiting the time in which a candidate for apostlehood must have received a resurrection appearance to only the ἡμερῶν τεσσεράκοντα ("forty days") after the resurrection (Acts 1:3). Luke's limitation to the symbolic "forty days" further undergirds the institution of this special small group as witnesses to the resurrection.[24] Because these requirements restrict later church leaders from claiming apostolic status for themselves, such a limitation of the qualifying appearances of Christ had momentous consequences.[25] As Elaine Pagels points out, "the question revolves around whether direct access to Christ is available by means of special revelation 'through visions long after the resurrection' and whether such revelations are granted only to certain persons and not to others."[26] Indeed, according to the Lukan requirements, even Paul himself does not qualify for apostleship. Of the twenty-eight occurrences of the word ἀπόστολος in Acts, in fact, only two instances occurring in one particular passage refer to Paul, and in both cases the plural form is used, because Paul is named in conjunction with another ἀπόστολος, Barnabas (14:4, 14). This pair of exceptions, contrary to the standard usage of Luke–Acts, employs the term "apostle" in a different, broader sense to refer to persons sent on a mission (see Acts 13:2–3), not in the sense of the "twelve."[27] The exceptional usage may well reflect the incorporation of earlier source material into Acts.[28]

[24]Philippe H. Menoud, "Pendant quarante jours," in *Jésus-Christ et la Foi: Recherches néotestamentaires* (Bibliothèque théologique; Neuchâtel/Paris: Delachaux et Niestlé, 1975), 110–18.

[25]Karl Holl, "Der Kirchenbegriff des Paulus in seinem Verhältnis zu dem der Urgemeinde," in SBAW (Berlin: Verlag der Akademie der Wissenschaften, 1921), 920–47; and repr. in *Der Osten*, vol. 2 of *Gesammelte Aufsätze zur Kirchengeschichte* (Tübingen: Mohr [Siebeck], 1928), 44–67, esp. 50–51; repr. Darmstadt: Wissenschaftliche Buchgesellschaft, 1964), 44–67.

[26]Pagels, "Visions, Appearances, and Apostolic Authority," 424.

[27]Betz, "Apostle," *ABD* 1:310.

[28]Ernst Haenchen, *The Acts of the Apostles: A Commentary* (trans. Bernard Noble and Gerald Shinn; Philadelphia: Westminster, 1971), 420. Haenchen argues that Luke appropriated the expression in vs. 4 from vs. 14. Loisy argues otherwise; see Alfred Loisy, *Les Actes des Apôtres* (Paris: Rieder, 1925), 546.

Finally, the definition of "apostle" in Acts imposes a third restriction on the term that is not present in Pauline texts: the author makes the requirement for being an apostle gender-exclusive. In the definition in Acts 1:21, the author uses the word ἀνδρές ("men") instead of ἄνθρωποι ("people"). Such a restriction of the gender of apostles does not agree with Paul's concept of apostleship and leadership.[29] As noted above, in Romans Paul refers to both Andronicus and Junia as "outstanding among the apostles" (ἐπίσημοι ἐν τοῖς ἀποστόλοις)[30] and describes them as "my compatriots and fellow prisoners who became Christians before me."[31]

Thus by identifying the "twelve" as *the* "apostles," the author of Luke–Acts denies this title to many, including the female leaders of early Christianity.[32] Luke draws a narrower, more exclusive circle that includes neither Paul, nor James, the brother of Jesus (who was to rise to the head of the Jerusalem church),[33] nor any female apostles: Mary

---

[29]Lietzmann, *An die Korinther*, 41. Compare 2 Cor 8:23; 11:5, 13; 12:11,12.

[30]For further details for understanding the term ἀπόστολος, see Marie-Joseph Lagrange, *Saint Paul: Épître aux Romains* (EBib; Paris: Gabalda, 1931), 365–66. Already in the first decades of the last century he went against the grain of scholarly consensus at the time to argue that it was more prudent to interpret the Greek word as Junia, a female name, rather than Junias, an unattested male one. See also Brooten, " 'Junia . . . Outstanding among the Apostles,' " 142.

[31]τοὺς συγγενεῖς μου καὶ συναιχμαλώτους μου . . . οἳ καὶ πρὸ ἐμοῦ γέγοναν ἐν Χριστῷ (Rom 16:7).

[32]Schüssler Fiorenza, *In Memory of Her*, 334.

[33]Some scholars, such as Lietzmann (*An die Korinther*, 41), believe that the brothers of Jesus are included in the circle of the apostles. It may be that Paul believed James to be an apostle, but unfortunately Gal 1:19 is somewhat ambiguous. Paul says: εἰ μὴ Ἰάκωβον τὸν ἀδελφὸν τοῦ κυρίου. The expression εἰ μή can be interpreted in two different ways that either include James in the group of apostles or not: "I saw none of the other apostles—but I did see James, the Lord's brother" or "I saw none of the other apostles—only James, the Lord's brother." For more see John P. Meier, "The Circle of the Twelve: Did it Exist during Jesus' Public Ministry," *JBL* 116 (1997): 640; or Maximilian Zerwick, *Graecitas Biblica* (Engl. ed. adapted from 4th Latin ed.; Rome: Biblical Institute Press, 1963), 158. In determining the meaning of εἰ μή scholars usually refer to Matt 12:4 "the food was not for David, nor his companions, but only for the 'priest.' " In this case it is possible for εἰ μή to have an adversative meaning, but one must prove that it has such a meaning in Gal 1:19, because in Greek the more common meaning is one of exception within the same category. See, for example, 1 Cor 8:4: "nobody is god except the one God." This stated, then, nothing precludes us from believing that James was an apostle. In this case the meaning of an exception within the same category is the most probable one, that Paul believed James to be an apostle. See Betz, *Galatians*, 78.

Magdalene, the other women at the tomb, or Junia.[34] As a result, in the struggle for authority in the first and second century of Christianity, the later additional Lukan requirements add a certain rigidity and exclusivity not present in Paul.[35]

Significantly, despite the crucial differences concerning the qualifications for an ἀπόστολος in Acts, at least one element of the definition remains consistent with Paul's: the requirement that the candidate be a witness to the resurrection. Even though the author of Luke circumscribes who may be an ἀπόστολος in at least three significant ways, this requirement still applies: the group was looking for "a witness with us to this resurrection."[36] The verses that follow the Lukan definition in Acts further reinforce this connection between apostleship and the status of witness to the resurrection. When the group in Acts chooses a witness to the resurrection to replace Judas, it is for an expressly stated purpose: "to take over this apostolic ministry."[37]

As a work of persuasive literature, Luke–Acts achieves a particular objective by concentrating apostolic authority into the hands of only certain followers of Jesus, called the "twelve." The author does so by molding this group of the "twelve" into the group known as the "apostles" and presenting them as the link or bridge between Jesus and the birth of the church. The very first verses of the Lukan text reveal this objective through Luke's use of the bond between "the first eye-witnesses" and the earthly Jesus as a guarantee of the validity of the gospel (Luke 1:1–4).[38] With this passage the author of Luke–Acts not only presents the purpose

---

[34]See, for example, 1 Cor 15:7 in which the phrase "all the apostles" indicates a wider circle. Conzelmann summarizes some of the controversies among scholars (Conzelmann, *1 Corinthians*, 153). For example, Eduard Lohse, "Ursprung und Prägung des christlichen Apostolates," *TZ* 9 (1953): 259–75, esp. 267, understands apostles as an open term designating missionaries in general, while Klein (*Zwölf Apostel*, 56) argues that it is a term describing a restricted group. Lietzmann argues that the term "all the apostles" is a larger group than the "twelve," but it is nevertheless still a restricted group, limited to the personal disciples of Jesus. See Lietzmann, *An die Korinther*, 79.

[35]Kirk, "Apostleship Since Rengstorf," 252.

[36]μάρτυρα τῆς ἀναστάσεως αὐτοῦ σὺν ἡμῖν (Acts 1:22).

[37]λαβεῖν τὸν τόπον τῆς διακονίας ταύτης καὶ ἀποστολῆς (Acts 1:25).

[38]"Many have undertaken to draw up an account of the things that have been fulfilled among us, just as they were handed down to us by those who from the first were eyewitnesses and servants of the word . . . so that you may know the certainty of the things you have been taught" (Luke 1:1–2, 4).

of the text—to give an orderly account of the events of Jesus' life—but also identifies the reliable sources of this account as those who have been "eyewitnesses" from the beginning—those, that is, who constitute Jesus' special group of "twelve." In Luke–Acts this close connection between Jesus and the "twelve" qualifies them as the only proper and trustworthy witnesses of the resurrection and also insures that it is precisely their version of the whole life and teachings of Jesus that is the correct one.[39] Luke thus forges a correlation between the apostolicity of the "twelve" and the content of their message as proper preaching material.[40] Such a role by his witnesses is essential for Luke's own claim to be the transmitter of the true message.

A study of Luke's presentation of the "twelve" in Luke 6:12–13 as compared to the parallels in Mark 3:14 and Matt 10:1–5 also indicates Luke's rhetorical agenda by highlighting the additional emphasis that Luke places on this select group.[41] Five of the six occurrences of ἀπόστολος in Luke "apply clearly and unequivocally to the Twelve."[42] Only in Luke does Jesus specifically choose the "twelve" from a larger group of followers (a larger group not present in Mark and Matthew).[43] Luke attributes to them a special status as a select holy group that will act as witnesses until the end.[44] Whereas in Mark the calling of the "twelve" is

[39]Klein, *Zwölf Apostel,* 206–7.

[40]Ibid., 208.

[41]Karl Heinrich, "δώδεκα," *TDNT* 2:321–28; Lake, "The Twelve and the Apostles," 47; Ernest Best, "Mark's Use of the Twelve," *ZNW* 69 (1978): 11–35; Raymond E. Brown, "The Twelve and the Apostolate," *NJBC,* 1377–81 (§§135–57); Béda Rigaux, "Die Zwölf in Geschichte und Kerygma," in *Der historische Jesus und der kerygmatische Christus* (ed. Helmut Ristow and Karl Matthiae; Berlin: Evangelische Verlagsanstalt, 1962), 168–86; Karl Kertelge, "Die Funktion der 'Zwölf' im Markusevangelium," *TTZ* 78 (1969): 193–206; Raymond F. Collins, "Twelve, The," *ABD* 6:670–71; Klein, *Zwölf Apostel,* 203–4; Johannes Munck, "Paul, the Apostles, and the Twelve," *ST* 3 (1950): 96–110.

[42]Luke 6:13, 9:10; 17:5; 22:14; 24:10. Nicholas Koulomzine, "Peter's Place in the Primitive Church," in *The Primacy of Peter: Essays in Ecclesiology and the Early Church* (ed. John Meyendorff; Crestwood, N.Y.: St. Vladimir's Seminary Press, 1992), 24.

[43]Bovon, *Lukas,* 1:281. Only Luke considers it necessary to explain in his gospel that Christ himself bestowed the title ἀπόστολος on the "twelve." Koulomzine ("Peter's Place in the Primitive Church," 25) claims that "Matthew and Mark forgot to put this in."

[44]A close comparison with Mark reveals additional differences. For example, although the postresurrection symbolism of a sacred mountain occur in both Mark and Luke, Luke emphasizes the symbolism to a greater degree.

quite functional—they are chosen for a mission—Luke diminishes this connection between their calling and a particular mission and gives them instead a more symbolic presence.[45]

The author of Luke–Acts thus effectively portrays the "twelve apostles" as the initial leaders of the Jerusalem Church—in which "twelve" led by Peter have precedence over all the other leaders, including Paul (see Acts 4:35–37; 5:2, 27–32; 6:6; 8:1, 14, 18; 9:27; 11:1; 15:1–6, 22–23; 16:4).[46] Luke's identification of the "twelve" with "the apostles" is endowed with even more meaning by the portrayal of the special ministry of the "twelve" in the early Jerusalem church.[47] This group of "twelve" appears at key moments in the text: at Pentecost (2:14)[48] and in the selection of the seven table-servers (6:2; in 6:6, the table-servers are then presented to "the apostles").[49] In light of these references, the "twelve" become ever more essential in the establishment of authority within a specific group of the first generation after Jesus.[50]

Once the author of Acts has established a link between Jesus and these "twelve" as the source of the true traditions, the text then turns to Paul and predictably the term ἀπόστολος rarely appears.[51] As a result, the Lukan presentation of the group of apostles differentiates clearly between them

---

[45]Jacques Dupont, "Le nom d'apôtres: a-t-il été donné aux Douze par Jésus?" *OrSyr* 1 (1956): 267–90; repr. *Études sur les Évangiles Synoptiques* (2 vols.; Leuven: Leuven University Press, 1985), 976–1018. On Luke's stricter definition, see also Ernst Haenchen, *Apostelgeschichte* (Göttingen: Vandenhoeck, 1959), 126.

[46]Betz, "Apostle," *ABD* 1:310.

[47]Fitzmyer, *Luke,* 1:254.

[48]"Then Peter stood up with the Eleven, raised his voice, and addressed the crowd" (Acts 2:14).

[49]"So the Twelve (δώδεκα) gathered all the disciples together" (Acts 6:2). "They presented these men to the apostles" (Acts 6:6). See Fitzmyer, *Luke,* 1:253.

[50]Klein argues against those who would say that Acts 1:21, 10:39, and 13:31 are all pre-Lukan. Certain tendencies appear to be clearly attributable to the author of Acts when one discerns them both in Acts and in Luke: "daβ die Verankerung des Apostolats im Frühstadium der historia Jesu eine lukanische Spezialität ist" (Klein, *Zwölf Apostel,* 204).

[51]Fitzmyer (*Luke,* 1:255) points out that after the "Council" of Jerusalem, Luke does not refer to the "apostles" in the Jerusalem church. Their last appearance is in Acts 16:4, where Paul, Silas, and Timothy announced to the churches in Asia Minor the decisions reached by "the apostles and elders in Jerusalem." No mention of apostles is made after that point. When Paul returns to Jerusalem at the end of the third mission he goes up to greet James and "all the elders" (21:18).

and Paul, whom the author of Luke portrays in a role subordinate to those at the Jerusalem church.[52] In Luke's presentation Paul must still come to Jerusalem to secure final approval of his plans or to defend his actions. Although the Lukan construction of leadership nevertheless honors Paul in portraying both the "twelve" and Paul over all the rest of the church leaders, it also makes clear that Paul's arrival on the apostolic scene is a belated one. He is not an eyewitness of Jesus' life, and although he is a prominent spokesperson for the tradition as a whole, he does not precisely fit Luke's definition of apostle.[53]

Priority and Authoritative Implications

The various understandings of the word ἀπόστολος evolved dramatically in the next decades, until eventually, in the century following the first generation of apostles, most early Christians no longer even dared to apply the title "apostle" to their church leaders, but instead limited their terminology to the adjective "apostolic."[54] Rather than describing themselves as apostles: "they are simply the successors, at most, the representatives of the apostles. . . ."[55] Today even the Roman Catholic pope himself does not bear the title of "apostle" but sits in an apostolic chair and continues a line of apostolic succession. Thus aspects of apostolic succession, especially Peter's, continue to make an impact even today.[56]

[52]Klein, *Zwölf Apostel*, 211.

[53]Ibid. See also Jacques Dupont, "Les ministères de l'Église naissante d'après les Actes des Apôtres," in *Nouvelles Études sur les Actes des apôtres* (LD 118; Paris: Cerf, 1984), 133–185. Dupont further examines the way that Luke constructs the twelve apostles and their authority.

[54]Ehrhardt, *Apostolic Ministry*, 5. This development is evident even in the Christian creed that refers to the "apostolic" church.

[55]Campenhausen, *Ecclesiastical Authority and Spiritual Power*, 22; Pagels, "Visions, Appearances, and Apostolic Authority," 416.

[56]For more information on apostolic succession, see Wolfgang Bienert, "Successio apostolica," *LTK* 9 (Freiburg: Herder, 2000), col. 1080–1083; and Karl Baus, "Wesen und Funktion der apostolischen Sukzession in der Sicht des heiligen Augustinus," in *Ekklesia: Festschrift für Bischof Matthias Wehr* (ed. Theologischen Fakultät Trier; Trierer Theologische Studien 15; Trier: Paulinus Verlag, 1962), 137–48. Also, Einar Molland ("Le développement de l'idée de succession apostolique," *RHPR* 34 [1954]: 1–29) provides a nice summary of the term and defines three primary concepts of succession. The Roman Catholic view includes the succession of the bishop with historical and juridical succession and the primacy of both Rome and the bishop. The Lutheran (or Protestant)

Because the term "apostle" is used so sparingly including the reluctance to apply it to even the highest church leaders, it is all the more important to discern who qualified in the first century. With time the close link between the terms "twelve" and "apostles" has gained such prominence even in contemporary settings that "a present-day Christian, when the apostles are mentioned, thinks first and foremost of the 'twelve apostles.' "[57] Thanks to the work of many New Testament scholars, including the foundational efforts of J. B. Lightfoot, this does not have to be the case. Lightfoot was one of the first to point out this Lukan construction and thus separate the "twelve" from the group called the "apostles."[58] In his wake, numerous critical studies have emerged supporting his insights, including those of Hans Conzelmann and Günter Klein who maintain that it is difficult—even impossible—to trace the origins of the "twelve apostles" within Jesus' ministry.[59] Despite this scholarly consensus, there are still those who,

---

view includes the witness of faith existing in every generation, which is not necessarily, however, by means of an ontological succession with an unbroken historical link every time. This view honors the apostolic heritage but believes that transmission is not necessarily without interruption. The third view, represented by the Anglicans, develops a theory of the continuation of ordination from the apostles—a view which from Molland's point of view was not present in antiquity, but provides an Anglican solution to the issue of having a bishop. The Lutheran view is present in antiquity with Clement and Origen. The succession of witnesses is one of faith, but it is not connected with ministry and not with an absolute historical continuity. The Roman Catholic view is present in Hegesippus, Irenaeus, and Tertullian but with two major differences from the modern Catholic view: Rome and Peter are not the absolute center or leader, but there does exist an interest in the lists of bishops and their connections to ministry. Originally, the bishop lists were not tightly connected to Matt 16:16 and the succession of Peter. Thus they were also not so closely connected to the transmission of power.

[57]Scholars such as Bruce Chilton and Jacob Neusner in their latest book on authority in the early Christian speak of "the emergence of the apostolate as a consequence of Jesus' ministry" without sufficiently establishing the historical connection of the apostolate to Jesus. See Bruce Chilton and Jacob Neusner, *Types of Authority in Formative Christianity and Judaism* (London and New York: Routledge, 1999), 56.

[58]John B. Lightfoot, *The Epistle of St. Paul to the Galatians* (10th ed.; Grand Rapids, Mich.: Zondervan, 1957), 92–100.

[59]Klein (*Die Zwölf Apostel*) traces the location and origin of the concept of the "twelve apostles." This historical question has significant theological implications if it places the "twelve apostles" chronologically before the foundation of the church. There is much to commend Klein's work. Schmithals points out one of the weaknesses in his argument by saying that "the later emergences of the twelve-apostles idea cannot consistently be traced back to Luke" (Schmithals, *Office,* 272). For those who point out the reference to the "twelve" in Matt 19:28, Klein explains that this reference cannot be traced back

nevertheless, attempt to establish the "twelve apostles" as a historical entity dating back to Jesus himself.[60] Such a claim is difficult to maintain, however, especially since Paul's authoritative list of leaders and witnesses in 1 Corinthians seems to represent the "twelve" and the "apostles" as two distinct groups, listing the "twelve" in 1 Cor 15:5 separately from the "apostles" in 1 Cor 15:7.[61] Whether or not this distinctive group existed in Jesus' lifetime is not, however, so much the issue here as is its effect on apostolic authority. As Conzelmann states, it is precisely the restriction of apostleship to the "twelve" that is significant for Luke.[62] Rengstorf likewise asserts that only Luke links the "twelve" closely with the "apostles."[63] With time this narrower Lukan definition took precedence in some churches—especially those that do not ordain women.

Although the reference to the resurrection appearance to Simon (Peter) alone in Luke has no parallel in the other canonical gospels, it does appear in the tradition Paul quotes in 1 Cor 15:5, where Mary's name does not appear at all. Because Paul transmits this list, and it must therefore be early, some scholars claim primacy for the individual resurrection appearance to Peter. The location of Peter's name at the head of Paul's list of epiphany recipients, however, does not necessarily mean that narratives about Peter chronologically precede the resurrection traditions involving Mary Magdalene in the competition for primacy of apostolic

---

to Jesus because the vocabulary in this text, including the term παλιγγενεσία ("new birth"), stems from later church issues and does not ring authentic to the concerns of the historical Jesus.

[60] For example, Rengstorf, "ἀπόστολος," 429. For a summary of the arguments, see Meier, "The Circle of the Twelve," 635–72. "It may well be that these narratives have been influenced by the concept of apostleship, which has been retrojected onto the Twelve." (Campenhausen, *Ecclesiastical Authority and Spiritual Power*, 15).

[61] If Jesus himself chose the "twelve," he likely intended them as representatives of the twelve tribes, not "apostles" at all.

[62] Hans Conzelmann, *The Theology of St Luke* (trans. Geoffrey Buswell; London: Faber and Faber, 1960), 216 n. 1.

[63] Against this argument for the exclusively Lukan construct of the twelve apostles, scholars have mentioned Matt 10:2 and Rev 21:14; neither of these references proves an early existence of the phrase, however, during the lifetime of Jesus. Nor does the reference in Matt 10:2 imply an exclusive equation of the "the twelve" and "the apostles" as it does in Luke. The use of the terms "apostles" and "disciples" in Matthew and Mark supports this. "When commissioned, the disciples of Matt 10:1 become the apostles of 10:2 (cf. Mark 6:30)," Rengstorf explains; "But on their return they become disciples again throughout the rest of these Gospels" (Rengstorf, "ἀπόστολος," 1:427).

witness. It only indicates that Paul received the particular tradition that favored Peter, and that the diverging, competing traditions concerning Peter and Mary Magdalene may have been early. The priority of Peter in Paul's list is likely attributable to the prominence of this specific tradition in Jerusalem, where Peter and James served as "pillars" and where Paul received his initial indoctrination into the early Christian church (see Gal. 1:18, in which Paul indicates that he visited with Peter [ἰστορῆσαι Κηφᾶν][64] and Gal. 1:19 that he met also with James, the Lord's brother). Paul has sometimes been criticized for not including Mary Magdalene in this list, but in Jerusalem, where Peter's role was quite significant, we can only guess what resurrection narratives Paul received. Significantly, all three gospel narratives that give prominence to Mary Magdalene direct the disciples to meet Jesus in Galilee, not Jerusalem as the Gospel of Luke mandates. There appears to be a geographic component to this apostolic competition.[65]

On the basis of Peter's priority in the list of 1 Corinthians, some scholars claim that the archaic nature of Luke 24:33–34 means that the Emmaus account in Luke provides supporting evidence for the primacy of the appearance of Jesus to Peter over the priority of the appearance to Mary Magdalene. However, the Emmaus account fails to support the appearance to Peter as the most archaic resurrection tradition for a number of reasons.[66] First, embedded within the Emmaus story are traces of the tradition of the women's visit to the tomb (Luke 24:22–23) as well as an angelophany to them (Luke 24:24). "This too indicates the very probable fact that in the earliest tradition a visit to the tomb by Mary Magdalene and the other women was well known and thus was combined with the

---

[64]The verb ἰστορέω that describes Paul's encounter with Peter is much debated. According to Liddell and Scott ἰστορέω means to inquire about a person or to visit a person for the purpose of inquiry (Liddell and Scott, s.v. "ἰστορέω"). George D. Kilpatrick, "Galatians 1,18, ἰστορῆσαι Κηφᾶν," in *NT Essays: Studies in Memory of T. W. Manson* (Manchester University, 1959), 144–49, gives a history of interpretation of this passage. The oldest Patristic interpretation of the word is "to see." He points out that Chrysostom, in his homily to the Galatians, said that Paul did more than just to "see" Peter, but denies that Paul actually acquired learning from Peter—according to Chrysostom, he only paid his respects.

[65]See discussion of the geographic component in O'Collins and Kendall, "Mary Magdalene as Major Witness to Jesus' Resurrection," 640 n. 35. See response by Schüssler Fiorenza, *Jesus: Miriam's Child*, 124.

[66]Jeremias, *Neutestamentliche Theologie*, 291.

actual Easter story and angelophany."[67] Perhaps by the time Luke writes, the tradition of Mary's visit to the tomb was so widely known that it needed to be included to some degree in an account of the resurrection, even if it was given a decidedly Petrine retelling.

According to Jeremias the resurrection appearance to Mary Magdalene is the most archaic one for two reasons: No one would invent a story of an appearance to a woman in this culture because women's role as witnesses may have had a marginalizing effect. Second, the negative reaction of the disciples portrayed in Luke 24:10–11 and 23—that no one really believes them—also adds to the probability of the priority of Mary's tradition because people are not likely to have created this tradition.[68]

Exclusionary traditions such as the claim to authority for the "twelve" apostles seek to suppress the inclusionary tradition's claim that gives the mandate to women to preach or proclaim the good news. Exclusionary traditions tend to discount the role of women as witnesses receiving the resurrection announcement, especially Mary Magdalene.[69] Christ then especially sends her to proclaim what is the standard apostolic announcement of the resurrection: "I have seen the Lord."[70] Brown describes the situation thus, "True, this is not a mission to the whole world; but Mary Magdalene comes *close* to meeting the basic Pauline requirements of an apostle."[71] Then he acknowledges that "it is she, not Peter, who is the first to see the risen Jesus."[72] Brown's analysis of the discrepancies in the reports and the primacy of Mary Magdalene are well done, but he stops short by declaring Mary Magdalene "close" to meeting the requirements of an apostle. This chapter has shown, however, if one takes into account the majority of the resurrection accounts, Mary Magdalene is certainly due apostolic authority.

This examination has shown, however, that other definitions existed in the first stages of Christianity, so that early church leaders besides the

---

[67]Atwood, *Mary Magdalene in the New Testament Gospels and Early Tradition*, 126.

[68]Jeremias, *Neutestamentliche Theologie*, 291.

[69]Hengel ("Maria Magdalena und die Frauen als Zeugen," 256) states "deren einzigartige Stellung dadurch begründet ist, daß sie der Auferstandene als erste seiner Erscheinung gewürdigt hat."

[69]Brown, *Community of the Beloved Disciple*, 189.

[70]Ibid.

[71]Ibid. (italics mine).

[72]Ibid.

"twelve" could and did qualify for the title of "apostle." One can therefore not use the nomenclature of the "twelve apostles," a later development within early Christianity, to deny apostolic status to either Paul or Mary Magdalene.

CHAPTER NINE

Conclusion:
Recovering Lost Apostolic Traditions

This study began by noting that some early Christians respected Mary Magdalene so much that they even bestowed upon her the title of "apostle of the apostles," and we return now to that title. Although its origins are not entirely clear, this tradition appears in the writings of Hippolytus, bishop and martyr of Rome (d. 235/6).[1] He describes this honorific title as one that the "risen Christ himself gave her, that being the *apostola apostolorum*" ("apostle of the apostles").[2] Legends about Mary Magdalene's career after the resurrection flourished in later centuries.[3]

---

[1] Hippolytus wrote the earliest commentary on *The Song of Songs*. See also Katherine Ludwig Jansen, "Maria Magdalena: *Apostolorum Apostola*," in *Women Preachers and Prophets through Two Millennia of Christianity* (ed. Beverly Mayne Kienzle and Pamela J. Walker; Berkeley and Los Angeles: University of California Press, 1998), 80; and Atwood, *Mary Magdalene*, 218.

[2] See Nürnberg, "Apostolae Apostolorum," 228–42. Haskins (*Mary Magdalen*, 58–97) devotes the entire third chapter of her book to an exploration of this title. Further documentation for Mary's title of "*apostola apostolorum*" can be found in Brown, *Community of the Beloved Disciple*, 190 n. 336. The term is often translated "apostle to the apostles" though, technically, "apostle of the apostles" is more correct. Kienzle explains that the "of" designates first an objective genitive (the one who brings the news of the Resurrection to the apostles), but also with a taste of "foremost" because she gets the word first. The preposition "of" more adequately conveys both meanings. For an excellent discussion of the portrayals of Peter and Mary Magdalene through the centuries, see Beverly Mayne Kienzle, "Penitents and Preachers: The Figure of Saint Peter and His Relationship to Saint Mary Magdalene," in *La figura di san Pietro nelle fonti del medioevo: Atti del convegno tenutosi in occasione dello Studiorum universitatum docentium congressus (Viterbo e Roma 5–8 settembre 2000)* (ed. Loredana Lazzari and Anna Maria Valente Bacci; Textes et études du moyen âge 17; Louvain-la-Neuve: F.I.D.E.M., 2001), 248–72.

[3] Paul-Marie Guillaume, "Marie-Madeleine," in *Dictionnaire de Spiritualité, Ascétique et Mystique: Doctrine et Histoire* (16 vols.; Paris: Beauchesne, 1937–94), 10:559–75. See also

She is venerated as a saint in the Roman Catholic Church, the Eastern Orthodox Church, and some Protestant circles. She is also depicted as a reformed prostitute and penitential sinner.[4] Mary Magdalene has thus been venerated and denigrated throughout the ages. Yet, despite numerous challenges to her status in the first century of the Christian church and since, the tradition honoring Mary Magdalene as the first resurrection witness has remained unshaken over time.

Because a resurrection appearance was so integral to establishing a figure's apostolic authority, indeed serving as a hallmark of such authority in early Christian texts, this discussion asks why, in spite of her meeting eligibility for apostolicity, Mary Magdalene's status nevertheless remains ambiguous or unacknowledged in many Christian churches even today. There are those who, despite the strong accolades for Mary Magdalene in some parts of Christendom, do not remember her as an apostle, much less an "apostle of the apostles." Part of the reason for such a broad spectrum of esteem for her emerges from the way at least two significantly different definitions for apostleship appear in the variety of texts that became the New Testament. This range of opinions has roots also in the variety of canonical and noncanonical texts that recount the first appearance of the risen Christ to his followers: in some texts Mary Magdalene is a/the privileged recipient of that first appearance, while in other texts it is Peter who receives that privilege. These two discrepancies are related because the Pauline definition would/could include Mary, while the Lukan definition would certainly exclude her as she is 1) a woman and 2) superfluous to the "twelve." Thus in no text do both Mary Magdalene and Peter enjoy the same status as witnesses. Indeed, this study has shown that as one of these two figures gains prominence, the status of the other often declines.

Implicit Challenges to Apostolic Authority

This study begins with the assertion that variations among the names of resurrection witnesses are particularly useful in revealing the politics and polemics that color early Christian literature, especially as the

---

King, "Prophetic Power and Women's Authority," 357–66. For more on Mary Magdalene in the late medieval religious culture, see Jansen, *The Making of the Magdalen.* There is even legendary material that describes her making a missionary journey to France.

    [4]The intersection of culture, art, and history are portrayed, for example, in Haskins, *Mary Magdalen* and Maisch, *Mary Magdalene.*

church debated the role of women. A review of these variations in the literary traditions allows us to identify specific strategies that authors and translators employed.

Diminishing Mary's Status as a Witness

We have seen the ways in which authors and redactors both subtly and overtly sculpted the primary figures in their texts to reflect their views on gender roles and inclusivity. Thus the tradition, reflected in three canonical gospels, that the risen Jesus appeared first to Mary Magdalene, is directly contradicted by another tradition that appears in a few other texts: the risen Jesus first appeared to Peter. The Markan and Matthean versions of the sepulchre scenes both portray epiphanies to Mary Magdalene, along with other women, and, even more importantly, both portray Mary Magdalene as receiving the mandate to go and spread the good news to others.[5] As Bovon states, "Mary Magdalene had an important role to play at the dawn of Christianity, particularly on Easter Day and during the early stages of the Church."[6] Particularly crucial to this role is the inestimable significance of commissioning scenes.

The competing portrayal of Peter as the first resurrection witness is one of the greatest challenges to Mary Magdalene's position as an apostle. As Raymond Brown points out—a "key to Peter's importance in the apostolate was the tradition that he was the first to see the risen Jesus."[7] This prominence of Peter is best represented by the Gospel of Luke, a text that reverses the portrayal of apostolic authority represented by the other three canonical gospels in a twofold way: by granting an individual resurrection appearance to Peter and not reporting any type of commission to Mary Magdalene. Because it is possible to isolate tendencies in Luke through comparison to the parallel traditions preserved in Matthew and Mark, the ways in which the author of Luke has shaped narrative materials are readily evident. In Luke, for example, the author reduces or eliminates traditions concerning Peter that could be interpreted as negative. Thus the Lukan author is silent on points such as Peter's rebuke of Jesus, Jesus' consequent reference to Peter as "Satan," Peter's cursing in the courtyard, and Peter's misunderstandings of Jesus' mission or intentions. Even more significant than these omissions, however, are the presence in Luke of pro-

---

[5]For more discussion, see Atwood, *Mary Magdalene*, 215.
[6]Bovon, "Mary Magdalene's Paschal Privilege," 147.
[7]Brown, *Community of the Beloved Disciple*, 189.

Petrine traditions that do not appear in the other canonical gospels, such as a commissioning for Peter (Luke 22:32), and especially the individual resurrection appearance to Simon (Peter) in Luke 24:33–34.

It is surely not coincidental that Luke is exceptional among the canonical gospels not only in its portrayal of Peter, but so, too, in its portrayal of Mary Magdalene. Only Luke, for example, introduces her into the gospel as a person possessed by seven demons who, therefore, required Jesus' healing. Only Luke minimizes the role of Mary Magdalene and the other women at the cross by importing other "acquaintances" into the crucifixion scene, acquaintances whose mention precedes that of the women. And only Luke fails to provide the names of the women in the scene at the cross. In fact, Luke refers to this group of women four times in the passion narrative, but names them only once, at the very point in the narrative where the male disciples evaluate the witness of these women as "foolish, idle talk."[8] But again, most importantly, the Gospel of Luke makes no reference to Jesus' resurrection appearance to Mary Magdalene or to her commissioning by either an angel or Jesus. The most significant feature of Luke's version of the resurrection narrative is a portrayal of Mary Magdalene that no longer reflects any primacy in her apostolic witness. This feature accords well with the overall program of the author: an emphasis on Peter that seems to have a corresponding inverse effect upon the portrayal of the status of Mary Magdalene.

The *Gospel of Peter,* a text that similarly reflects this reshaping, also stresses Peter's authority and grants him prominence over Mary Magdalene. The *Gospel of Peter* focuses on Peter by portraying him witnessing and narrating the entire resurrection event; moreover, like that of Luke, this gospel portrays neither a resurrection appearance to Mary Magdalene nor her commissioning. Narrative elements unique to the *Gospel of Peter* include the description of guards at the tomb who, in conjunction with Peter, witness the resurrection, with the result that Mary Magdalene and the other women are but secondary witnesses, in time as well as in status: their presence in the narrative is effectively rendered superfluous. The rhetorical result of these subtle changes of the sequence of events and the lack of commissionings in both the Gospel of Luke and the *Gospel of*

---

[8]John's gospel, on the other hand, does name these women and portrays them in even closer proximity to the cross (within speaking distance) than do other accounts (John 19:25–27).

Peter removes any possibility that women could use these accounts of the resurrection to claim that they, too, had a mandate to preach and to teach. Significantly, this diminishment of the women's role is compensated by the amplified role that Peter plays in both of these two texts; to paraphrase the words of John the Baptist (John 3:30), "She must decrease, while he must increase."

On the other hand, the Gospel of John shows signs of shaping the resurrection narrative in the opposite direction. In the rivalry for apostolic authority between Mary Magdalene and Peter, this gospel supports the status of Mary Magdalene by featuring her prominently in its resurrection appearance narrative and portraying her character in dialogue with Jesus. Further evidence that the author of John may have shaped an existing tradition lies in the words that Mary speaks to the other disciples. John's version presents Mary Magdalene initially alone at the tomb, but when she speaks to the others, she uses the plural pronoun "we," clearly a remnant of the tradition that the other women had accompanied her. Thus John's narrative places a special focus on Mary Magdalene, as Jesus appears to and converses with her alone and imparts to her alone the commission to spread the news.

As Mary's prominence in John increases, so Peter's status decreases, and I submit that the correlation is not merely coincidental. As explicated in chapter 3, the Gospel of John seems to diminish the status of Peter by indicating that he became one of Jesus' followers through his brother, Andrew, who discovered Jesus first and brought Peter to him. Moreover, in John's gospel, Peter is not the first disciple called, he never appears in a select group, his confession is less stellar than Martha's, he voices his misunderstanding of the nature of Jesus' ministry at the footwashing, and at the Last Supper he communicates with Jesus through an intermediary, the Beloved Disciple. Finally, at the end of this gospel, Peter receives no individual resurrection appearance from Jesus as he does in Luke. (It is only in chapter 21, viewed by many as an appendix, that Peter is represented as a leader of the group.) Although the Gospel of John apparently arose independently of Mark and Matthew, it supports the primacy of Mary Magdalene as the first apostolic witness of the resurrection. The contrasting evaluations by Luke and John of the apostolic status of Mary Magdalene and Peter are but two examples of authors attributing authority and credibility to one early Christian figure and withholding them from another.

Diminishing Mary's Presence as a Witness

The way that Luke portrays Mary Magdalene and Peter, in contrast to the other canonical gospels, preserves some of the earliest hints of implicit challenges to Mary's authority. The following examination identifies at least three other implicit, subtle strategies that have undermined Mary's status and diminished her role as a witness, role model, and apostle. The first of these strategies achieves a diminution of Mary Magdalene's qualifications for apostolic authority by replacing her with a substitute in certain narratives. One intriguing example of such narrative replacement occurs in the Coptic version of the *Acts of Philip*, which alters the earlier Greek version. In the Greek version, Mary is included among the apostles, and Jesus sends her alongside Philip to strengthen him on his journey. In the Coptic version, however, Mary is eliminated from the narrative, and it is Peter who accompanies Philip on his missionary journey.

Even more intriguing than this narrative replacement is a more subtle displacement of Mary Magdalene effected in certain resurrection narratives that depict Jesus first appearing in the garden not to Mary Magdalene but to Mary, his mother.[9] These narratives, preserved in later Greek, Coptic, and Syriac texts or fragments, present a resurrection appearance story strikingly similar to the account of Mary Magdalene at the sepulchre in John 20. They cannot be construed simply as alternative resurrection appearance narratives, because they reproduce a dialogue similar to that of Jesus with Mary Magdalene, in which he warns her not to touch him because he has not yet ascended. Scholars have sometimes assumed that this change in Mary's identity is merely the result of confusion or carelessness on the part of the authors of the later versions. The rhetorical result of these changes is significant, however, because the versions that feature Mary, Jesus' mother, grant to her the privilege of being the first resurrection witness.[10] And as one might suspect, in the versions that eliminate Mary Magdalene in favor of Mary, the mother of Jesus, the role of Peter is consistently elevated. In fact, in one such version, Peter is called "the great interpreter of Jesus" and even receives the title "Archbishop of the whole

[9]Ciro Giannelli, "Témoignages patristiques grecs en faveur d'une apparition du Christ ressuscité à la Vierge Marie," in *Mélanges Martin Jugie* = *REByz* 11 (1953): 106–19.

[10]Revillout, *Les Évangiles des douze apôtres et de Saint Barthélemy,* 169–70. See ch. 7, above.

world"; in another, Jesus addresses Simon as "the foundation of the holy Church" and "the fountainhead out of which my doctrine is drawn."

In general, texts that stress the authority of Peter tend to diminish the role of women, with one exception: Mary, mother of Jesus. Thus the pro-Petrine Gospel of Luke highlights her more than any other woman in the text and presents traditions of her that no other gospel preserves. A number of noncanonical texts also feature Mary, Jesus' mother, as a primary figure. In the *Questions of Bartholomew,* for example, she acknowledges the authority of Peter, calls him the chief and great pillar, and, more tellingly, declares her wish to defer to him because he is a male.[11] Scholars have suggested that the author of this scenario may be employing the mother of Jesus as a foil for Mary Magdalene and using her words to prescribe what women should be doing. Texts such as the Coptic *Acts of Philip* and the *Questions of Bartholomew* indicate that when an author or redactor or translator chooses to feature or eliminate a character appearing in the tradition, such choices are not arbitrary or random but significant clues to the politics of the text.

In order to explore further this clear correlation between pro-Petrine traditions and the reduction of women's leadership roles, this study examined another text that relies heavily upon the authority of Peter: the *Acts of Peter.* A comparison of this text with another from the same period, the *Acts of Paul,* with a particular eye to the interactions of both apostles with other characters in the texts, shows that the *Acts of Peter* accords women visibility and even narrative utility, but it definitely does not affirm them in leadership roles. Thus, while the *Acts of Paul* associates Paul's apostleship with strong female leadership, as seen in the figure of Thecla, by contrast the *Acts of Peter* forges no such association. In fact, in typical pro-Petrine texts, the diminished role of women does not appear as an issue of contention to be addressed in a work of persuasive narrative literature—indeed it is usually presented as a foregone conclusion. The *Acts of Peter* and the *Acts of Paul* symbolize two clashing representations of female religious leadership, and the differences in the worldviews that these two texts advocate are critical to an understanding of gender politics in the early church.

[11]*Questions of Bartholomew* in Elliott, *Apocryphal New Testament,* 652–72, esp. 658–61.

Diminishing Mary's Status as a Role Model

In the secular political arena, one of the more effective ways to under-mine opponents is by demeaning their reputations or besmirching their morals. The same is true in the politics of the church. Although over time Mary of Nazareth's portrayal in the church tended towards greater perfection and idealism, Mary Magdalene's reputation over the years became ever more tarnished in certain circles. Such tarnish resulted not from open slander but from the exegetical habit of conflating Mary Magdalene with the unnamed woman of Luke 7:36–50 who is portrayed as a sinner and often interpreted as a prostitute. This account of the woman who washed Jesus' feet is immediately followed by the passage in which Mary of Magdala is first introduced by name. As Thompson points out, "It seems unlikely that the same woman be named in the second of two passages that follow each other and remain unnamed in the first,"[12] but this unlikelihood did not deter exegetes.

Pope Gregory the Great (540–604), who most notably conflated the Marys, is one of the sources of this misidentification. He made the con-flation official when he preached a sermon in Rome that established for Western Christendom a new Magdalene, "indeed a figure who would have been almost entirely unrecognizable to her colleagues in the primitive church."[13] This sermon thus helped institutionalize the conflation and negatively affected her role as an apostle or leader.[14] Scholars have already discussed this portrayal of Mary Magdalene as a prostitute thoroughly and cogently elsewhere,[15] but I mention it here because it provides another

[12]Thompson, *Mary of Magdala*, 13–14.

[13]Jansen, "Maria Magdelena: *Apostolorum Apostola*," 60. This occurred on September 21, 591 C.E., in the Basilica of San Clemente.

[14]Those that did not maintain the differences may have been confused in part as a result of the harmonizations of the unction stories. See Thompson, *Mary of Magdala*, 3. "Some scholars speculate that the interpretation of Luke 8:2 as a reference to immoral behavior and hence to Mary of Magdala as prostitute, can be traced to the early fourth century of the Christian era. It is found in the writings of Ephraim the Syrian, 306–373 C.E." (Thompson, *Mary of Magdala*, 14). In a comparison of Luke 7:36–50 with Mark 14:3–11 and John 12: 1–8, Elisabeth Schüssler Fiorenza explains that "Luke especially stresses over and over again that Jesus called sinners to repentance so it was probably he who characterized the woman, as 'a woman of the city, a sinner,' that is a prostitute." See her book, *In Memory of Her*, 129; Schaberg, "How Mary Magdalene Became a Whore," 37.

[15]See Jane Schaberg, for example, who blames male bias for the practice of identifying Mary Magdalene as a whore, thus "fulfill[ing] the desire—or the need—to downgrade

essential factor in the diminishment of Mary Magdalene's apostolic authority. It is also a more insidious tool of diminishing her status because it operates within the confines of the established canon. As Rosemary Ruether explains, "The tradition of Mary Magdalene as a sinner was developed in orthodox [western] Christianity primarily to displace the apostolic authority claimed for women through her name."[16] Karen King argues, along with other scholars, for the abandonment of the identification of Mary Magdalene as the sinful woman because it is unscriptural.[17] For students of western Christianity, "Probably the most important working principle in the attempt to discern the role of Mary of Magdala in the first-century church is to reject the tradition that characterizes her as the sinful woman."[18]

This kind of confusion did not occur among certain early church figures, such as Origen, or Chrysostom, nor did it occur in the Eastern Orthodox Church, because it maintained the difference between Mary Magdalene and Mary of Bethany and the sinful woman.[19] Interestingly, Peter never gained the same ascendancy and primacy in the eastern half of early Christendom as he did in the western. Because the Eastern Orthodox Church never concurred with this conflation that Gregory and others helped instigate, its liturgies celebrate Mary of Magdala and Mary of Bethany with separate feasts.[20]

Diminishing Mary's Status as an Apostle

Another strategy for excluding Mary Magdalene from any authoritative position was to redefine who qualifies to be an apostle. For instance, Acts defines an apostle as someone who had been there from the begin-

---

the Magdalene, as well as the desire to attach to female sexuality the notions of evil, repentance and mercy." Schaberg, "How Mary Magdalene Became a Whore," 30–37, 51–52, esp. 37.

[16]Rosemary Ruether, *Women-Church* (San Francisco: Harper & Row, 1985), 286 n. 1.

[17]King, "Prophetic Power and Women's Authority," 357–66.

[18]Thompson, *Mary of Magdala*, 13–14. Thompson also argues the importance of not identifying Mary of Magdala with Mary of Bethany, making the argument in part on the basis of geography: Mary of Bethany was obviously a Judean while Mary of Magdala was just as clearly a Galilean.

[19]Schaberg, "How Mary Magdalene Became a Whore," 37.

[20]June 4 for Mary of Bethany and June 30, July 22, and August 4 for Mary Magdalene (Victor Saxer, "Les saintes Marie Madeleine et Marie de Béthanie dans la tradition liturgique et homilétique orientale," *RevScRel* 32 [1958]: 1–37; see also Jansen, "Maria Magdalena: *Apostolorum Apostola*, 82 n. 18).

ning and is one of twelve men (1:21, 22, and 26). The Lukan exclusivity represented by the "twelve" apostles is another strategy that effectively functions to diminish those independent of this select group. Other than the Petrine influence, it is not entirely clear why Luke–Acts presents this diminished role for women. Perhaps this author perceived a need to distance the status of the resurrection witness in the early churches from Mary Magdalene's testimony in response to some of the harsh critics of Christianity in the first centuries. The kinds of attacks that faced early Christians included the charge of Celsus "that belief in the risen Jesus was based on the testimony of a 'hysterical female.' "[21] Although Luke's motives remain a matter of conjecture, we can see that the "orderly presentation" that Luke professes includes a programmatic mitigation of some of the revolutionary content of the gospel; thus Luke's Romans are less culpable in Jesus' death, and Luke's women play roles that conform to patriarchal expectations.

The diminishment of Mary's role as a resurrection witness, however, did not end in the first centuries of Christianity, and may be traced in the interpretation of these narratives in this past century. Some New Testament scholars, especially form critics, differentiated between certain kinds of resurrection narratives, associating the "empty tomb narratives" with the female disciples, and the epiphanies of Jesus with the male disciples, especially the "twelve." Such a false dichotomy needs reexamination for several reasons. First, this dichotomy does not adequately account for the number of narratives that recount epiphanies to the women, as well as the number of narratives in which the male disciples encounter the empty tomb.[22] If one closely examines the "empty tomb" stories, for instance, Peter, alone or in the company of other male disciples, encounters an empty tomb almost as often as the women do (Luke 24:12, 24; John 20: 6–10). Furthermore, with respect to the women, the designation of "empty tomb" story less than adequately represents the dynamic of these stories, whereas a term such as "resurrection-announcement" story actually more accurately conveys the import of these traditions.[23]

---

[21]Origen, for example, had to argue to refute this charge. See *Contra Celsum* 2.55 (trans. Henry Chadwick; Cambridge: Cambridge University Press, 1953), 109–10. See also O'Collins and Kendall, "Mary Magdalene as Major Witness to Jesus' Resurrection," 631.

[22]See Atwood's dissertation, *Mary Magdalene in the New Testament Gospels and Early Tradition.*

[23]Alsup, *Post Resurrection Appearances*, 88 n. 266.

Another false dichotomy perpetuated in scholarship on these narratives is that Mary Magdalene became an authority figure for heretics, especially those called "gnostics," while Peter became the hero for those who eventually declared their traditions "orthodox." This study, however, has gone to special lengths to show that the claim for Mary Magdalene's apostolic status, rooted as it is in three of the four canonical gospels, is as "orthodox" as Peter's. In only one of those four gospels does she not receive a commission to tell others the good news.

Explicit Challenges to Apostolic Authority

The contradictions among resurrection appearance narratives reveal some of the implicit, subtle challenges to Mary's leadership role that were later presented explicitly in controversy dialogues. The number of extant portrayals of overt challenges to Mary Magdalene's role has increased with the discovery of new manuscripts over the last two centuries, including texts such as the *Gospel of Mary*, the *Gospel of Thomas*, the *Gospel of Philip*, and *Pistis Sophia*. Scholarly examinations of such texts have also brought greater recognition of the contributions that women in leadership roles made to the early church.[24] The *Gospel of Mary*, for example, preserves a portrait of Mary's leadership as she comforts and rallies the other disciples after a vision from Jesus. It also preserves Peter's objection that Jesus would not have revealed to her what he did not reveal to them. As Karen King writes, "The *Gospel of Mary* now provides direct evidence of early Christian arguments in favor of the leadership of women and allows us to see that views excluding women were but one side of a hotly debated issue."[25] Other texts, such as the *Gospel of Thomas* and *Pistis Sophia*, likewise portray Mary's role and also contain explicit objections to her authority made by Peter. In the controversy dialogues, when Peter attacks or confronts Mary, either a disciple or Jesus himself inevitably comes to her defense.

It is significant, then, that these controversy passages concerning Mary's leadership appear in texts that construct Mary, Judas Thomas, or Philip as an authority figure. This select grouping of names appears as well in other

---

[24]Beginning with the groundbreaking work of Schüssler Fiorenza (*In Memory of Her*) and Pagels (*Gnostic Gospels*).

[25]King, "Gospel of Mary Magdalene," *Searching the Scriptures*, 2:601.

early Christian texts that depict Mary as part of an inner circle of disciples. The *Dialogue of the Savior,* for example, focuses on Mary, Matthew, and Judas (Thomas), describing her as the one who "knows the all" or "who understands completely." Another text, *Sophia of Jesus Christ,* likewise highlights Mary, along with Matthew, Thomas, Philip, and Bartholomew. Thus these verbal challenges and controversy scenes that portray Peter as the opponent of Mary Magdalene tend to occur in precisely those texts for which Peter is not one of the primary authority figures. In a side note, it is interesting that in the *Acts of Paul,* a text that highlights Thecla's missionary activity, Paul describes his indoctrination into the church as coming not from Peter but from Judas, the brother of the Lord.[26] So again it appears that the constellations and choices of names within texts provide hints to political struggles within the early churches.[27]

In the realm of early Christian literature, Peter most frequently serves as Mary Magdalene's antagonist, perhaps because his name was somehow already linked to the party that opposed the role of women as leaders. Let us return now to Gregory of Antioch's words, quoted in the first chapter, when he describes Jesus appearing to Mary Magdalene and the other Mary at the tomb and saying to them: "Be the first teachers of the teachers. So that Peter who denied me learns that I can also choose women as apostles" (πρῶται γίνεσθε τῶν διδασκάλων διδάσκαλοι. μαθέτω Πέτρος ὁ ἀρνησάμενος με ὅτι δύναμαι καὶ γυναῖκας ἀποστόλους χειροτονεῖν).[28] We may now appreciate more fully why it is that Gregory invokes Peter when he imagines Jesus asserting his right to choose as his apostles women as well as men.

---

[26]Paul states, "I entered into a great church through (?) the blessed Judas, the brother of the Lord, who from the beginning gave me the exalted love of faith." From the Coptic fragment of the *Acts of Paul* not yet published, English translation from the *Acts of Paul* in NTApoc[5].

[27]Scripture itself bears witness to this phenomena to the rivalry among early believers with respect to the names of their leaders. Paul, for example, admonishes the Corinthians with the words: λέγω δὲ τοῦτο, ὅτι ἕκαστος ὑμῶν λέγει, ἐγὼ μέν εἰμι Παύλου, ἐγὼ δὲ Ἀπολλῶ, ἐγὼ δὲ Κηφᾶ, ἐγὼ δὲ Χριστοῦ ("What I mean is this: One of you says, 'I follow Paul'; another, 'I follow Apollos'; another, 'I follow Cephas'; still another, 'I follow Christ' "; 1 Cor 1:12).

[28]Gregory of Antioch, *Oratio in Mulieres Unguentiferas. XI* PG 88.1863–64, cited in Haskins, *Mary Magdalen,* 92.

Recovering Apostolic Status

On the basis of the literary evidence of explicit and implicit challenges to Mary's authority alone, one cannot make the sociological leap that automatically pits a Petrine group against a Mary Magdalene group. Each of these leadership figures and their respective traditions, no doubt, functioned authoritatively for more than one Christian group. Sometimes a controversy narrative may have even represented an inner-group controversy. However, what is beyond dispute is that in addition to any number of other theological or philosophical differences, the divergent authoritative traditions associated with these two figures differed on at least one critical issue — whether Christ included women in the mandate to preach and proclaim the good news. The texts that call upon Mary Magdalene as the guarantor of their tradition consistently charge female leaders with significant words or visions to share with others. The texts for which Peter functions as the authority figure consistently do not. Nor do they tend to provide even the grounds upon which one might begin to claim female eligibility for leadership roles; rather they primarily model the roles of women as supportive (especially financially), if not submissive, silent, or altogether absent.

Innumerable challenges to the apostolic roles of Mary Magdalene and other women as preachers and proclaimers of the good news have thus occurred.[29] Unfortunately, over time the more exclusive definition of apostolic eligibility has gained undue influence in many Christian circles against its earlier and more inclusive counterpart.[30] An examination of a greater range of early Christian texts, however, makes possible a more complete reconstruction of the early leadership exerted by women such as Mary Magdalene and thus assists in countering the attenuation of her authority. Karen King notes that a "critical reconstruction of the past aims to present a more accurate and complete accounting of the past at the forks

[29]Karen King ("Prophetic Power and Women's Authority," 29) points out, "We are now in a position to address the question of why every prominent stream of theology and practice within early Christianity that supported women's leadership was sharply opposed, even decried as heretical."

[30]See Eisen, *Women Officeholders in Early Christianity,* 58 n. 17, especially her reference to von Harnack's summary that shows how the more restrictive definition of apostleship overshadowed its rival.

where historical accuracy meets equity and justice."[31] Thus historical accountability includes "re-membering" Mary's role in early Christian texts and recognizing the various strategies that some Christians have used to undermine women's early apostolic status.[32]

Historical studies of the tensions within early Christian circles reveal that the idyllic picture of a completely unified early church simply does not do justice to the complexity of the movement even from the beginning. Then, as now, the questions of authority, apostolic status, and women's ordination have proven to be not only highly relevant but also controversial for some. In describing my research to those who inquired, I often found that this topic touched a nerve, and I received in response an amazing number of narratives from those who had also faced strong resistance to their right to proclaim the gospel message. To cite just one example of many, a woman explained how she had devoted more than six months of her life to organizing a peace conference for her church body, carrying it through from her own initial vision to its final, detailed execution, but was then denied the right to speak so much as a prayer at it. Those who oppose the right of women to lead public prayer, to preach, or to be ordained often do so because they claim a lack of precedent.[33] This study calls into question such a perceived lack of precedent by reexamining early Christian definitions of "apostle" and the authority that accompanies a divine commissioning for that purpose.

Looking back on the past may help us see with more clarity the possibilities for the future. It is my hope that revealing some of the implicit and explicit challenges to Mary Magdalene's leadership authority will help

---

[31]King, "The Gospel of Mary Magdalene," *Searching the Scriptures,* 2:601.

[32]Schüssler Fiorenza (*Rhetoric and Ethic,* 95) writes, "If the goal of a critical feminist rhetoric of liberation is to change relations of domination and the knowledge that keeps them in place, then feminist scholars cannot but engage with discourses and traditions of exclusion and domination."

[33]Mary Ann Rossi, "Priesthood, Precedent, and Prejudice: On Recovering the Women Priests of Early Christianity," *JFSR* 7 (1991): 74. She offers a translation of the work of Giorgio Otranto, the director of the Istituto di Studi classici e cristiani in the Università degli studi-Bari, and a scholar interested in the issue of women's priesthood. He calls into question the monolithic solidity of arguments from scripture and tradition. Rossi describes the way in which "Otranto provides ample grounds for reconsidering the role of women in the priesthood of early Christianity, and he challenges scholars dealing with the problem to question the omission of such evidence, and to search for the reasons for its omission."

recover a greater appreciation for her role as the first apostle. Furthermore, I hope it will thereby give inspiration and authority to all Christians who, regardless of their gender, may be strengthened by her example to pursue their callings to teach and proclaim the good news of Jesus' love for all.

Bibliography

A. Reference Works

Aland, Kurt, Matthew Black, Carlo M. Martini, Bruce M. Metzger, and Allen Wikgren, eds. *Novum Testamentum Graece*. Stuttgart: Deutsche Bibelgesellschaft, 1963.

Bauer, W., W. F. Arndt, F. W. Gingrich, and F. W. Danker. *Greek-English Lexicon of the New Testament and Other Early Christian Literature*. 2d ed. Chicago: University of Chicago Press, 1979.

Blass, Friedrich, and Albert Debrunner. *A Greek Grammar of the New Testament and Other Early Christian Literature*. Translated and edited by Robert W. Funk. Chicago: University of Chicago Press, 1961.

The Computer-Konkordanz zum Novum Testamentum Graece. Berlin/New York: de Gruyter, 1980.

Crum, Walter E. *Catalogue of the Coptic Manuscripts in the British Museum*. London: British Museum, 1905.

——. A Coptic Dictionary. Oxford: Clarendon, 1939.

Hatch, Edwin, and Henry A. Redpath. *A Concordance to the Septuagint and the Other Greek Versions of the Old Testament*. 3 vols. in 2. Grand Rapids, Mich.: Baker, 1987.

Lampe, Geoffrey W. H. *A Patristic Greek Lexicon*. Oxford: Clarendon, 1961.

Liddell, Henry George, and Robert Scott. *A Greek-English Lexicon*. Oxford: Clarendon, 1968.

Moulton, William F., and Alfred S. Geden. *A Concordance to the Greek Testament*. Edinburgh: T&T Clark, 1978.

Smyth, Herbert Weir. *Greek Grammar*. Cambridge: Harvard University Press, 1984.

Zerwick, Maximilian. *Graecitas Biblica*. Engl. ed. adapted from 4th Latin ed. Rome: Biblical Institute Press, 1963.

B. General Bibliography

Abogunrin, Samuel O. "The Three Variant Accounts of Peter's Call: A Critical and Theological Examination of the Texts." *NTS* 31 (1985): 587–602.

Agnew, Francis H. "On the Origin of the Term *Apostolos*." *CBQ* 38 (1976): 49–53.

———. "The Origin of the NT Apostle-Concept: A Review of Research." JBL 105 (1986): 75–96.

Agourides, Savvas. "Peter and John in the Fourth Gospel." In *SE* 4, edited by Frank L. Cross, 3–7. TU 102. Berlin: Akademie, 1968.

Albright, W. F., and C. S. Mann, *Matthew*. AB 26. Garden City, N.Y.: Doubleday, 1971.

Allberry, C. R. C. *A Manichaean Psalm-Book, Part II*. Manichaean Manuscripts in the Chester Beatty Collection 2. Stuttgart: Kohlhammer, 1938.

Allen, Edgar Leonard. "The Lost Kerygma." *NTS* 3 (1956–57): 349–53.

Alsup, John E. *The Post-Resurrection Appearance Stories of the Gospel Tradition: A History-of-Tradition Analysis with Text-Synopsis*. Stuttgart: Calwer, 1975.

Amsler, Frédéric. *Acta Philippi: Commentarius*. CCSA 12. Turnhout: Brepols, 1999.

Anderson, Hugh. *The Gospel of Mark*. NCBC. Grand Rapids, Mich.: Eerdmans, 1976.

Anderson, Janice Capel. "Matthew: Gender and Reading." *Semeia* 28 (1983): 3–27.

Anderson, Paul N. "The *Sitz im Leben* of the Johannine Bread of Life Discourse and Its Evolving Context." In *Critical Readings of John 6*, edited by R. Alan Culpepper, 1–59. Leiden: Brill, 1997.

Annand, Rupert. "'He was seen of Cephas': A Suggestion about the First Resurrection Appearance to Peter." *SJT* 11 (1958): 180–87.

Arai, Sasagu. "'To Make Her Male': An Interpretation of Logion 114 in Gospel of Thomas." In StPatr 24, edited by Elizabeth A. Livingstone, 373–76. Leuven: Peeters, 1993.

Arendzen, John P. "An Entire Syriac Text of the Apostolic Church Order." *JTS* 3 (1902): 59–80.

Atwood, Richard. *Mary Magdalene in the New Testament Gospels and Early Tradition*. European University Studies 457. Bern: Peter Lang, 1993.

Baarda, Tjitze. *Aphrahat's Text of the Fourth Gospel*. Vol. 1 of *The Gospel Quotations of Aphrahat the Persian Sage*. Amsterdam: Vrije Universiteit Amsterdam, 1975.

———. "Jesus and Mary (John 20, 16f) in the Second Epistle on Virginity Ascribed to Clement." In *Studien zum Text und zur Ethik des Neuen Testaments* (Fs. Heinrich Greeven), edited by W. Schrage, 11–34. BZNW 47. Berlin: de Gruyter, 1986.

Bakhtin, Mikhail. "Forms of Time and Chronotope in the Novel." In *The Dialogic Imagination*, edited by Michael Holquist, 84–258. Austin, Tex.: University of Texas Press, 1981.

Barrett, Charles K. "The Apostles in and after the New Testament." *SEÅ* 21 (1957): 30–49.

———. *The Gospel According to St. John: An Introduction with Commentary and Notes on the Greek Text*. 2d ed. Philadelphia: Westminster Press, 1978.

———. *The Signs of an Apostle*. London: Epworth Press, 1970.

———. ΨΕΥΔΑΠΟΣΤΟΛΟΙ (2 Cor 11.13). In *Mélanges Bibliques* (Fs. B. Rigaux), edited by A. Descamps and A. de Halleux, 377–96. Gembloux: Duculot, 1970.

Bauer, Walter. *Das Leben Jesu im Zeitalter der Neutestamentlichen Apokryphen*. Tübingen: Mohr, 1909.

———. *Orthodoxy and Heresy in Earliest Christianity*. Edited by Robert Kraft and Gerhard Kradel; translated by members of the Philadelphia Seminar on Christian Origins. Translation of *Rechtgläubigkeit and Ketzerei im ältesten Christentum* (1934). Philadelphia: Fortress, 1979.

Baus, Karl. "Wesen und Funktion der apostolischen Sukzession in der Sicht des heiligen Augustinus." In *Ekklesia: Festschrift für Bischof Matthias Wehr*, edited by Theologischen Fakultät Trier, 137–48. Trierer Theologische Studien 15. Trier: Paulinus Verlag, 1962.

Benoit, André. "Le 'Contra Christianos' de Porphyre: où en est la collecte des fragments?" In *Paganisme, Judaïsme, Christianisme: Influences et affrontements dans le monde antique* (Fs. Marcel Simon), 261–75. Paris: De Boccard, 1978.

Best, Ernest. "Mark's Use of the Twelve." *ZNW* 69 (1978): 11–35.

Betz, Hans Dieter. "Apostle." *ABD* 1:309–11.

———. *2 Corinthians 8 and 9: A Commentary on Two Administrative Letters of the Apostle Paul*. Edited by George W. MacRae. Hermeneia. Philadelphia: Fortress, 1985.

Betz, Hans Dieter. *Galatians: A Commentary on Paul's Letter to the Churches.* Philadelphia: Fortress, 1979.

Bieberstein, Sabine. *Verschwiegene Jüngerinnen—vergessene Zeuginnen: Gebrochene Konzepte im Lukasevangelium.* NTOA 38. Freiburg: Universitätsverlag; Göttingen: Vandenhoeck & Ruprecht, 1998.

Bienert, Wolfgang A. "The Picture of the Apostle in Early Christian Tradition." In *Writings Related to the Apostles, Apocalypses and Related Subjects.* Vol. 2 of *New Testament Apocrypha,* edited by Wilhelm Schneemelcher, 5–27. 2 vols. Translated by R. McL. Wilson. Rev. ed. Cambridge: James Clark and Co.; Louisville, Ky.: Westminster/John Knox, 1992.

———. "Successio apostolica." *LTK* 9. Freiburg: Herder, 2000, col. 1080–1083.

Blinzler, Josef. *Die Brüder und Schwestern Jesu.* SBS 21. Stuttgart: Katholisches Bibelwerk, 1967.

Bloch, Maurice, ed. *Political Language and Oratory in Traditional Society.* New York: Academic Press, 1975.

Bock, Darrell L. *Luke.* Baker Exegetical Commentary on the New Testament. 2 vols. Grand Rapids, Mich.: Baker Books, 1996.

Boer, Esther de. *Mary Magdalene: Beyond the Myth.* Translated by John Bowden. Harrisburg, Pa.: Trinity Press, 1997.

Bornhäuser, Karl. *Studien zum Sondergut des Lukas.* Gütersloh: Bertelsmann, 1934.

Boughton, Lynne C. "From Pious Legend to Feminist Fantasy: Distinguishing Hagiographical License from Apostolic Practice in the *Acts of Paul/Acts of Thecla.*" *JR* 71 (1991): 362–83.

Bouvier, Bertrand, and François Bovon, "Actes de Philippe, I, d'après un manuscrit inédit." In *Oecumenica et Patristica: Festschrift für Wilhelm Schneemelcher,* 367–94. Edited by Damaskinos Papandreou, Wolfgang A. Bienert, and Knut Schäferdiek. Geneva: Metropolie der Schweiz, 1989.

Bovon, François. "Les Actes de Philippe." In *ANRW* 2:25/6.4432–4525. Berlin: de Gruyter, 1988.

———. *Das Evangelium nach Lukas.* 3 vols. EKKNT 3. Zürich: Benziger/Neukirchen-Vluyn: Neukirchener Verlag, 1989–96. (ET: *Luke 1: A Commentary on the Gospel of Luke 1:1–9:50.* Hermeneia. Translated by Christine M. Thomas. Minneapolis: Augsburg Fortress, 2002.)

———. "The Gospel According to John, Access to God, at the Obscure Origins of Christianity." *Diogenes* 146 (1990): 36–50.

Bovon, François. "Jesus' Missionary Speech as Interpreted in the Patristic Commentaries and the Apocryphal Narratives." In *Texts and Contexts: Biblical Texts in Their Textual and Situational Contexts*, edited by Tord Fornberg and David Hellhom, 871–86. Oslo: Scandinavian University Press, 1995.

———. "Le privilège pascal de Marie-Madeleine." *NTS* 30 (1984): 50–64. (ET: "Mary Magdalene's Paschal Privilege." In *New Testament Traditions and Apocryphal Narratives,* translated by Jane Haapiseva-Hunter, 147–57. PTMS 36. Allison Park, Pa.: Pickwick, 1995.)

———. "The Synoptic Gospels and the Noncanonical Acts of the Apostles." *HTR* 81 (1988): 19–36.

———. "La vie des apôtres: traditions bibliques et narrations apocryphes." In *Les Actes apocryphes des apôtres: christianisme et monde païen,* 141–58. Geneva: Labor et Fides, 1981. (ET: "The Life of the Apostles." In *New Testament Traditions and Apocryphal Narratives*, translated by Jane Haapiseva-Hunter, 159–75. Allison Park, Pa.: Pickwick, 1995.)

Bovon, François, Bertrand Bouvier, and Frédéric Amsler, eds. *Acta Philippi: Textus.* CCSA 11. Turnhout: Brepols, 1999.

———, Bertrand Bouvier, and Frédéric Amsler, trans. *Actes de l'apôtre Philippe.* With introduction and notes by Frédéric Amsler. Apocryphes 8. Turnhout: Brepols, 1996.

——— and Pierre Geoltrain, eds. *Écrits apocryphes chrétiens I.* La Pléiade. Paris: Gallimard, 1997.

Brock, Ann Graham. "Genre of the *Acts of Paul:* One Tradition Enhancing Another." *Apocrypha: Revue internationale des littératures apocryphes* 5 (1994): 119–36.

———. "Peter, Paul, and Mary: Canonical vs. Non-Canonical Portrayals of Apostolic Witnesses." In *Society of Biblical Literature: 1999 Seminar Papers,* edited by David L. Tiede, 173–202. Atlanta: Scholars Press, 1999.

———. "Political Authority and Cultural Accommodation: Social Diversity in the *Acts of Paul* and the *Acts of Peter.*" In *The Apocryphal Acts of the Apostles: Harvard Divinity School Studies,* edited by François Bovon, Ann Graham Brock, and Christopher R. Matthews, 145–69. Cambridge: Harvard University Center for the Study of World Religions, 1999.

———. "Setting the Record Straight—The Politics of Identification: Mary Magdalene and Mary the Mother in *Pistis Sophia.*" In *Which Mary?: The Marys of Early Christian Tradition,* edited by F. Stanley Jones, 43–52. SBLSymS 19. Atlanta: Society of Biblical Literature, 2002.

Brooten, Bernadette. "Early Christian Women and Their Cultural Context: Issues of Method in Historical Reconstruction." In *Feminist Perspectives on Biblical Scholarship*, edited by Adela Yarbro Collins, 65–91. Society of Biblical Literature Centennial Publications. Chico, Calif.: Scholars Press, 1985.

———. "'Junia . . . Outstanding among the Apostles' (Romans 16:7)." In *Women Priests: A Catholic Commentary on the Vatican Declaration*, edited by Leonard Swidler and Arlene Swidler, 141–44. New York: Paulist, 1977.

———. *Women Leaders in the Ancient Synagogue*. Chico, Calif.: Scholars Press, 1982.

Brown, Raymond E. *The Community of the Beloved Disciple*. New York: Paulist, 1979.

———. *The Gospel According to John*. 2 vols. AB 29–30. Garden City, N.Y.: Doubleday, 1966–70.

———. "The *Gospel of Peter* and Canonical Gospel Priority." *NTS* 33 (1987): 321–43.

———. "'Other Sheep Not of this Fold': The Johannine Perspective on Christian Diversity in the Late First Century." *JBL* 97 (1978): 5–22.

———. "Roles of Women in the Fourth Gospel." *TS* 36 (1975): 688–99.

———. "The Twelve and the Apostolate." *NJBC* 1377–81 (§§135–57).

Brown, Raymond E., Karl Donfried, and John Reumann, eds. *Peter in the New Testament*. Minneapolis/New York: Augsburg/Paulist Press, 1973.

Bruyne, Donatien De. "*Epistula Titi, discipuli Pauli, De dispositione sanctimonii.*" *RBén* 37 (1925): 47–72.

Buckley, Jorunn Jacobson. *Female Fault and Fulfilment in Gnosticism*. SR. Chapel Hill: University of North Carolina Press, 1986.

———. "An Interpretation of Logion 114 in *The Gospel of Thomas*." *NovT* 27 (1985): 245–72.

Budge, E. A. W. *The Contendings of the Apostles*. 2 vols. Amsterdam: Philo, 1976.

———. *Coptic Apocrypha in the Dialect of Upper Egypt*. London: British Museum, 1913.

Bultmann, Rudolf. *The Gospel of John: A Commentary*. Translated by G. R. Beasley-Murray. Translation of *Das Evangelium des Johannes* (1964). Philadelphia: Westminster, 1971.

Burgess, Joseph A. *A History of the Exegesis of Matthew 16:17–19 from 1781 to 1965*. Ann Arbor, Mich.: Edwards Brothers, 1976.

Burrus, Virginia. *Chastity as Autonomy: Women in the Stories of the Apocryphal Acts*. Studies in Women and Religion 23. Lewiston, N.Y.: Mellen Press, 1987.

Byrne, Brendan. "The Faith of the Beloved Disciple and the Community in John 20." *JSNT* 23 (1985): 83–97.

Cameron, Ron. *The Other Gospels: Non-Canonical Gospel Texts*. Philadelphia: Westminster, 1982.

Campagnano, Annarosa, ed. *Ps. Cirillo di Gerusalemme: Omelie copte sulla Passione, sulla Croce e sulla Vergine*. Milan: Cisalpino-Goliardica, 1980.

Campenhausen, Hans von. *Der Ablauf der Osterereignisse und das leere Grab*. 3d ed. Heidelberg: Carl Winter Universitätsverlag, 1966.

———. *Ecclesiastical Authority and Spiritual Power in the Church of the First Three Centuries*. Translated by J. A. Baker. Translation of *Kirchliches Amt und Geistliche Vollmacht*. Peabody, Mass.: Hendrickson, 1997.

———. "Der urchristliche Apostelbegriff." *ST* 1 (1947): 96–130.

Campenhausen, Hans von, and Henry Chadwick. *Jerusalem and Rome: The Problem of Authority in the Early Church*. Philadelphia: Fortress, 1966. Facet Books, Historical Series, No. 4.

Castelli, Elizabeth. "Virginity and its Meaning for Women's Sexuality in Early Christianity." *JFSR* 2 (1986): 61–88.

Chadwick, Henry. *The Circle and the Ellipse: Rival Concepts of Authority in the Early Church: Inaugural Lecture delivered to Oxford before the University of Oxford on 5 May 1959*. Oxford: Clarendon, 1959.

———, trans. *Contra Celsum*. Cambridge: Cambridge University Press, 1953.

Charlesworth, James H. *The Beloved Disciple: Whose Witness Validates the Gospel of John?* Valley Forge, Pa.: TPI, 1995.

Chilton, Bruce, and Jacob Neusner. *Types of Authority in Formative Christianity and Judaism*. London and New York: Routledge, 1999.

Clifford, Anne M. *Introducing Feminist Theology*. Maryknoll, N.Y.: Orbis, 2001.

Collins, Raymond F. "Mary." *ABD* 4:584–86.

Collins, Raymond F. "Twelve, The." *ABD* 6:670–71.

Connolly, Richard Hugh. *Didascalia Apostolorum: The Syriac Version Translated and Accompanied by the Verona Latin Fragments*. Oxford: Clarendon, 1929.

Conzelmann, Hans. *1 Corinthians*. Hermeneia. Philadelphia: Fortress, 1975.

——. *The Theology of St. Luke*. Translated by Geoffrey Buswell. Translation of *Mitte der Zeit: Studien zur Theologie des Lukas* (1954). London: Faber and Faber, 1960.

——. "Zu Mythos, Mythologie und Formgeschichte, geprüft an der dritten Praxis der Thomas-Akten." *ZNW* 67 (1976): 111–22.

Cooper, Kate. "Apostles, Ascetic Women, and Questions of Audience: New Reflections on the Rhetoric of Gender in the Apocryphal Acts." In *Society of Biblical Literature: 1992 Seminar Papers,* edited by Eugene H. Lovering, Jr., 147–53. Atlanta: Scholars Press, 1992.

Coyle, J. Kevin. "The Fathers on Women and Women's Ordination." *EgT* 9 (1978): 51–101.

——. "Mary Magdalene in Manichaeism?" *Mus* 104 (1991): 39–55.

Cribbs, F. Lamar. "St. Luke and the Johannine Tradition." *JBL* 90 (1971): 422–50.

Crossan, John Dominic. *The Birth of Christianity*. San Francisco: HarperSan Francisco, 1998.

——. *The Cross that Spoke: The Origins of the Passion Narrative*. San Francisco: Harper & Row, 1973.

——. "The Gospel of Peter & the Canonical Gospels: Independence, Dependence, or Both?" *Forum* 1 (1998): 7–51.

Cullmann, Oscar. *Der johanneische Kreis: Sein Platz im Spätjudentum, in der Jüngerschaft Jesu und im Urchristentum: Zum Ursprung des Johannesevangeliums*. Tübingen: Mohr (Siebeck), 1975. (ET: *The Johannine Circle: Its Place in Judaism among the Disciples of Jesus and in early Christianity*. Translated by John Bowden. Philadelphia: Westminster, 1976.)

——. *Peter: Disciple, Apostle, Martyr: A Historical and Theological Study*. 2d ed. Philadelphia: Westminster, 1962.

Culpepper, R. Alan. *Anatomy of the Fourth Gospel: A Study in Literary Design*. Philadelphia: Fortress, 1983.

——. *John, the Son of Zebedee: The Life of a Legend*. Columbia, S.C.: University of South Carolina Press, 1994.

D'Angelo, Mary Rose. "Re-membering Jesus: Women, Prophecy, and Resistance in the Memory of the Early Churches." *Horizons* 19.2 (1990): 199–218.

——. "Women in Luke–Acts: A Redactional View." *JBL* 109 (1990): 441–61.

Dart, John. "The Two Shall Become One." *ThTo* 35 (1978–1979): 321–25.

Dauer, Anton. *Johannes Und Lukas*. FB 50. Würzburg: Echter Verlag, 1984.

Davies, Stevan. *The Gospel of Thomas and Christian Wisdom*. New York: Seabury, 1983.

Davies, William David. "Church Life in the New Testament." *Christian Origins and Judaism: The Jewish People: History, Religion, Literature*. Philadelphia: Westminster Press, 1962.

De Conick, April D. *Seek to See Him: Ascent and Vision Mysticism in the Gospel of Thomas*. VCSup 33. Leiden: Brill, 1996.

Delorme, Jean. "Luc V.1–11: Analyse structurale et histoire de la rédaction." *NTS* 18 (1971/1972): 331–50.

Denis, Albert Marie. "L'investiture de la fonction apostolique par 'apocalypse.'" *RB* 64 (1957): 335–62, 492–515.

Denker, Jünger. *Die theologiegeschichtliche Stellung des Petrusevangeliums: Ein Beitrag zur Frühgeschichte des Doketismus*. EHS.T 36. Bern and Frankfurt: Lang, 1975.

Derrett, J. Duncan M. "Miriam and the Resurrection (John 20,16)." *DRev* 111 (1993): 174–86.

Desjardins, Michel R. "Where Was the Gospel of Thomas Written?" *TJT* 8 (1992): 121–33.

Dewey, Arthur J. "Time to Murder and Create: Visions and Revisions in the *Gospel of Peter*." *Semeia* 49 (1990): 101–27.

Dibelius, Martin. *Die Formgeschichte des Evangeliums*. 3d. ed. Tübingen: Mohr (Siebeck), 1959.

———. *James*. Rev. Heinrich Greeven. Hermeneia. Philadelphia: Fortress, 1976.

Dietrich, Wolfgang. *Das Petrusbild der lukanischen Schriften*. BWANT 5, Heft 14. Stuttgart: Kohlhammer, 1972.

Dillon, Richard J. *From Eye-Witnesses to Ministers of the Word: Tradition and Composition in Luke 24*. AnBib 82. Rome: Biblical Institute Press, 1978.

Dobschütz, Ernst von. *Ostern und Pfingsten*. Leipzig: Hinrichs, 1903.

Dodd, Charles Harold. "The Appearances of the Risen Christ: An Essay in Form-Criticism of the Gospels." In *Studies in the Gospels*, edited by D. E. Nineham, 9–35. Oxford: Oxford University Press, 1957.

———. *Historical Tradition in the Fourth Gospel*. Cambridge: Cambridge University Press, 1963.

———. *The Interpretation of the Fourth Gospel*. Cambridge: Cambridge University Press, 1953.

Dornish, Loretta. *A Woman Reads the Gospel of Luke.* Collegeville, Ind.: Liturgical Press, 1996.

Dubisch, Jill. *Gender and Power in Rural Greece.* Princeton, N.J.: Princeton University Press, 1986.

Dunn, James D. G. *Unity and Diversity in the New Testament: An Inquiry into the Character of Earliest Christianity.* 2d ed. London: SCM, 1990.

Dunn, Peter. "Women's Liberation: The *Acts of Paul,* and Other Apocryphal Acts of the Apostles." *Apocrypha* 4 (1993): 245–61.

Dupont, Jacques. "Les discours de Pierre." In *Nouvelles Études sur les Actes des apôtres,* 58–111. LD 118. Paris: Cerf, 1984.

———. "Le nom d'apôtres: a-t-il été donné aux Douze par Jésus?" *OrSyr* 1 (1956): 267–90; reprint, in *Études sur les Évangiles Synoptiques,* edited by F. Neirynck, 976–1018. 2 vols. Leuven: Leuven University Press, 1985.

———. "Les ministères de l'Église naissante d'après les Actes des Apôtres." In *Nouvelles études sur les Actes des Apôtres,* 133–85. LD 118. Paris: Cerf, 1984.

Ehlers, Barbara. "Kann das Thomasevangelium aus Edessa stammen?" *NovT* 12 (1970): 70–77.

Ehrhardt, Arnold. *The Apostolic Ministry.* Edinburgh: Oliver and Boyd, 1958.

Eisen, Ute E. *Amtsträgerinnen im frühen Christentum: Epigraphische und literarische Studien.* Forschungen zur Kirchen-Dogmengeschichte 61. Göttingen: Vandenhoeck & Ruprecht, 1996. (ET: *Women Officeholders in Early Christianity: Epigraphical and Literary Studies.* Translated by Linda M. Maloney. Collegeville, Minn.: Liturgical Press, 2000.)

Elliott, James Keith, ed. *The Apocryphal New Testament: A Collection of Apocryphal Christian Literature in an English Translation.* Oxford: Clarendon Press, 1993.

Elliott, Neil. *Liberating Paul: The Justice of God and the Politics of the Apostle.* Maryknoll, N.Y.: Orbis, 1994.

Ellis, I. P. "'But Some Doubted.'" *NTS* 14 (1967/1968): 574–80.

Emmel, Stephen, ed. *Nag Hammadi Codex III,5: The Dialogue of the Savior.* With an introduction by Helmut Koester and Elaine Pagels. NHS 26. Leiden: Brill, 1984.

Erbetta, Mario. *Atti e Leggende.* Gli Apocrifi del Nuovo Testamento. Vol. 2/2. Turin: Marietti, 1966.

———. *Vangeli.* Gli Apocrifi del Nuovo Testamento. Vol. 1/2. Turin: Marietti, 1981.

Esbroeck, Michel van. "Le roi Sanatrouk et l'apôtre Thaddée." *Revue des Études Arméniennes* 9 (1973): 141–283.

Evans, Christopher F. "I Will Go Before You Into Galilee." *JTS* 5 (1954): 3–18.

———. *Saint Luke.* TPINTC. London: SCM, 1990.

———. *Resurrection and the New Testament.* SBT, 2nd Series, 12. London: SCM, 1970.

Evelyn-White, Hugh. *The Monasteries of the Wadi 'n Natrûn* 1/2: 38–43. Metropolitan Museum of Art Egyptian Expedition. New York: n.p., 1926.

Finegan, Jack. *Die Überlieferung der Leidens- und Auferstehungsgeschichte Jesu.* Beihefte zur Zeitschrift für die neutestamentliche Wissenschaft und die Kunde der älteren Kirche 15. Gießen, Germany: Töpelman, 1934.

Fitzmyer, Joseph A. *The Gospel According to Luke.* 2 vols. AB 28–28A. Garden City, N.Y.: Doubleday, 1985.

Flender, Helmut. *St. Luke, Theologian of Redemptive History.* Translated by Reginald H. and Ilse Fuller. Translation of *Heil und Geschichte in der Theologie des Lukas* (1965). Philadelphia: Fortress, 1967.

Fortna, Robert T. "Christology in the Fourth Gospel: Redaction-Critical Perspectives." *NTS* 21 (1974–75): 489–504.

———. *The Gospel of Signs.* SNTSMS 11. Cambridge: Cambridge University Press, 1970.

Frank, Chrysostom. "Petrine Texts in Byzantine Homilies on the Dormition." *Eastern Churches Journal* 6 (1999): 67–84.

Fuller, Reginald H. *The Formation of the Resurrection Narratives.* New York: Macmillan, 1971.

Furnish, Victor Paul. *II Corinthians.* AB 32A. New York: Doubleday, 1984.

Gardner-Smith, Percival. "The Date of the Gospel of Peter." *JTS* 27 (1926): 401–7.

Gaventa, Beverly Roberts. *Mary: Glimpses of the Mother of Jesus.* Columbia, S.C.: University of South Carolina Press, 1995. Repr., Minneapolis: Fortress, 1999.

Giannelli, Ciro. "Témoignages patristiques grecs en faveur d'une apparition du Christ ressuscité à la Vierge Marie." In *Mélanges Martin Jugie = REByz* 11 (1953): 106–19.

Geisler, Norman L. *The Battle for the Resurrection.* Nashville: Thomas Nelson, 1989.

Good, Deirdre. "Pistis Sophia." In *A Feminist Commentary.* Vol. 2 of *Searching the Scriptures,* edited by Elisabeth Schüssler Fiorenza, 678–707. 2 vols. New York: Crossroad, 1994.

Goodspeed, Edgar Johnson. *The Twelve: The Story of Christ's Apostles.* Philadelphia: J. C. Winston, 1957.

Goulder, Michael D. *Luke: A New Paradigm.* JSNTSup 20. 2 vols. Sheffield: JSOT Press, 1989.

Grant, Robert M. "Two Gnostic Gospels." *JBL* 79 (1960): 1–11.

Grappe, Christian. *Images de Pierre aux deux premiers siècles.* EHPR 75. Paris: Presses Universitaires de France, 1995.

Graβ, Hans. *Ostergeschehen und Osterberichte.* 4th ed. Göttingen: Vandenhoeck, 1970.

Green, Joel B. "The Gospel of Peter: Source for a Pre-Canonical Passion Narrative?" *ZNW* 78 (1987): 293–301.

Grundmann, Walter. *Das Evangelium nach Lukas.* THKNT 3. 5th ed. Berlin: Evangelische Verlagsanstalt, 1969.

———. *Das Evangelium nach Matthäus.* THKNT 1. 5th ed. Berlin: Evangelische Verlagsanstalt, 1981.

Guidi, Ignazio. "Frammenti Copti, nota IIª." *Rendiconti della R. Academia dei Lincei* 3/2 (1887): 20–23.

Guillaume, Jean-Marie. *Luc interprète des anciennes traditions sur la résurrection de Jésus.* EBib. Paris: Gabalda, 1979.

Guillaume, Paul-Marie. "Marie-Madeleine." In *Dictionnaire de Spiritualité, Ascétique et Mystique: Doctrine et Histoire.* 16 vols. Paris: Beauchesne, 1937–94.

Gunther John J. "The Relation of the Beloved Disciple to the Twelve." *TZ* 37 (1981): 129–48.

Haenchen, Ernst. *The Acts of the Apostles: A Commentary.* Trans. Bernard Noble and Gerald Shinn. Translated from *Die Apostelgeschichte* (1968). Philadelphia: Westminster, 1971.

———. *Die Apostelgeschichte.* Göttingen: Vandenhoeck, 1959.

———. "Petrus-Probleme." *NTS* 7 (1960–61): 187–97.

Hahn, Ferdinand. *Christologische Hoheitstitel: Ihre Geschichte im frühen Christentum.* FRLANT 83. 4th ed. Göttingen: Vandenhoeck & Ruprecht, 1974.

———. "Der Apostolat im Urchristentum." *KD* 20 (1974): 54–77.

Harnack, Adolf von. "Ein jüngst entdeckter Auferstehungsbericht." ThSt. *Festschrift für Bernhard Weiss.* Göttingen: Vandenhoeck & Ruprecht, 1897.

Harnack, Adolf von. *Die Lehre der zwölf Apostel.* TU 2, 5. Leipzig, 1884.

———. *Die Mission und Ausbreitung des Christentums in den ersten drei Jahrhunderten.* Wiesbaden: VMA, 1924.

Harnack, Adolf von. *Untersuchungen über das gnostische Buch* Pistis Sophia. TU 7/2. Leipzig: Hinrichs, 1891.

Hartenstein, Judith. *Die zweite Lehre: Erscheinungen des Auferstandenen als Rahmenerzählungen frühchristlicher Dialoge.* TUGAL 146. Berlin: Akademie, 2000.

Haskins, Susan. *Mary Magdalen: Myth and Metaphor.* New York: Harcourt Brace, 1993.

Hedrick, Charles, and Robert Hodgson, Jr., eds. *Nag Hammadi, Gnosticism, and Early Christianity.* Peabody, Mass.: Hendrickson, 1986.

Heine, Susanne. *Frauen der frühen Christenheit: Zur historischen Kritik einer feministischen Theologie.* Göttingen: Vandenhoeck & Ruprecht, 1986. (ET: *Women and Early Christianity: Are the Feminist Scholars Right?* Translated by John Bowden. London: SCM, 1987.)

Heinrich, Karl. "δώδεκα." In *TDNT* 2:321–28.

Hengel, Martin. "Maria Magdalena und die Frauen als Zeugen." In *Abraham unser Vater: Juden und Christen im Gespräch über die Bibel* (Fs. Otto Michel), edited by Otto Betz, Martin Hengel, Peter Schmidt, 243–56. Leiden: Brill, 1963.

Hoffmann, Paul. "Der Petrus-Primat im Matthäusevangelium." In *Neues Testament und Kirche* (Fs. R. Schnackenburg), edited by J. Gnilka, 94–114. Freiburg: Herder, 1974.

Holl, Karl. "Der Kirchenbegriff des Paulus in seinem Verhältnis zu dem der Urgemeinde (1921)." Reprinted in *Der Osten,* vol. 2 of *Gesammelte Aufsätze zur Kirchengeschichte,* 44–67. Tübingen: Mohr (Siebeck), 1928.

Holzmeister, Urban. "Die Magdalenenfrage in der kirchlichen Überlieferung." *ZKT* 46 (1922): 402–22, 556–84.

Ide, Arthur Frederick. *Woman as Priest, Bishop & Laity in the Early Catholic Church to 440 A.D.: With a critical commentary on Romans 16 and other relevant Scripture and patrological writings on women in the early Christian Church.* Mesquite, Tex.: Ide House, 1984.

Isenberg, Wesley W. "Gospel of Philip." In *NHL,* edited by James M. Robinson, 139–60. San Francisco: Harper & Row, rev. ed., 1988.

James, M. R. *The Apocryphal New Testament.* Oxford: Clarendon, 1924.

Jansen, Katherine Ludwig. *The Making of the Magdalen: Preaching and Popular Devotion in the Later Middle Ages*. Princeton: Princeton University Press, 2000.

Jansen, Katherine Ludwig. "Maria Magdalena: *Apostolorum Apostola*." In *Women Preachers and Prophets through Two Millennia of Christianity*, edited by Beverly Mayne Kienzle and Pamela J. Walker, 57–96. Berkeley and Los Angeles: University of California Press, 1998.

Jasper, Alison. "Interpretative Approaches to John 20.1–18: Mary at the Tomb of Jesus." *ST* 47 (1993): 107–18.

Jeremias, Joachim. *Neutestamentliche Theologie. I. Die Verkündigung Jesu.* Gütersloh: Mohn, 1971.

———. *The Parables of Jesus*. New York: Scribner, 1963.

———. *Die Sprache des Lukasevangeliums: Redaktion und Tradition im Nicht-Markusstoff des dritten Evangeliums*. Göttingen: Vandenhoeck & Ruprecht, 1980.

Junod, Éric, trans. "Évangile de Pierre." In *Écrits apocryphes chrétiens*, edited by François Bovon and Pierre Geoltrain, 241–54. La Pléiade. Paris: Gallimard, 1997.

Kaestli, Jean-Daniel. "Les principales orientations de la recherche sur les Actes apocryphes des apôtres." In *Les Actes apocryphes des apôtres: christianisme et monde païen*, edited by François Bovon et al., 49–67. Geneva: Labor et Fides, 1981.

———. "Questions de Barthélemy." In *Écrits apocryphes chrétiens*, edited by François Bovon and Pierre Geoltrain, 267–95. La Pléiade. Paris: Gallimard, 1997.

Kaestli, Jean-Daniel, and Pierre Cherix. *L'Évangile de Barthélemy d'après écrits apocryphes*. Apocryphes 1. Turnhout: Brepols, 1993.

———. "Livre de la résurrection de Jésus-Christ par l'apôtre Barthélemy." In *Écrits apocryphes chrétiens*, edited by François Bovon and Pierre Geoltrain, 299–356. La Pléiade. Paris: Gallimard, 1997.

Karris, Robert J. "Women and Discipleship in Luke." *CBQ* 56 (1994): 1–20.

Käsemann, Ernst. *Commentary on Romans*. Translated by Geoffrey W. Bromiley. Translation of *An die Römer* (1973). Grand Rapids, Mich.: Eerdmans, 1980.

Kennedy, George A. *New Testament Interpretation through Rhetorical Criticism*. Chapel Hill: University of North Carolina Press, 1984.

Kertelge Karl. "Die Funktion der 'Zwölf' im Markusevangelium." *TTZ* 78 (1969): 193–206.

Kessler, William Thomas. *Peter as the First Witness of the Risen Lord: An Historical and Theological Investigation.* Tesi Gregoriana, Serie Teologia 37. Rome: Pontificia Universita Gregoriana, 1998.

Kienzle, Beverly Mayne. "Penitents and Preachers: The Figure of Saint Peter and His Relationship to Saint Mary Magdalene." In *La Figura di san Pietro nelle fonti del medioevo: Atti del convegno tenutosi in occasione dello Studiorum universitatum docentium congressus (Viterbo e Roma 5–8 settembre 2000),* edited by Loredana Lazzari and Anna Maria Valente Bacci, 248–72. Textes et études du moyen âge, 17. Louvain-la-Neuve: F.I.D.E.M., 2001.

Kilpatrick, George D. "Galatians 1,18, ἱστορῆσαι Κηφᾶν." In *NT Essays: Studies in Memory of T. W. Manson,* 144–49. Manchester: Manchester University, 1959.

King, Karen. "Canonization and Marginalization: Mary of Magdala." In *Women's Sacred Scriptures,* edited by Kwok Pui-Lan and Elisabeth Schüssler Fiorenza, 29–36. *Concilium: Revue internationale de Théologie* 1998/3. London: SCM Press; Maryknoll: Orbis Books, 1998.

———. "The Gospel of Mary Magdalene." In *A Feminist Commentary.* Vol. 2 of *Searching the Scriptures,* edited by Elisabeth Schüssler Fiorenza, 601–34. New York: Crossroad, 1994.

———. *The Gospel of Mary.* Sonoma, Calif.: Polebridge, forthcoming (2003).

———, ed. *Images of the Feminine in Gnosticism.* Philadelphia: Fortress, 1988.

———. "Introduction" [to the *Gospel of Mary* (BG 8502, 1)]. In *Nag Hammadi Library in English,* edited by James M. Robinson, 523–24. 3d ed. San Francisco: Harper and Row, 1988.

———. "The Gospel of Mary." In *The Complete Gospels: Annotated Scholars Version,* edited by Robert J. Miller, 357–66. Revised and expanded edition. Sonoma, Calif.: Polebridge, 1994.

———. "Prophetic Power and Women's Authority: The Case of the *Gospel of Mary* (Magdalene)." In *Women Preachers and Prophets through Two Millennia of Christianity,* edited by Beverly Mayne Kienzle and Pamela J. Walker, 357–66. Berkeley and Los Angeles: University of California Press, 1998.

———. "Why All the Controversy: Mary in the *Gospel of Mary.*" In *Which Mary?: The Marys of Early Christian Tradition,* edited by F. Stanley Jones, 53–74. SBLSymS 19. Atlanta: Society of Biblical Literature, 2002.

Kingsbury, Jack Dean. "The Figure of Peter in Matthew's Gospel as a Theological Problem." *JBL* 98 (1979): 67–83.

Kirk, J. Andrew. "Apostleship since Rengstorf: Towards a Synthesis." *NTS* 21 (1975): 249–64.

Kittel, Gerhard. "Die Auferstehung Jesu." *DT* 4 (1937): 133–68.

Kitzberger, Ingrid Rosa. "Mary of Bethany and Mary of Magdala—Two Female Characters in the Johannine Passion Narrative: A Feminist, Narrative-Critical Reader-Response." *NTS* 41 (1995): 564–86.

Klein, Günter. "Die Berufung des Petrus." *ZNW* 58 (1967): 1–44.

———. "Die Verleugnung des Petrus: Eine traditionsgeschichtliche Untersuchung." *ZTK* 58 (1961): 285–328.

———. *Die zwölf Apostel: Ursprung und Gehalt einer Idee.* FRLANT 77. Göttingen: Vandenhoeck & Ruprecht, 1961.

Klijn, Albertus F. J. "Christianity in Edessa and the Gospel of Thomas." *NovT* 14 (1972): 70–77.

Koester, Helmut. *Ancient Christian Gospels: Their History and Development.* Philadelphia: Trinity Press, 1992.

———. "Apocryphal and Canonical Gospels." *HTR* 73 (1980): 105–30.

———. "Gnostic Sayings and Controversy Traditions in John 8:12–59." In *Nag Hammadi, Gnosticism, and Early Christianity*, edited by Charles Hedrick and Robert Hodgson, 97–110. Peabody, Mass.: Hendrickson, 1986.

———. "Introduction [to *The Gospel according to Thomas*]." In *Nag Hammadi Codex, II, 2–7,* edited by Bentley Layton, 38–49. NHS 20. Leiden: Brill, 1989.

———. "La tradition apostolique et les origines du gnosticisme." *RTP* 119 (1987): 1–16.

———. "The Story of the Johannine Tradition." *STRev* 36 (1992): 17–32.

———. "Three Thomas Parables." In *The New Testament and Gnosis* (Fs. Robert McL. Wilson), edited by A. H. B. Logan and A. J. M. Wedderburn, 195–203. Edinburgh: T&T Clark, 1983.

———. "Writings and the Spirit: Authority and Politics in Ancient Christianity." *HTR* 84 (1991): 353–72.

Koester, Helmut, and Elaine Pagels. "Introduction." In *Nag Hammadi Codex, III,5: The Dialogue of the Savior*, edited by Stephen Emmel, 1–17. NHS 26. Leiden: Brill, 1984.

Koulomzine, Nicholas. "Peter's Place in the Primitive Church." In *The Primacy of Peter: Essays in Ecclesiology*, edited by John Meyendorff, 1–29. Crestwood, N.Y.: St. Vladimir's Seminary Press, 1992.

Kraemer, Ross Shepard. "The Conversion of Women to Ascetic Forms of Christianity." *Signs* 6 (1980/81): 298–307.

——. *Her Share of the Blessings: Women's Religions among Pagans, Jews, and Christians in the Greco–Roman World*. Oxford: Oxford University Press, 1992.

Kraus, Thomas, J., and Tobias Nicklas, eds. *Griechische Fragmente des sog. "Petrusevangeliums"/ Griechische Fragmente des sog. "Offenbarung des Petrus."* GCS n.s. 7. Berlin: De Gruyter, forthcoming (2003).

Kredel, Elmar M. "Der Apostelbegriff in der neueren Exegese: Historisch-kritische Darstellung." *ZKT* 78 (1956): 169–93, 257–305.

Kugener, Marc-Antoine, and E. Triffaux, eds. *Les Homiliae cathédrales de Sévère d'Antioche*. Homélie 77. PO 16:5. Paris, 1922. Repr., Turnhout: Brepols, 1976.

Kundsin, Karl. *Topologische Überlieferungsstoffe im Johannes-Evangelium: Eine Untersuchung*. FRLANT Neue Folge, 22. Göttingen: Vandenhoeck & Ruprecht, 1925.

Küng, Hans. *Die Kirche*. Freiburg: Herder, 1967.

Kurz, William S. *Reading Luke-Acts: Dynamics of Biblical Narrative*. Louisville, Ky.: Westminster/John Knox Press, 1993.

Kysar, Robert. *The Fourth Evangelist and His Gospel: An Examination of Contemporary Scholarship*. Minneapolis: Augsburg, 1975.

——. "The Gospel of John in Current Research." *RelSRev* 9 (1983): 314–23.

Lacau, Pierre. *Fragments d'apocryphes coptes*. Cairo: Institut français d'archéologie orientale, 1904.

Lagrange, Marie-Joseph. *Évangile selon saint Marc*. EBib. Paris: Gabalda, 1929.

——. *Saint Paul: Épître aux Romains*. EBib. Paris: Gabalda, 1931.

Lake, Kirsopp. "The Twelve and the Apostles." In *The Beginnings of Christianity*, edited by F. J. Foakes-Jackson and K. Lake, 5:37–59. 5 vols. London: Macmillan, 1933.

Lambdin, Thomas O., trans. "The Gospel according to Thomas." In *Nag Hammadi Codex, II, 2–7,* edited by Bentley Layton, 38–49. NHS 20. Leiden: Brill, 1989.

Lamy, Thomas J., ed. *Sancti Ephraem Hymni et Sermones*. 4 vols. Mecheln: H. Dessain, 1882–1902.

Layton, Bentley, ed. *Nag Hammadi Codex II, 2–7.* 2 vols. Leiden: Brill, 1989.

——, trans. *The Gnostic Scriptures.* Garden City, N.Y.: Doubleday, 1987.

Leloir, Louis. *Éphrem de Nisibe, Commentaire de l'évangile concordant ou Diatessaron: Traduit du Syriaque et de l'Arménien.* SC 121. Paris: Cerf, 1966.

——, ed. Saint Ephrem, *Commentaire l'Évangile concordant.* CSCO Scr. Arm. II. Louvain: Durbecq, 1954.

Lelyfeld, Marguerite. *Les logia de la vie dans l'Évangile selon Thomas: A la recherche d'une tradition et d'une rédaction.* NHS 34. Leiden: Brill, 1987.

Lemm, Oscar von. "Koptische Apokryphe Apostelakten." *Mélanges Asiatiques* 10 (1890–92): 110–47.

Lietzmann, Hans. *An die Korinther.* HNT 9. 2d ed. Tübingen: Mohr (Siebeck), 1923.

Lightfoot, John B. *The Epistle of St. Paul to the Galatians.* 10th ed. Grand Rapids, Mich.: Zondervan, 1957.

Linnemann, Eta. "Die Verleugnung des Petrus." *ZTK* 63 (1966): 1–32.

Lipsius, Richard Albert. *Die apokryphen Apostelgeschichten und Apostellegenden.* 2 vols. in 3 and supp.; 1883–90. Repr., Amsterdam: Philo, 1976.

——, ed. *Acta Thaddaei.* In *Acta Apostolorum Apocrypha,* edited by R. A. Lipsius and M. Bonnet, 1:273–78. 3 vols. Leipzig: Mendelssohn, 1891–1903. Reprint Darmstadt: Wissenschaftliche Buchgesellschaft, 1959.

Lipsius, Richard Albert, and Maximilianus Bonnet. *Acta Apostolorum Apocrypha.* 2 vols in 3. Leipzig: Mendelssohn, 1891–1903. Repr. Darmstadt: Wissenschaftliche Buchgesellschaft, 1959.

Lohmeyer, Ernst. *Galiläa und Jerusalem.* FRLANT 34. Göttingen: Vandenhoeck & Ruprecht, 1936.

Lohse, Eduard. "Ursprung und Prägung des christlichen Apostolates." *TZ* 9 (1953): 259–75.

Loisy, Alfred. *Les Actes des Apôtres.* Paris: Rieder, 1925.

Lucchesi, Enzo. "Évangile selon Marie ou Évangile selon Marie-Madeleine?" *AnBoll* 103 (1985): 366.

Lüdemann, Gerd. *The Resurrection of Jesus: History, Experience, Theology.* Minneapolis: Fortress, 1994.

Lührmann, Dieter. "Die griechischen Fragmente des Mariaevangeliums POxy 3525 und PRyl 463." *NovT* 30 (1988): 321–38.

——. *Das Markusevangelium.* HNT 3. Tübingen: Mohr, 1987.

——. "POx 4009: Ein neues Fragment des Petrusevangelium?" *NovT* 35 (1993): 390–410.

Luttikhuizen, Gerard P. "The Evaluation of the Teaching of Jesus in Christian Gnostic Revelation Dialogues." *NovT* 30 (1988): 158–68.

Luz, Ulrich. *Das Evangelium nach Matthäus.* EKKNT 1. Zürich: Benziger/ Neukirchen-Vluyn: Neukirchener Verlag, 1985–2002.

Maas, Paul, and Constantine A. Trypanis, eds. *Sancti Romani Melodi Cantica.* Oxford: Clarendon, 1963.

MacDonald, Dennis R. *"The Acts of Paul* and *The Acts of Peter:* Which Came First?" In *Society of Biblical Literature 1992 Seminar Papers,* edited by Eugene H. Lovering, Jr., 214–24. Atlanta: Scholars Press, 1992.

——. *The Legend and the Apostle: The Battle for Paul in Story and Canon.* Philadelphia: Westminster, 1983.

——, ed. *The Apocryphal Acts of the Apostles. Semeia* 38. Decatur, Ga.: Scholars Press, 1986.

MacDonald, Margaret Y. *Early Christian Women and Pagan Opinion: The Power of the Hysterical Woman.* Cambridge: Cambridge University Press, 1996.

MacKay, Thomas W. "Observations on P. Bodmer X (Apocryphal Correspondence between Paul and the Corinthian Saints)." In *Actes du Xve Congrès International de Papyrologie.* Vol. 3 of Papyrologica Bruxellensia 18, 119–28. Bruxelles: Fondation Egyptologique Reine Elisabeth, 1979.

——. "Response." *Semeia* 38 (1986): 145–49.

MacRae, George W. "The Fourth Gospel and Religionsgeschichte." *CBQ* 32 (1970): 13–24.

——. *Invitation to John: A Commentary in the Gospel of John with Complete Text from the Jerusalem Bible.* Garden City, N.Y.: Image Books, 1978.

——. *Studies in the New Testament and Gnosticism.* Wilmington, Del.: Glazier, 1987.

MacRae, George W., and Robert McL. Wilson, trans. "The Gospel of Mary." In *Nag Hammadi Library in English,* ed. James M. Robinson, 524–27. 3d ed. San Francisco: Harper and Row, 1988.

Maisch, Ingrid. *Maria Magdalena: Zwischen Verachtung und Verehrung: Das Bild einer Frau im Spiegel der Jahrhunderte.* ET: *Mary Magdalene: The Image of a Woman through the Centuries.* Translated by Linda M. Maloney. Collegeville, Minn.: Liturgical Press, 1998.

Malan, Solomon C. *The Conflicts of the Holy Apostles: An Apocryphal Book of the Early Eastern Church Translated from an Ethiopic Manuscript.* London, 1871.

Maly, Eugene H. "Women and the Gospel of Luke." *BTB* 10 (1980): 99–104.

Mánek, Jindřich. "Fishers of Men." *NovT* 2 (1958): 138–41.

Mara, Maria Grazia, trans. *Évangile de Pierre.* SC 201. Paris: Cerf, 1973.

Mariès, Louis, and Charles Mercier, trans. *Hymnes de Saint Éphrem conservées en version arménienne.* PO 30. Paris: Firmin-Didot, 1961.

Marjanen, Antii. *The Woman Jesus Loved: Mary Magdalene in the Nag Hammadi Library and Related Documents.* NHMS 40. Leiden: Brill, 1996.

Marsh, *Gospel of St. John.* New York: Viking, 1968.

Marshall, I. Howard. *The Gospel of Luke: A Commentary on the Greek Text.* Grand Rapids, Mich.: Eerdmans, 1978.

Martyn, James Louis. *The Gospel of John in Christian History: Essays for Interpreters.* New York: Paulist, 1979.

Marxsen, Willi. *The Resurrection of Jesus of Nazareth.* Philadelphia: Fortress, 1970.

Masson, Charles. "Le tombeau vide." *RTP* 32 (1944): 161–74.

Matthews, Christopher R. *Philip: Apostle and Evangelist.* NovTSup. Leiden: Brill, 2002.

Maurer, Christian, and Wilhelm Schneemelcher. "The Gospel of Peter." In *Gospels and Related Writings,* Vol. 1. of *New Testament Apocrypha,* edited by Wilhelm Schneemelcher, 216–27. Translated by R. McL. Wilson. Rev. ed. Cambridge: James Clark and Co.; Louisville, Ky.: Westminster/John Knox, 1991.

Maynard, Arthur H. "The Role of Peter in the Fourth Gospel." *NTS* 30 (1984): 531–48.

McCant, Jerry W. "The Gospel of Peter: Docetism Reconsidered." *NTS* 30 (1984): 258–73.

McCarthy, Carmel. *Saint Ephrem's Commentary on Tatian's Diatessaron: An English Translation of Chester Beatty Syriac MS 709 with Introduction and Notes.* JSSSup 2. Oxford: Oxford University Press, 1993.

McKnight, Edgar V., and Elizabeth Struthers Malbon, eds. *New Literary Criticism and the New Testament.* Sheffield, Eng.: Sheffield Academic Press, 1994. Repr., Valley Forge, Pa.: Trinity Press International, 1994.

Meeks, Wayne. "'Am I a Jew?' Johannine Christianity and Judaism." *Christianity, Judaism and Other Greco-Roman Cults.* Vol 1. Leiden: Brill, 1975.

———. "Galilee and Judea in the Fourth Gospel." *JBL* 85 (1966): 159–69.

Meeks, Wayne. "Image of the Androgyne: Some Uses of a Symbol in Earliest Christianity." *HR* 13 (1973–74): 165–208.

———. *The Prophet-King: Moses Traditions and the Johannine Christology.* NovTSup 14. Leiden: Brill, 1967.

Meier, John P. "The Circle of the Twelve: Did it Exist during Jesus' Public Ministry." *JBL* 116 (1997): 635–72.

Ménard, Jacques-É. *L'Évangile selon Thomas.* NHS 5. Leiden: Brill, 1975.

Menoud, Philippe H. "Pendant Quarante Jours." In *Jésus-Christ et la Foi: Recherches néotestamentaires,* 110–18. Bibliothèque théologique. Neuchâtel/Paris: Delachaux et Niestlé, 1975.

Meyer, Marvin W., trans. and introduction. *The Gospel of Thomas: The Hidden Sayings of Jesus.* Interpreted by Harold Bloom. New York: HarperSanFrancisco, 1992.

———, introduction. "Letter of Peter to Philip (VIII,2)." Translated by Frederik Wisse. In *NHL,* edited by James M. Robinson, 431–37. San Francisco: Harper & Row, rev. ed., 1988.

———. "Making Mary Male: The Categories 'Male' and 'Female' in the Gospel of Thomas." *NTS* 31 (1985): 554–70.

Meynet, Roland. *L'Évangile selon Saint Luc: Analyse rhétorique.* 2 vols. Paris: Cerf, 1988.

Michaelis, Wilhelm. *Die Erscheinungen des Auferstandenen.* Basel: Heinrich Majer, 1944.

Michel, Otto. "Ein johanneischer Osterbericht." In *Studien zum Neuen Testament und zur Patristik: Festschrift für Erich Klostermann,* 35–42. TU 77. Berlin: Akademie-Verlag, 1961.

Minear, Paul S. "'We don't know where. . .' John 20:2." *Int* 30 (1976): 125–39.

Minnerath, Roland. *De Jérusalem à Rome: Pierre et l'unité de l'Église apostolique.* ThH 101. Paris: Beauchesne, 1994.

Mohri, Erika. *Maria Magdalena: Frauenbilder in Evangelientexten des 1. bis 3. Jahrhunderts.* Marburg: Elwert Verlag, 2000.

Molland, Einar. "Le développement de l'idée de succession apostolique." *RHPR* 34 (1954): 1–29.

Moltmann-Wendel, Elisabeth. *The Women around Jesus.* New York: Crossroad, 1982.

Moore, Stephen D. *Mark and Luke in Poststructuralist Perspectives: Jesus Begins to Write.* New Haven/London: Yale University Press, 1992.

Morard, Françoise. "Un Évangile écrit par une femme?" *BCPE* 49.2–3 (May, 1997): 27–34.

Mosbech, Holger. "Apostolos in the New Testament." *ST* 2 (1948): 166–200.

Moxnes, Halvor. *Economy of the Kingdom: Social Conflict and Economic Relations in Luke's Gospel.* Philadelphia: Fortress, 1988.

Munck, Johannes. "Paul, the Apostles, and the Twelve." *ST* 3 (1950): 96–110.

Murray, Robert. *Symbols of Church and Kingdom: A Study in Early Syriac Tradition.* Cambridge: Cambridge University Press, 1975.

Nauck, Wolfgang. "Die Bedeutung des leeren Grabes für den Glauben an den Auferstandenen." *ZNW* 47 (1956): 243–67.

Norelli, Enrico. "Situation des apocryphes pétriniens." *Apocrypha* 2 (1991): 31–83.

Nürnberg, Rosemarie. "Apostolae Apostolorum. Die Frauen am Grab als erste Zeuginnen der Auferstehung in der Väterexegese." In *Stimuli, Exegese und ihre Hermeneutik in Antike und Christentum*s (Fs. Ernst Dassmann), edited by Georg Schöllgen and Clemens Scholten, 228–42. JAC.E 23. Münster: Aschendorff, 1996.

O'Collins, Gerald, and Daniel Kendall. "Mary Magdalene as Major Witness to Jesus' Resurrection." *TS* 48 (1987): 631–46.

Otto, Johann Carl Theodor von. *Corpus Apologetarum Christianorum.* Jena: Prostat in Libraria H. Dufft, 1847–72.

Paffenroth, Kim. *The Story of Jesus according to L.* JSNTSup 147. Sheffield: Sheffield Academic Press, 1997.

Pagels, Elaine H. *The Gnostic Gospels.* New York: Vintage Books, 1981.

——. "Visions, Appearances, and Apostolic Authority: Gnostic and Orthodox Traditions." In *Gnosis,* Fs. Hans Jonas, edited by Barbara Aland, 415–30. Göttingen: Vandenhoeck & Ruprecht, 1978.

Painter, John. *Just James: The Brother of Jesus in History and Tradition.* Columbia, S.C.: University of South Carolina Press, 1997.

Parrott, Douglas M. "Gnostic and Orthodox Disciples in the Second and Third Centuries." In *Nag Hammadi, Gnosticism, & Early Christianity*, edited by Charles W. Hedrick and Robert Hodgson, Jr., 193–219. Peabody, Mass.: Hendrickson, 1986.

——, trans. "Sophia of Jesus Christ (III,4 and BG 8502,3). In *Nag Hammadi Library in English*, edited by James M. Robinson, 220–43. 3d ed. San Francisco: Harper & Row, 1988.

Parsons, P. J. "3525. Gospel of Mary." In *The Oxyrhynchus Papyri, Volume 50*, 12–14. Graeco-Roman Memoirs, No. 70. London: Egypt Exploration Society, 1983.

Parvey, Constance F. "The Theology and Leadership of Women in the New Testament." In *Religion and Sexism*, edited by Rosemary Radford Ruether, 139–49. New York: Simon & Schuster, 1974.

Pasquier, Anne. "L'eschatologie dans l'Évangile selon Marie: Étude des notions de nature et d'image." In *Colloque International sur les Textes de Nag Hammadi (Québec, 22–25 août 1978)*, edited by B. Barc, 390–404. Québec-Louvain: Presses de l'Université Laval, 1981.

———. *L'Évangile selon Marie*. BCNH; Section "Textes" 10. Québec: Les presses de l'Université Laval, 1983.

Patterson, Stephen J. *The Gospel of Thomas and Jesus*. Sonoma, Calif.: Polebridge, 1993.

Pelikan, Jaroslav. *Mary through the Centuries*. New Haven: Yale University Press, 1996.

Perkins, Pheme. *The Gnostic Dialogue: The Early Church and the Crisis of Gnosticism*. Theological Inquiries. New York: Paulist Press, 1980.

———. *Gnosticism and the New Testament*. Minneapolis: Fortress, 1993.

———. "Gospel of Thomas." In *A Feminist Commentary*. Vol. 2 of *Searching the Scriptures*, edited by Elisabeth Schüssler Fiorenza, 535–60. New York: Crossroad, 1994.

———. "Mary, Gospel of." In *The Anchor Bible Dictionary*, edited by David Noel Freedman, 4:583–84. New York: Doubleday, 1992.

———. *Peter: Apostle for the Whole Church*. Columbia, S.C.: University of South Carolina Press, 1994.

Pervo, Richard I. *Profit With Delight: The Literary Genre of the Acts of the Apostles*. Philadelphia: Fortress, 1987.

Pesch, Rudolf. *Das Markusevangelium: Kommentar zu Kap. 8,27–16,20*. HTKNT 2.2. Freiburg: Herder, 1977.

———. "La rédaction lucanienne du logion des pêcheurs d'homme (Lc. V,10c)." *ETL* 46 (1970): 413–32.

———. "Zur Enstehung des Glaubens an die Auferstehung Jesu." *TQ* 153 (1973): 201–28.

Petersen, Silke. *"Zerstört die Werke der Wieblichkeit!": Maria Magdalena, Salome und andere Jüngerinnen Jesu in christlich-gnostischen Schriften*. NHMS 48. Leiden: Brill, 1999.

Petersen, William L. *Tatian's Diatessaron: Its Creation, Dissemination, Significance, and History in Scholarship*. Leiden: Brill, 1994.

Petersen, William L. *The Diatessaron and Ephrem Syrus as Sources of Romanos the Melodist*. CSCO 475. Subsidia 74. Louvain: Peeters, 1985.

Petzke, Gerd. *Das Sondergut des Evangeliums nach Lukas*. Zürcher Werkkommentare zur Bibel. Zürich: Theologischer Verlag, 1990.

Pilhofer, Peter. "Justin und das Petrusevangelium." *ZNW* 81 (1990): 60–78.

Plevnik, Joseph. " 'The Eleven and Those with Them' according to Luke." *CBQ* 40 (1978): 205–11.

Plummer, Alfred. *A Critical and Exegetical Commentary on the Gospel according to St. Luke*. New York: Scribner's Sons, 1896.

Poupon, Gérard. "Les 'Actes de Pierre' et leur remaniement." In *ANRW* 2: 25/6. 4363–83. Berlin: De Gruyter, 1988.

———. "Encore une fois: Tertullien, *De baptismo* 17, 5." In *Nomen Latinum* (Fs. André Schneider), 199–203. Neuchâtel: Faculté de Lettres, 1997.

Powell, Mark Allan. *What is Narrative Criticism?* Minneapolis: Fortress, 1990.

Price, Robert M. "Mary Magdalene: Gnostic Apostle?" *Grail* 6 (1990): 54–76.

Puech, Henri-Charles. "Gnostische Evangelien und verwandte Dockumente." In *Evangelien*. Vol. 1 of *Neutestamentliche Apokryphen in deutscher Übersetzung*, edited by Edgar Hennecke and Wilhelm Schneemelcher, 285–329. 2 vols. 3d ed. Tübingen: Mohr (Siebeck), 1959–1964.

———. *En quête de la Gnose: Sur l'Évangile selon Thomas: Esquisse d'une interprétation systématique*. Paris: Gallimard, 1978.

———. "Das Thomas-Evangelium." In *Evangelien*. Vol. 1 of *Neutestamentliche Apokryphen in deutscher Übersetzung*, edited by Edgar Hennecke and Wilhelm Schneemelcher, 199–223. 2 vols. 3d ed. Tübingen: Mohr (Siebeck), 1959–1964.

———. "The Gospel of Mary." Revised by Beate Blatz. In *Gospels and Related Writings*. Vol. 1 of *New Testament Apocrypha*, edited by Wilhelm Schneemelcher, 391–95. Translated by Robert McL. Wilson. Rev. ed. Cambridge: James Clark and Co.; Louisville, Ky.: Westminster/John Knox, 1991.

Quast, Kevin. *Peter and the Beloved Disciple: Figures for a Community in Crisis*. JSNTSup 32. Sheffield: JSOT Press, 1989.

Reeves, Keith Howard. *The Resurrection Narrative in Matthew: A Literary-Critical Examination*. Lewiston, N.Y.: Mellen Biblical Press, 1993.

Rehkopf, Friedrich. *Die lukanische Sonderquelle*. WUNT 5. Tübingen: Mohr, 1959.

Reid, Barbara E. *Choosing the Better Part? Women in the Gospel of Luke.* Collegeville, Minn.: Liturgical Press, 1996.

Reid, Barbara E. "A Colloquy on the Women in Luke–Acts: Choosing the Better Part." *BR* 42 (1997): 23–31.

Reidl, J. "'Wirklich, der Herr ist auferweckt worden und dem Simon erschienen' (Lk 24,34): Entstehung und Inhalt des neutestamentlichen Osterglaubens." *BLit* 40 (1967): 81–110.

Reinhartz, Adele. "The Gospel of John." In *A Feminist Commentary.* Vol. 2 of *Searching the Scriptures*, edited by Elisabeth Schüssler Fiorenza, 561–600. New York: Crossroad, 1994.

Rengstorf, Karl Heinrich. "ἀποστέλλω." *TDNT* 1:398–406.

——. "ἀπόστολος." *TDNT* 1:407–47.

——. "*apóstolos.*" In *TDNT: Abridged in One Volume*, abridged by Geoffrey W. Bromiley, 69–75. Grand Rapids, Mich.: Eerdmans, 1985.

——. *Die Auferstehung Jesu: Form, Art und Sinn der urchristlichen Osterbotschaft.* Witten/Ruhr: Luther-Verlag, 1960.

——. "δώδεκα." *TDNT* 2:321–28.

——. "Urchristliches Kerygma und 'gnostische' Interpretation in einigen Sprüchen des Thomas evangeliums." In *Le Origini dello Gnosticimo: Colloquio di Messina 13–18 Aprile 1966: Testi e Discussioni*, edited by Ugo Bianchi, 563–74. SHR, Numen Sup 12. Leiden: Brill, 1967.

Revillout, Eugène, ed. *Les Évangiles des douze apôtres et de saint Barthélemy.* Les apocryphes coptes I. In PO 2.2, edited by R. Graffin and F. Nau, 169–70. Paris: Firmin-Didot, 1904.

Ricci, Carla. *Mary Magdalene and Many Others: Women Who Followed Jesus.* Translated by Paul Burns. Translation of *Maria Magdala e le molte altre* (1991). Minneapolis: Fortress, 1994.

Rice, George E. "Luke's Thematic Use of the Call to Discipleship." *AUSS* 19 (1981): 51–58.

Rigaux, Béda. "Die Zwölf in Geschichte und Kerygma." In *Der historische Jesus und der kerygmatische Christus*, edited by Helmut Ristow and Karl Matthiae, 168–86. Berlin: Evangelische Verlagsanstalt, 1962.

Riley, Gregory J. *Resurrection Reconsidered: Thomas and John in Controversy.* Minneapolis: Fortress, 1995.

Rimoldi, Antonio. *L'apostolo san Pietro fondamento della Chiesa, principe degli Apostoli ed ostiario celeste nella Chiesa primitiva dalle origini al Concilio di Calcedonia.* Roma: Universitas Gregoriana, 1958.

Roberts, Colin H. "463: The Gospel of Mary." In *Catalogue of the Greek Papyri in the John Rylands Library*, 3:18–23. 4 vols. Manchester: University Press, 1911–52.

Robinson, James M. "Basic Shifts in German Theology." *Int* 16 (1962): 76–97.

——, ed. *Nag Hammadi Library in English*. 3d ed. San Francisco: Harper and Row, 1988.

Robinson, James M., and Helmut Koester. *Trajectories through Early Christianity*. Philadelphia: Fortress, 1971.

Roloff, Jürgen. *Apostolat–Verkündigung–Kirche: Ursprung, Inhalt und Funktion des kirchlichen Apostelamtes nach Paulus, Lukas und den Pastoralbriefen*. Gütersloh: Mohn, 1965.

Rordorf, Willy. "Tradition and Composition in the *Acts of Thecla*." *Semeia* 38 (1986): 43–52.

Rossi, Mary Ann. "Priesthood, Precedent, and Prejudice: On Recovering the Women Priests of Early Christianity." *JFSR* 7 (1991): 73–93.

Rostalski, Friedrich. *Die Sprache der griechischen Paulusakten: mit Berücksichtigung ihrer lateinischen Übersetzungen*. Myslowitz: Max Rolle, 1913.

Ruether, Rosemary. *Women-Church*. San Francisco: Harper & Row, 1985.

Ruschmann, Susanne. *Maria von Magdala im Johannesevangelium: Jüngerin—Zeugin—Lebensbotin*. Neutestamentliche Abhandlungen 40. Münster: Aschendorff, 2002.

Sanders, Joseph N. "Who Was the Disciple Whom Jesus Loved?" In *Studies in the Fourth Gospel*, edited by Frank L. Cross, 72–82. London: A. R. Mowbray, 1957.

——. *A Commentary on the Gospel according to St. John*. Peabody, Mass.: Hendrickson, 1968.

Santos Otero, Aurelio de. "Later Acts of Apostles." In *Writings Related to the Apostles, Apocalypses and Related Subjects*. Vol. 2 of *New Testament Apocrypha*, edited by Wilhelm Schneemelcher, 426–82. 2 vols. Translated by R. McL. Wilson. Rev. ed. Cambridge: James Clark and Co.; Louisville, Ky.: Westminster/John Knox, 1992.

Saxer, Victor. "Les saintes Marie Madeleine et Marie de Béthanie dans la tradition liturgique et homilétique orientale." *RevScRel* 32 (1958): 1–37.

Schaberg, Jane. "How Mary Magdalene Became a Whore: Mary Magdalene is in fact the primary witness to the fundamental data of early Christian faith." *BRev* 8 (1992): 30–37, 51–52.

Schaberg, Jane. "Luke." In *The Women's Bible Commentary*, edited by Carol A. Newsom and Sharon H. Ringe, 275–92. Louisville, Ky.: Westminster/John Knox, 1992.

———. *The Resurrection of Mary Magdalene: Legends, Apocrypha, and the Christian Testament*. New York: Continuum, 2002.

———. "Thinking Back through the Magdalene." *Continuum* 1.2 (1991): 71–90.

Schaff, Philip, ed. In *Epistolam ad Romanos, Homilia* 31, 2 (PG 60, 669-70). English translation from *The Homilies of St. John Chrysostom, The Epistle to the Romans*, Homily XXXI; Nicene and Post-Nicene Fathers, series I; Peabody, Mass.: Hendrickson, 1994.

Schenke, Hans-Martin. "Bemerkungen zum koptischen Papyrus Berolinensis 8502." In *Festschrift zum 150 jährigen Bestehen des Berliner Ägyptischen Museums*, 315–22. Mitteilungen aus der Ägyptischen Sammlung 8. Berlin: Akademie Verlag, 1974.

Schmid, Renate. *Maria Magdalena in gnostischen Schriften*. Material-Edition 29. Munich: Arbeitsgemeinschaft für Religions- und Weltanschauungsfragen, 1990.

Schmidt, Carl. *Acta Pauli aus Heidelberger koptischen Papyrus Handschrift, Nr. 1*. Leipzig, Hinrichs, 1904. Repr. Hildesheim: Georg Olms, 1965.

———, ed. *Pistis Sophia*. Translated by Violet MacDermot. NHS 9. Leiden: Brill, 1978.

———. *Pistis Sophia: Ein gnostisches Originalwerk des 3. Jahrhunderts aus dem Koptischen übersetzt*. Leipzig: Hinrichs, 1925.

———. "Die Urschrift der Pistis Sophia." *ZNW* 24 (1925): 218–40.

Schmidt, Carl, and Wilhelm Schubart. ΠΡΑΞΕΙΣ ΠΑΥΛΟΥ: *Acta Pauli nach dem Papyrus der Hamburger Staats- und Universitäts-Bibliothek*. Glückstadt/Hamburg: Augustin, 1936.

Schmidt, Carl, and Walter Till. *Die Pistis Sophia: Die beiden Bücher des Jeû: Unbekanntes altgnostisches Werk*. GCS 45. 3d ed. Berlin, 1954. Repr. 1959, 1962.

Schmidt, Karl Ludwig. *Der Rahmen der Geschichte Jesu*. Berlin: Trowitzsch und Sohn, 1919.

Schmithals, Walter. *Das kirchliche Apostelamt: Ein historische Untersuchung*. FRLANT 79, n.s., 61. Göttingen: Vandenhoeck & Ruprecht, 1961. (ET: *The Office of Apostle in the Early Church*. Translated by John E. Steely. Nashville and New York: Abingdon, 1969.)

Schnackenburg, Rudolf. "Apostles before and during Paul's time." In *Apostolic History and the Gospel*, edited by W. Ward Gasque and Ralph P. Martin, 287–303. Grand Rapids, Mich.: Eerdmans, 1970.

——. "Apostolicity—the Present Position of Studies." *OiC* 6 (1970): 243–73.

——. *The Gospel according to St. John*. 3 vols. New York: Crossroad, 1982.

——. "Der Jünger, den Jesus liebte." In *EKKNT: Vorarbeiten,* 2:97–117. Zürich: Neukirchener Verlag, 1970.

Schneemelcher, Wilhelm. "Introduction [The Gospel of Peter]." In *Gospels and Related Writings*. Vol. 1. of *New Testament Apocrypha*, edited by Wilhelm Schneemelcher, 216–27. 2 vols. Translated by Robert McL. Wilson. Rev. ed. Cambridge: James Clark and Co.; Louisville, Ky.: Westminster/John Knox, 1991.

——. "Second and Third Century Acts of Apostles: Introduction." In *Writings Related to the Apostles, Apocalypses and Related Subjects.* Vol. 2 of *New Testament Apocrypha,* edited by Wilhelm Schneemelcher, 75–86. 2 vols. Translated by Robert McL. Wilson. Rev. ed. Cambridge: James Clark and Co.; Louisville, Ky.: Westminster/John Knox, 1992.

Schneiders, Sandra M. "Women in the Fourth Gospel and the Role of Women in the Contemporary Church." *BTB* 12 (1982): 35–45.

Schottroff, Luise. "Maria Magdalena und die Frauen am Grabe Jesu." *EvT* 42 (1982): 3–25.

Schottroff, Luise, Silvia Schroer, and Marie-Theres Wacker. *Feminist Interpretation: The Bible in Women's Perspective*. Translated by Martin and Barbara Rumscheidt. Translation of *Feministische Exegese: Forschungserträge zur Bibel aus der Perspektive von Frauen*. Minneapolis: Fortress, 1998.

Schubert, Paul. "The Structure and Significance of Luke 24." In *Neutestamentliche Studien für Rudolf Bultmann,* edited by Walther Eltester, 165–86. BZNW 21. Berlin: Töpelmann, 1954.

Schüngel, Paul. "Ein Vorschlag, EvTho 114 neu zu übersetzen." *NovT* 36 (1994): 394–401.

Schürmann, Heinz. *Das Lukasevangelium*. HTKNT 3/1. Freiburg: Herder, 1969.

——. "La promesse à Simon-Pierre. Lc 5, 1–11." *AsSeign* 36 (1974): 63–70.

Schüssler Fiorenza, Elisabeth. *Bread Not Stone: The Challenge of Feminist Biblical Interpretation*. Boston: Beacon, 1984.

——. "A Feminist Critical Interpretation for Liberation: Martha and Mary: Luke 10:38–42." *Religion and Intellectual Life* 3 (1986): 21–35.

Schüssler Fiorenza, Elisabeth. *In Memory of Her: A Feminist Theological Reconstruction of Christian Origins*. New York: Crossroad, 1983.

——. *Jesus: Miriam's Child, Sophia's Prophet*. New York: Continuum, 1994.

——. "Mary Magdalene: Apostle to the Apostles." *Union Theological Seminary Journal* (April 1975): 22–24.

——. "The Quest for the Johannine School: The Apocalypse and the Fourth Gospel." *NTS* 23 (1977): 402–27.

——. *Rhetoric and Ethic: The Politics of Biblical Studies*. Minneapolis: Fortress, 1999.

——. "Rhetorical Situation and Historical Reconstruction in I Corinthians." *NTS* 33 (1987): 386–403.

——, ed. *A Feminist Commentary*. Vol. 2 of *Searching the Scriptures*. New York: Crossroad, 1994.

Schweizer, Eduard. *Matthäus und seine Gemeinde*. SBS 71. Stuttgart: Katholisches Bibelwerk, 1974.

Scopello, Maddalena. "Marie-Madeleine et la tour: *Pistis et sophia*." In *Figures du Nouveau Testament chez les Péres*, 179–96. CBPa 3. Strasbourg: Centre d'analyse et de documentation patristiques, 1991.

Scott, Martin. *Sophia and the Johannine Jesus*. JSNTSup 71. Sheffield, England: JSOT Press, 1992.

Sebastiani, Lilia. *Tra/Sfigurazione: Il personaggio evangelico di Maria di Magdala e il mito della peccatrice redenta nella tradizione occidentale*. Brescia: Queriniana, 1992.

Segovia, Fernando F. "Cultural Studies and Contemporary Biblical Criticism: Ideological Criticism as a Mode of Discourse." In *Social Location and Biblical Interpretation in Global Perspective*. Vol. 2 of *Reading from This Place*, edited by Fernando F. Segovia and Mary Ann Tolbert, 1–17. Minneapolis: Fortress, 1995.

Seim, Turid Karlsen. *The Double Message: Patterns of Gender in Luke–Acts*. Edinburgh: T&T Clark, 1994.

——. "A Colloquy on the Women in Luke–Acts: Searching for the Silver Coin." *BR* 42 (1997): 32–42.

Setzer, Claudia. "Excellent Women: Female Witness to the Resurrection." *JBL* 116 (1997): 259–72.

Shoemaker, Stephen J. *The Ancient Traditions of the Virgin Mary's Dormition and Assumption*. Oxford Early Christian Studies. Oxford: Clarendon Press, forthcoming.

——. "Mary and the Discourse of Orthodoxy: Early Christian Identity and the Ancient Dormition Legends." Ph.D. diss. Duke University, 1997.

Shoemaker, Stephen J. "Rethinking the 'Gnostic Mary': Mary of Nazareth and Mary of Magdala in Early Christian Tradition." *JECS* 9 (2001): 555–95.

Sim, David C. "The Women Followers of Jesus: The Implications of Luke 8: 1–3." *HeyJ* 30 (1989): 51–62.

Smith, Dwight Moody. *The Composition and Order of the Fourth Gospel: Bultmann's Literary Theory.* New Haven: Yale University Press, 1965.

———. *Johannine Christianity: Essays on Its Setting, Sources and Theology.* Columbia, S.C.: University of South Carolina Press, 1984.

Smith Lewis, Agnes. *The Mythological Acts of the Apostles.* HSem 4. London: Clay, 1904.

Smith, Terence. *Petrine Controversies in Early Christianity: Attitudes towards Peter in Christian Writings of the First Two Centuries.* WUNT 2.15. Tübingen: Mohr (Siebeck), 1985.

Snyder, Graydon F. "John 13:16 and the Anti-Petrinism of the Johannine Tradition." *BR* 16 (1971): 5–15.

Spencer, F. Scott. *The Portrait of Philip in Acts: A Study of Roles and Relations.* JSNTSup 67. Sheffield: Sheffield Academic Press, 1992.

Stichele, Caroline Vander. "A Disciple of the Lord and Her Friends: Women in the Gospel of Peter." SBL Annual Meeting, 1997.

Stoops, Robert F., Jr. "Patronage in the *Acts of Peter*." *Semeia* 38 (1986): 91–100.

———. "Peter, Paul, and Priority in the Apocryphal Acts." In *SBL 1992 Seminar Papers,* edited by Eugene H. Lovering, Jr., 225–33. Atlanta: Scholars Press, 1992.

Struthers Malbon, Elizabeth. "Galilee and Jerusalem: History and Literature in Marcan Interpretation." *CBQ* 44 (1982): 242–55.

Swidler, Leonard. *Biblical Affirmations of Women.* Philadelphia: Westminster, 1979.

Synek, Eva M. " 'Die andere Maria.' Zum Bild der Maria von Magdala in den östlichen Kirchentraditionen." *OrChr* 79 (1995): 181–96.

Tardieu, Michel. *Écrits Gnostiques: Codex de Berlin.* Sources gnostiques et manichéennes 1. Paris: Cerf, 1984.

Tardieu, Michel, and Jean-Daniel Dubois. *Introduction à la littérature gnostique* I. Paris: Cerf and CNRS, 1986.

Taylor, Vincent. *The Passion Narrative of St. Luke: A Critical and Historical Investigation.* Edited by O. E. Evans. SNTSMS 19. Cambridge: Cambridge University Press, 1972.

Theissen, Gerd. *Soziologie der Jesusbewegung*. ET: *Sociology of Early Palestinian Christianity*. Translated by John Bowden. Philadelphia: Fortress, 1978.

Theissen, Gerd. "Autoritätskonflikte in den Johanneischen Gemeinden: Zum 'Sitz im Leben' des Johannesevangeliums." *Diakonia*. Thessalonike, 1988.

Thiede, Carston. *Simon Peter: From Galilee to Rome*. Grand Rapids, Mich.: Academie Books, 1988.

Thimmes, Pamela. "Memory and Re-vision: Mary Magdalene Research since 1975." *CurBS* 6 (1998): 193–226.

Thomas, Christine M. "The Acts of Peter." In *The Apocryphal Acts of the Apostles: Harvard Divinity School Studies*, edited by François Bovon, Ann Graham Brock, and Christopher R. Matthews, 39–62. Cambridge: Harvard University Center for the Study of World Religions, 1999.

——. *The Acts of Peter, Gospel Literature, and the Ancient Novel: Rewriting the Past*. Oxford: Oxford University Press, forthcoming (2003).

Thompson, Mary R. *Mary of Magdala: Apostle and Leader*. New York: Paulist Press, 1995.

Till, Walter C. "Die Berliner gnostische Handschrift." In *Europäischer Wissenschafts-Dienst* 4 (1944): 19–21.

——. "Εὐαγγέλλιον κατὰ Μαριάμ." *La parola del passato* 1 (1946): 260–65.

——. *Das Evangelium nach Philippos*. PTS 2. Berlin: de Gruyter, 1963.

——. "Die Gnosis in Aegypten." *La parola del passato* 4 (1949): 230–49.

——. *Pistis Sophia*. 3d ed. Berlin: Akademischer Verlag, 1962.

Till, Walter C., and Hans-Martin Schenke. *Die gnostischen Schriften des koptischen Papyrus Berolinensis 8502*. TU 60. 2d ed. Berlin: Akademie Verlag, 1972.

Torjesen, Karen Jo. *When Women were Priests: Women's Leadership in the Early Church and the Scandal of their Subordination in the Rise of Christianity*. San Francisco: Harper & Row, 1993.

Trompf, G. W. "The First Resurrection Appearance and the Ending of Mark's Gospel." *NTS* 18 (1972): 308–30.

Turner, Max. "The Spirit of Prophecy and the Power of Authoritative Preaching in Luke–Acts: A Question of Origins." *NTS* 38 (1992): 66–88.

Vaganay, Léon. *L'Évangile de Pierre*. EBib. Paris: Gabalda, 1930.

Valantasis, Richard. "Narrative Strategies and Synoptic Quandaries: A Response to Dennis MacDonald's Reading of *Acts of Paul* and *Acts of Peter*." In *Society of Biblical Literature 1992 Seminar Papers*, edited by Eugene H. Lovering, Jr., 234–39. Atlanta: Scholars Press, 1992.

Via, E. Jane. "Women in the Gospel of Luke." In *Women in the World's Religions: Past and Present*, edited by Ursula King, 38–55. New York: Paragon House, 1987.

Vielhauer, Philipp. "ΑΝΑΠΑΥΣΙΣ, Zum gnostischen Hintergrund des *Thomasevangeliums*." In *Apophoreta: Festschrift für Ernst Haenchen*, ed. W. Eltester, 281–99. BZNW 30. Berlin: Töpelmann, 1964.

———. *Aufsätze zum Neuen Testament*. TB 31. Munich: Kaiser, 1965.

———. *Geschichte der urchristlichen Literatur*. Berlin: de Gruyter, 1975.

Völter, Daniel. "Petrusevangelium oder Ägypterevangelium." *ZNW* 6 (1905): 368–72.

Vööbus, Arthur, ed. *Didascalia Apostolorum in Syriac: Chapter XI-XXVI*. CSCO Scriptores Syri 180. Louvain: Secrétariat du CSCO, 1979.

Vouaux, Léon. *Les Actes de Paul et ses lettres apocryphes*. Les apocryphes du Nouveau Testament. Paris: Letouzey et Ané, 1913.

———. *Les Actes de Pierre: Introduction, textes, traduction et commentaire*. Les apocryphes du Nouveau Testament. Paris: Letouzey et Ané, 1922.

Wagenmann, Julius. *Die Stellung des Apostels Paulus neben den Zwölf in den ersten zwei Jahrhunderten*. BZNW 3. Berlin: de Gruyter, 1926.

Wainwright, Elaine Mary. "Gospel of Matthew." In *A Feminist Commentary*. Vol. 2 of *Searching the Scriptures*, edited by Elisabeth Schüssler Fiorenza, 635–77. 2 vols. New York: Crossroad, 1994.

———. *Towards a Feminist Critical Reading of the Gospel according to Matthew*. BZNW 60. Berlin: de Gruyter, 1991.

Wanke, Joachim. *Die Emmauserzählung: Eine redaktionsgeschichtliche Untersuchung zu Lk 24, 13–35*. Erfurter Theologische Studien 31. Leipzig: St. Benno, 1973.

Widengren, Geo. "Les origines du gnosticisme et l'histoire des religions." In *Le Origini dello Gnosticismo. Colloquio di Messina 13–18 Aprile 1966. Testi e Discussioni*, edited by Ugo Bianchi, 28–60. SHR, *Numen Sup* 12. Leiden: Brill, 1967.

———. *Religionsphänomenologie*. Berlin: De Gruyter, 1969.

Wiefel, Wolfgang. *Das Evangelium nach Lukas*. THKNT. Berlin: Evangelische Verlagsanstalt, 1988.

Wilckens, Ulrich. *Auferstehung: Das biblische Auferstehungszeugnis historisch untersucht und erklärt.* Gütersloh: Mohn, 1974. (ET: *Resurrection: Biblical Testimony to the Resurrection: An Historical Examination and Explanation.* Translated by A. M. Stewart. Atlanta: John Knox, 1978.)

Wilcox, Max. "Peter and the Rock: A Fresh Look at Matthew xvi. 17–19." *NTS* 22 (1975/76): 73–88.

Williams, Francis E., ed. "The Apocryphon of James." In *Nag Hammadi Codex I (The Jung Codex): Introductions, Texts, Translations, Notes,* edited by Harold W. Attridge, 13–53. NHS 22. Leiden: Brill, 1985.

Wilson, Robert McL. *Gnosis: A Selection of Gnostic Texts.* Edited by Werner Foerster. 2 Vols. Oxford: Clarendon, 1972–1974.

———. "The New Testament in the Gnostic Gospel of Mary." *NTS* 3 (1956/1957): 236–43.

———. *The Gospel of Philip.* New York: Harper & Row, 1962.

Wilson, Robert McL., and George W. MacRae. "BG,1: The Gospel According to Mary." In *Nag Hammadi Codices V, 2–5 and VI with Papyrus Berolinensis 8502, 1 and 4,* edited by Douglas M. Parrott, 453–71. NHS 11. Leiden: Brill, 1979.

Witherington, Ben, III. "On the Road with Mary Magdalene, Joanna, Susanna, and Other Disciples—Luke 8:1–3." *ZNW* 70 (1979): 243–48.

Wright, William. *Apocryphal Acts of the Apostles. Syriac and English.* Vol. 1: *The Syriac Texts.* Vol. 2: *The English Translations.* Amsterdam: Philo, 1968.

Zillessen, Klaus. "Das Schiff des Petrus und die Gefährten vom anderen Schiff." *ZNW* 57 (1966): 137–39.

Zumstein, Jean. "Der Prozess der Relecture in der johanneischen Literatur." *NTS* 42 (1996): 394–411.

Index of Modern Authors

Index of Ancient Sources

Canonical and Deuterocanonical

Gospel of John

See esp. Chapter 3

Noncanonical Sources

Index of Subjects

Harvard Theological Studies

51. Brock, Ann Graham. *Mary Magdalene, The First Apostle: The Struggle for Authority*, 2003.

50. Trost, Theodore Louis. *Douglas Horton and the Ecumenical Impulse in American Religion*, 2002.

49. Huang, Yong. *Religious Goodness and Political Rightness: Beyond the Liberal-Communitarian Debate*, 2001.

48. Rossing, Barbara R. *The Choice between Two Cities: Whore, Bride, and Empire in the Apocalypse*, 1999.

47. Skedros, James Constantine. *Saint Demetrios of Thessaloniki: Civic Patron and Divine Protector, 4th–7th Centuries C.E.*, 1999.

46. Koester, Helmut, ed. *Pergamon, Citadel of the Gods: Archaeological Record, Literary Description, and Religious Development*, 1998.

45. Kittredge, Cynthia Briggs. *Community and Authority: The Rhetoric of Obedience in the Pauline Tradition*, 1998.

44. Lesses, Rebecca Macy. *Ritual Practices to Gain Power: Angels, Incantations, and Revelation in Early Jewish Mysticism*, 1998.

43. Guenther-Gleason, Patricia E. *On Schleiermacher and Gender Politics*, 1997.

42. White, L. Michael. *The Social Origins of Christian Architecture*. Vol. I and II, 1997.

41. Koester, Helmut, ed. *Ephesos, Metropolis of Asia: An Interdisciplinary Approach to its Archaeology, Religion, and Culture*, 1995.

40. Guider, Margaret Eletta. *Daughters of Rahab: Prostitution and the Church of Liberation in Brazil*, 1995.

39. Schenkel, Albert F. *The Rich Man and the Kingdom: John D. Rockefeller, Jr., and the Protestant Establishment*, 1995.

38. Hutchinson, William R. and Hartmut Lehmann, eds. *Many Are Chosen: Divine Election and Western Nationalism*, 1994.

37. Lubieniecki, Stanislas. *History of the Polish Reformation and Nine Related Documents*. Translated and interpreted by George Huntston Williams, 1995.

– Davidovich, Adina. *Religion as a Province of Meaning: The Kantian Foundations of Modern Theology*, 1993.

36. Thiemann, Ronald F., ed. *The Legacy of H. Richard Niebuhr*, 1991.

35. Hobbs, Edward C., ed. *Bultmann, Retrospect, and Prospect: The Centenary Symposium at Wellesley*, 1985.

34. Cameron, Ron. *Sayings Traditions in the Apocryphon of James*, 1984.

33. Blackwell, Albert L. *Schleiermacher's Early Philosophy of Life: Determinism, Freedom, and Phantasy*, 1982.

32. Gibson, Elsa. *The "Christians for Christians" Inscriptions of Phrygia: Greek Texts, Translation and Commentary*, 1978.

31. Bynum, Caroline Walker. Docere Verbo et Exemplo: *An Aspect of Twelfth-Century Spirituality*, 1979.

30. Williams, George Huntston, ed. *The Polish Brethren: Documentation of the History and Thought of Unitarianism in the Polish-Lithuanian Commonwealth and in the Diaspora 1601–1685*, 1980.

29. Attridge, Harold W. *First-Century Cynicism in the Epistles of Heraclitus*, 1976.

28. Williams, George Huntston, Norman Pettit, Winfried Herget, and Sargent Bush, Jr., eds. *Thomas Hooker: Writings in England and Holland, 1626–1633*, 1975.

27. Preus, James Samuel. *Carlstadt's* Ordinaciones *and Luther's Liberty: A Study of the Wittenberg Movement, 1521–22*, 1974.

26. Nickelsburg, George W. E. *Resurrection, Immortality, and Eternal Life in Intertestamental Judaism*, 1972.

25. Worthley, Harold Field. *An Inventory of the Records of the Particular (Congregational) Churches of Massachusetts Gathered 1620–1805*, 1970.

24. Yamauchi, Edwin M. *Gnostic Ethics and Mandaean Origins*, 1970.

23. Yizhar, Michael. *Bibliography of Hebrew Publications on the Dead Sea Scrolls 1948–1964*, 1967.

22. Albright, William Foxwell. *The Proto-Sinaitic Inscriptions and Their Decipherment*, 1966.

21. Dow, Sterling, and Robert F. Healey. *A Sacred Calendar of Eleusis*, 1965.

20. Sundberg, Jr., Albert C. *The Old Testament of the Early Church*, 1964.

19. Cranz, Ferdinand Edward. *An Essay on the Development of Luther's Thought on Justice, Law, and Society*, 1959.

18. Williams, George Huntston, ed. *The Norman Anonymous of 1100 A.D.: Towards the Identification and Evaluation of the So-Called Anonymous of York*, 1951.

17. Lake, Kirsopp, and Silva New, eds. *Six Collations of New Testament Manuscripts*, 1932.

16. Servetus, Michael. *The Two Treatises of Servetus on the Trinity: On the Errors of the Trinity, 7 Books, A.D. 1531. Dialogues on the Trinity, 2 Books. On the Righteousness of Christ's Kingdom, 4 Chapters, A.D. 1532*. Translated by Earl Morse Wilbur, 1932.

15. Casey, Robert Pierce, ed. Serapion of Thmuis's *Against the Manichees*, 1931.

14. Ropes, James Hardy. *The Singular Problem of the Epistles to the Galatians*, 1929.

13. Smith, Preserved. *A Key to the Colloquies of Erasmus*, 1927.

12. Spyridon of the Laura and Sophronios Eustratiades. *Catalogue of the Greek Manuscripts in the Library of the Laura on Mount Athos,* 1925.

11. Sophronios Eustratiades and Arcadios of Vatspedi. *Catalogue of the Greek Manuscripts in the Library of the Monastery of Vatopedi on Mt. Athos*, 1924.

10. Conybeare, Frederick C. *Russian Dissenters*, 1921.

9. Burrage, Champlin, ed. *An Answer to John Robinson of Leyden by a Puritan Friend: Now First Published from a Manuscript of A.D. 1609*, 1920.

8. Emerton, Ephraim. The *Defensor pacis of Marsiglio of Padua: A Critical Study*, 1920,

7. Bacon, Benjamin W. *Is Mark a Roman Gospel?* 1919.

6. Cadbury, Henry Joel. 2 vols. *The Style and Literary Method of Luke*, 1920.

5. Marriott, G. L., ed. Macarii Anecdota: *Seven Unpublished Homilies of Macarius*, 1918.

4. Edmunds, Charles Carroll and William Henry Paine Hatch. *The Gospel Manuscripts of the General Theological Seminary*, 1918.

3. Arnold, William Rosenzweig. *Ephod and Ark: A Study in the Records and Religion of the Ancient Hebrews*, 1917.

2. Hatch, William Henry Paine. *The Pauline Idea of Faith in its Relation to Jewish and Hellenistic Religion*, 1917.

1. Torrey, Charles Cutler. *The Composition and Date of Acts*, 1916.

Harvard Dissertations in Religion

In 1993, Harvard Theological Studies absorbed
the Harvard Dissertations in Religion series.

31. Baker-Fletcher, Garth. *Somebodyness: Martin Luther King, Jr. and the Theory of Dignity*, 1993.

30. Soneson, Jerome Paul. *Pragmatism and Pluralism: John Dewey's Significance for Theology*, 1993.

29. Crabtree, Harriet. *The Christian Life: The Traditional Metaphors and Contemporary Theologies*, 1991.

28. Schowalter, Daniel N. *The Emperor and the Gods: Images from the Time of Trajan*, 1993.

27. Valantasis, Richard. *Spiritual Guides of the Third Century: A Semiotic Study of the Guide-Disciple Relationship in Christianity, Neoplatonism, Hermetism, and Gnosticism*, 1991.

26. Wills, Lawrence Mitchell. *The Jews in the Court of the Foreign King: Ancient Jewish Court Legends*, 1990.

25. Massa, Mark Stephen. *Charles Augustus Briggs and the Crisis of Historical Criticism*, 1990.

24. Hills, Julian Victor. *Tradition and Composition in the* Epistula apostolorum, 1990.

23. Bowe, Barbara Ellen. *A Church in Crisis: Ecclesiology and Paraenesis in Clement of Rome,* 1988.

22. Bisbee, Gary A. *Pre-Decian Acts of Martyrs and* Commentarii, 1988.

21. Ray, Stephen Alan. *The Modern Soul: Michel Foucault and the Theological Discourse of Gordon Kaufman and David Tracy,* 1987.

20. MacDonald, Dennis Ronald. *There Is No Male and Female: The Fate of a Dominical Saying in Paul and Gnosticism,* 1987.

19. Davaney, Sheila Greeve. *Divine Power: A Study of Karl Barth and Charles Hartshorne,* 1986.

18. LaFargue, J. Michael. *Language and Gnosis: The Opening Scenes of the Acts of Thomas,* 1985.

12. Layton, Bentley, ed. *The Gnostic Treatise on Resurrection from Nag Hammadi,* 1979.

11. Ryan, Patrick J. *Imale: Yoruba Participation in the Muslim Tradition: A Study of Clerical Piety,* 1977.

10. Neevel, Jr., Walter G. *Yamuna's Vedanta and Pancaratra: Integrating the Classical and the Popular,* 1977.

9. Yarbro Collins, Adela. *The Combat Myth in the Book of Revelation,* 1976.

8. Veatch, Robert M. *Value-Freedom in Science and Technology: A Study of the Importance of the Religious, Ethical, and Other Socio-Cultural Factors in Selected Medical Decisions Regarding Birth Control,* 1976.

7. Attridge, Harold W. *The Interpretation of Biblical History in the* Antiquitates judaicae *of Flavius Josephus,* 1976.

6. Trakatellis, Demetrios C. *The Pre-Existence of Christ in the Writings of Justin Martyr,* 1976.

5. Green, Ronald Michael. *Population Growth and Justice: An Examination of Moral Issues Raised by Rapid Population Growth,* 1975.

4. Schrader, Robert W. *The Nature of Theological Argument: A Study of Paul Tillich,* 1976.

3. Christensen, Duane L. *Transformations of the War Oracle in Old Testament Prophecy: Studies in the Oracles Against the Nations,* 1975.

2. Williams, Sam K. *Jesus' Death as Saving Event: The Background and Origin of a Concept,* 1972.

1. Smith, Jane I. *An Historical and Semantic Study of the Term "Islam" as Seen in a Sequence of Qur'an Commentaries,* 1970.

This book was produced at the offices of Harvard Theological Studies, located at the Harvard Divinity School, Cambridge, Massachusetts:

Managing Editor: Margaret Studier

Copy editors: Gene McGarry
                     Lyn Miller

Typesetters: Margo McLoughlin
                     Mindy Newman
                     Greg Goering

The indexes were prepared by David R. Brock. The Syriac, Greek, Coptic, and Hebrew fonts (EEstrangelo, SymbolGreekII, CopticLS, and New Jerusalem) used to print this work are available from Linguist's Software, Inc. PO Box 580, Edmonds, WA 98020-0580 USA tel (425) 775-1130 www.linguistsoftware.com.